"With Bodilie Eyes"

Eschatological Themes in Puritan Literature and Gravestone Art

Studies in the Fine Arts: Iconography, No. 3

Linda Seidel, Series Editor

Associate Professor of Art History
University of Chicago

Other Titles in This Series

"With Bodilie Eyes"
Eschatological Themes in Puritan Literature and Gravestone Art

by
David H. Watters

UMI RESEARCH PRESS
Ann Arbor, Michigan

Produced and distributed by
UMI Research Press
an imprint of
University Microfilms International
Ann Arbor, Michigan 48106

Library of Congress Cataloging in Publication Data

Watters, David H.
   "With bodilie eyes."

   (Studies in the fine arts. Iconography ; no. 3)
   Revision of thesis (Ph.D.)–Brown University, 1978.
   Bibliography: p.
   Includes index.
   1. Eschatology–History of doctrines. 2. Puritans–
New England. 3. Sepulchral monuments–New England.
I. Title. II. Series.

BT819.5.W37 1981   236   81-16466
ISBN 0-8357-1249-4   AACR2

For Janice

Contents

List of Illustrations

Acknowledgments

It is impossible to acknowledge the people who really made this study possible, the New Englanders who decided not to use gravestones for landfill. I can thank the staffs of libraries who have preserved and shared other kinds of knowledge, at The John Carter Brown Library, The John Hay Library, the American Antiquarian Society, the Houghton Library, and the Beinecke Library. My research was aided by grants from Brown University and the University of New Hampshire. If the illustrations capture anything of the beauty of the objects discussed in this book, it is due to the expertise of Amy Johnsen-Harris. Of the people who visited innumerable graveyards vicariously by commenting on drafts of this work, I would like to thank David L. Parker, Barton St. Armand, and Barbara K. Lewalski for their insight and guidance. Mason Lowance's inspiration will be apparent to those who know his work, but his friendship and support contributed in untold ways to the completion of this study. I would also like to thank Boston University Scholarly Publications for materials which previously appeared in *Puritan Gravestone Art II*; the Westfield Athenaeum for passages quoted from Edward Taylor's "Publick Records of the Church at Westfield;" the American Antiquarian Society for passages quoted from Cotton Mather's "Problema Theologicum" and "Triparadisus;" The Museum of Art, Rhode Island School of Design, The Wadsworth Athenaeum, and Brown University Library, Special Collections for the use of photographs of items in their collections.

Introduction

BW

DIED SEP 12 1680
WHAT ONCE WAS WRIT
BY ONE UPON THIS STONE
HE HEARS IS NOW WASHT OUT
AND LOST AND GONE
TWAS WRIT HOPING IN
TIME HE MIGHT IT FIND
NOT ON THIS STONE
BUT ON THE REDERS MIND

—Windsor, CT

This study treats the aesthetics of New England Puritan literature and gravestone carving. In discussing Increase Mather's term, "bodilie eyes," I propose that Puritan literature and art were profoundly affected by the anticipation of the moment during the Resurrection when saintly humans would see, with human but glorified eyes, the beauties of Christ and the Millennium. The expectation of this apocalyptic moment sent ripples throughout the Puritan imagination, influencing thinking about literature and art at all levels of New England culture.

While Puritan doctrines of the last things—death, judgment, heaven, and hell—were endlessly debated in England and New England in the seventeenth and eighteenth centuries, in New England ideas about the visionary qualities of "bodilie eyes" formed the mainstream of Puritan aesthetics. I will trace the development of Puritan eschatology in the seventeenth century, with particular reference to strategies of visualizing the last things. I will then examine how Increase Mather and New England stonecarvers use the concept of "bodilie eyes" to develop their prophetic images of the end of the world, and I will discuss Edward Taylor's poetry to show the influence of such prophetic images on his understanding of metaphorical language. Finally, I will trace the legacy of Puritan aesthetics after the Great Awakening.

The significance of "bodilie eyes" in Puritan eschatology is two-fold. First, they reveal the christological focus of Puritan doctrines of the last things. Since Christ would be seen in human form by human, glorified eyes, the end of the world is viewed optimistically as a time of the ex-altation of the human body as the saints are resurrected in Christ's image. Prophecies of Christ's return, whether hidden in the figurative language of the Old Testament or the New, are passionately expounded until the texts form a canon of symbols which preacher and stonecarver alike can count on to strike a responsive chord in their audiences. Second, "bodilie eyes" are the centerpiece of an epistemology which defines man's ability to perceive divine things. Puritans believed that fallen humans see through a glass darkly, since language is only able to express in part the glory of heaven, but the elect were assured that a real, perceptible world would exist after the Resurrection, to be perceived with "bodilie eyes" as the substance of what language shadowed forth on earth. The rich figurative language of Scripture gains added significance as Puritans emphasized the reality of the heavenly world promised to believers by the Bible. During life Puritans were encouraged to "see" with eyes of faith what would be revealed to "bodilie eyes" during the Resurrection; such imag-inings during life are not vain, since they anticipate an apocalyptic reality. By understanding Puritan thinking on "bodilie eyes," we can understand the fundamentally prophetic nature of early New England aesthetic the-ory. Moreover, it becomes possible to view much of New England liter-ature and art as the result of a coherent, indigenous body of theory which values artistic expression, rather than as negative forms of expression constrained by a supposedly antiaesthetic plain style.

In illustrating this study of eschatological literature with gravestone art, I emphasize the continuities between these two forms of early Amer-ican expression. Lacking diaries or other statements written by gravestone carvers, it is impossible to trace lines of influence between ministers and carvers, so I proceed by presenting analogous materials, contiguous in time and region whenever possible. In discussing gravestones, I borrow an iconographic method from Erwin Panofsky and present the "intrinsic meaning or content" of the images found on the stones, "apprehending by ascertaining those underlying principles which reveal the basic atti-tudes of a nation, a period, a class, a religious or philosophical persuasion, unconsciously qualified by one personality and condensed into one work."[1] The difficulty in employing Panofsky's method lies in proving that certain principles do, in fact, underlie the basic attitudes of a nation, period, or religious persuasion. In the case of Puritan gravestone art, some critics refuse to believe that the tradition is anything but decorative, at best a primitive permutation of English traditions with little conscious or unconscious value.[2] As Panofsky notes, iconographical analysis "presupposes a familiarity with specific themes or concepts as transmitted through literary sources, whether acquired by purposeful reading or by oral tradition."[3] It is my contention that the popularity and coherency of Puritan gravestone designs can be explained through the aesthetics of "bodilie eyes," aesthetics that were transmitted both in print and orally throughout New England.

It is a peculiar twentieth-century bias to presume that folk cultures are incapable of treating sophisticated and abstract ideas in their art and oral tradition. As Henry Glassie has shown in his study of folk housing, once we understand the conceptual pattern of the particular folk community, its material culture can be seen as remarkably expressive.[4] Moreover, twentieth-century concerns over the distinctions between elite and popular culture should not blind us to the fact that early New England culture was remarkably unified by the Word, whether communicated in learned treatises, from the pulpit, or in the Bible itself. I will argue that whatever doctrinal differences may divide early New England communities or classes, a common resource of biblical imagery unifies them. By analyzing gravestones as well as printed matter, we are freed from an exclusively literate, ministerial perspective, and we may explore the imaginative ends to which the congregation used the Word.

I do not propose to survey New England stonecarving traditions comprehensively, for I am finally concerned with a Puritan imaginative structure which transcends most local concerns and historical events. I do not attempt, however, to resurrect the New England mind from various critical graveyards to explain away the diversity of New England, but I do argue that eschatological ideas are deeply conservative and resistant to change.[5] While other gravestone carving traditions, such as the *memento mori* tradition of Boston and the folk images of the soul in its separate state popular in Plymouth County are significant to all New England carving, I have limited my study to the most pervasive tradition which features prophetic images of the Resurrection and the aesthetics of "bodilie eyes."

The aesthetics of "bodilie eyes" are inextricably linked to Puritan theorizing on eschatology, which was a popular subject in Puritan Old and New England. In using this term, I refer to general and particular doctrines current in the seventeenth century, from the belief in Christ's Second Coming, the Resurrection of the dead, and the Millennium to the personal confrontation with death, judgment, heaven, and hell.[6] The more extreme manifestations of eschatological beliefs by such radical groups as the Fifth Monarchists have drawn attention from the simple belief held by the vast majority of Englishmen and Americans in the seventeenth century that Christ would indeed return and that a millennial reign either prior to or after His return would be realized on earth. Grounded in the biblical literalism of the Reformation and by a hundred-year exegetical tradition, eschatological fervor flowered in the mid-seventeenth century. The Westminster assembly gave these beliefs the status of dogma, and as Bryan W. Ball has shown in his exhaustive study, "There can be little doubt . . . that a large measure of conformity existed in the structures of the various eschatological schemes. Austere Anglican bishops and rabid Fifth Monarchy Men alike raised their hopes on similar foundations, and the finished fabric of each bore an observable resemblance."[7] Certainly there was endless debate and occasional violence over the nature of the Millennium. Within the context of shared beliefs, however, I will note only those distinctions between theories on the Millennium which are immediately relevant to my study. In general I will use the terms chiliasm and millennarianism to refer to the broadest belief that a thousand-year reign of the saints would occur on earth before the end of the world. Under these general headings the most-commonly made distinction is between pre- and postmillennialists who disagree on the time and form of Christ's appearance. Premillennialists felt Christ would arrive at the inauguration of the Millennium either in person or in the spirit personally to the saints. Postmillennialists put this appearance and the Last Judgment at the end of the Millennium, a Millennium distinguished by the progressive and general revelation of Christ's spiritual presence to the world. In either case, a cataclysmic break with human history was expected with the arrival of Christ. Both groups affirmed the Resurrection of the dead. But a prime subject of debate between these camps was the Resurrection—Who would be resurrected? When would the risen saints appear? and, What role would they play in the millennial reign?

Whatever intensity these distinctions generated in England at the time gravestone art appeared in New England, it seems that gravestone and literary imagery reflects commonly held beliefs.[8] James W. Davidson began his study of the "logic" of millennial thought with the assumption that such a logic did indeed exist and would conform to the commonly accepted distinctions between pre- and postmillennialism, liberalism, and orthodoxy. But he discovered that millennialists of all stripes shared basic assumptions in using figurative language from Scripture, and I suggest that viewing gravestones as expressions of mutually exclusive positions such as "orthodoxy," "unorthodoxy," a belief in spiritual or physical resurrection misses the point.[9] It is my purpose to show that literary and artistic visions of eschatological events gained popularity precisely because they resisted such categorization and thereby allowed the individual imagination room for play, speculation, and personality. Not only was it necessary that gravestone images and figurative language escape condemnation as idols and vain imaginings, but they also had to allow for a flexibility of interpretation that united rather than divided the community if they were to survive in a Puritan culture. I will show that congregations with opposing positions on church polity still shared eschatological beliefs and set gravestones with identical designs in their burying grounds. And I will argue that an aesthetic of the power of "bodilie eyes" was the means of transcending doctrinal boundaries.

Puritan eschatology involves a belief in the continuity between what can be perceived with eyes of faith in life and what will be perceived with "bodilie eyes" in the Resurrection world. Thus an image on a gravestone may refer at once to the restored soul in life and to the resurrected body, and the Puritan viewer of the image was cognizant of its various eschatological references. As we shall see in my discussions of Increase Mather and Edward Taylor, this multiplicity of reference lends an eschatological force to metaphoric language as well. While millennialism had profound political implications in seventeenth-century England, in America the legacy is political *and* aesthetic.

Previous studies of Puritan eschatology and funerary art have taken attitudes towards iconolatry and iconoclasm as their points of departure, and I will also discuss this subject in chapter one. John Phillips has written a perceptive and comprehensive study of Puritan iconoclasm in England to 1660, and it is regrettable the scope of his study could not include New England Puritanism after 1660.[10] Discussion of New England gravestones has been complicated by several critics' incomplete understanding of the iconoclastic impulse and the nature of American Puritanism. The earliest writers, including the pioneering Harriette Merrifield Forbes, assumed funerary art was in a decorative tradition since image-making could not have been condoned in an iconoclastic culture.[11] Allan Ludwig, James Deetz, and Edwin S. Dethlefsen must be credited for their original attempts to explain gravestone art as a reflection of cultural values.[12] Through a seriation study, Deetz and Dethlefsen claim that the change in design patterns from death's head to cherub to urn and willow correlates with changes in Puritan orthodoxy. Unfortunately, by equating grim death's heads with orthodoxy and cherubs with unorthodoxy, this study wrenches intellectual history to make Jonathan Edwards a liberal whose eschatology departed from that of orthodox Calvinism. Moreover, Deetz and Dethlefsen never explain why they assume the effigies popular from 1740 to 1760 are cherubs and therefore hopeful, and they neglect the fact that an effigy tradition in Essex County, Massachusetts, predates the popular-

ity of death's heads there. Given the evidence of eschatological conformity presented by Ball and Davidson, the extent of change in doctrinal
eschatology becomes moot.

Peter Benes, in his *Masks of Orthodoxy*, develops the seriation thesis
at great length in discussing Plymouth County carving. Benes' knowledge
of Puritanism surpasses that of Deetz and Dethlefsen, and he adds to the
thesis of eighteenth-century liberalism the important fact that assurance
becomes a sign of grace for radicals during the Great Awakening.[13] Thus
for Benes, cheerful effigies from 1739 to 1745 reflect a new optimism. But
Benes has not shown that eschatological optimism springs solely from
assurance, nor has he shown that hopes about the end of the world and
the Resurrection were different in the eighteenth century from those in
the seventeenth. Bryan W. Ball warns us against assuming that the Puritan
preoccupation with death and the end of the world was pessimistic. He
writes,

> Protestant eschatological optimism deriving from the Reformation achieved its most
> lucid expression with English theologians in the Puritan era. That optimism included
> the certainty that time would see the fulfillment of biblical prophecy, belief in the
> triumph of good over evil, and hope in the ultimate realisation of the will of God on
> earth. That such optimism was unfounded in the immediate historical context, and
> that it was sometimes expressed in forms unacceptable to a more mature theological
> orientation should not be allowed to preclude the more fundamental aspects of Chris-
> tian hope it sought to express.[14]

In his major study of New England funerary art, Allan Ludwig bases
his approach on the problem of an iconic carving tradition in an iconoclastic culture. Ludwig sets the context for the debate over Puritan iconoclasm in his discussion of Samuel Willard's intense assertion of God's
essential incommunicability:

> HENCE *how very unsutable it is to represent the Divine Nature by any Corporeal
> similitude*: I mean in Pictures or Images of any visible and bodily substance, and that
> whether it be for civility or devotion, *i.e.*, either merely as Ornamental, or as some
> pretend, to encrease devout Affections in any; how is it possible to rightly shadow a
> Spirit? Who was ever able rightly to decypher the form or shape of a being which is
> invisible! It is folly to pretend to afford us the Portraiture of an Angel, but it is madness
> and wickedness to offer any image or Representation of God: How many solemn
> cautions did God give his people against this by *Moses*, besides the express forbidding
> of in the second Command; and God declares it to be a thing Idolatrous.[15]

Although it can be argued just how representative Willard's conservatism is on the subject of idolatry, care must be taken in applying comments on idolatry to gravestone art. In the first place, the injunction

against representing the Divine Nature is not precisely applicable to gravestones, since it was not the subject of funerary art except in one late example.[16] Most gravestone effigies are representations of Death, the deceased, the deceased's soul, angels, or the resurrection body; Puritan theology, as we shall soon see, justifies such images. Williard's objection to the depiction of invisible beings such as angels needs further examination. There was considerable argument over just which heavenly beings were visible, and even invisible beings could be represented by emblems and through metaphors. Angels often took on human forms in Scripture, and it was possible they would don forms in heaven so that the saints could see them. By taking Willard's position as universally held doctrine, Ludwig can explain symbol-making only as the result of a radical split between the clergy and a populace which preferred images over words, immediacy over mediacy, in the religious experience.

Lacking sufficient evidence, it is difficult to prove or disprove Ludwig's thesis that there was a split between the clergy and the multitude. But his equation of this split with a divergence of word and image, mediacy and immediacy, goes against the grain of what we know about Puritanism. Ludwig sees gravestone carving as "a protest against the stifling verbalism of Puritan doctrine," "which denied believers the possibility of communication with the Godhead." Ludwig offers this explanation for the development of "realized eschatology" outside the pale of New England theology:

> visual imagery opened up the possibility of communication between contrite man and a benevolent, forgiving God. In sharp contrast to Puritan theology, which left no room for supplication, the gravestones are rich in these possibilities. The emerging formula concerning the use of symbols in New England seems to amount to this: the more transcendent the God, the greater the need for visual imagery. As the avenue of subjectivity in religion narrowed, a boulevard of symbolic imagery appeared. The more verbal the formulas of the institutionalized church the more the multitude strove to express the "nouminal" immediacy of spirit in their stone icons.[17]

I suspect the "boulevard of symbolic imagery" would have been seen by Puritans as a primrose path if it really did lead to an escape from the Word. The possibility of such an escape had been dealt with severely during the Antinomian Controversy thirty years before the appearance of gravestone images. Anne Hutchinson believed that the soul was nothing but light, and her Mortalist heresy of denying the immortality of the soul and the resurrection of the body horrified her inquisitors.[18] Moreover, Puritans habitually "read" both texts and images with the same method; although the Word was preeminent in Puritan theology, images were eminently useful as well. The popularity of the emblem tradition in Puritan

Old and New England alike, with its aesthetic basis in Horace's dictum, *Ut pictura poesis*, should warn the critic that Puritans did not neatly differentiate image and word.[19] Furthermore, as we shall see below in the sermons of Richard Sibbes and Richard Baxter, Puritan traditions of meditation encouraged the creation of mental pictures drawn from biblical texts. Especially in the gravestone tradition are word and image compatible, since, in true emblematic fashion, it is the conjunction of epitaph and image which defines the classic Puritan gravestone.

Nevertheless, Ludwig's underlying assumption, mediacy equals Word equals orthodoxy while immediacy equals image equals protest, is a provocative speculation on the meaning of symbols in the Puritan mind. His distinction between mediacy and immediacy is predicated on a Platonic model of symbol-making as modified by Jungian psychology. This is not the place to discuss exhaustively the applicability of Platonism to Puritanism, but Ludwig's distinction does raise several issues to which I will return throughout this study. First, many of the symbols found on gravestones refer to mediation in all its Puritan forms: the Sacrament, the Word, the church, and above all the Incarnation. I contend that even in funerary art the basis of Puritan epistemology is the doctrine of the means which holds that God accommodates Himself to the limits of human understanding in the language of the Bible. Ludwig has not demonstrated that the symbols on gravestones fall outside this context let alone protest against it. I have yet to find a gravestone image that does not have some analogous expression in metaphoric language in biblical texts. Second, it can be shown that Puritans were encouraged to use images much as they used other means to know God, even though images were excluded from formal worship.[20]

Mediation was not limited to man's earthly state, for, as we shall discover, many ministers felt means would be employed in heaven as well. Though the sacrament of the Lord's Supper would no longer be needed to commemorate Christ since He would be present in heaven, direct apprehension of the Godhead with human senses would be impossible. Christ's human form would still be the means of knowing God, and language would be retained as well. There were notable exceptions, however; Jesper Rosenmeier has shown that John Cotton's *A Practical Commentary . . . Upon the First Epistle Generall of John* emphasizes the mystical, ineffable communion of God and believer in heaven.[21]

Second, the Platonic-Jungian model of archetype and symbol requires modification because of Puritan incarnationalism and millennialism which affect the relationship of image to archetype. For Ludwig, the unknowable archetype symbolized in portrait effigies is the image of God in the soul. This relationship is complicated by the fact that Christ, like

Adam, was created in the image of God, and chiliasts in particular emphasized the fact that the image of God restored in man's soul and in the Resurrection body was in fact the image of Christ. As an archetype for the images of the resurrection bodies of saints, however, Christ is not nouminal, for He will be known and seen at the Resurrection. In Puritan symbolism, the archetype has a habit of coming down to earth, and metaphors and symbols of the saint's resurrection become indistinguishable from "factual" description of what will occur at the end of time. Images in literature and on gravestones both symbolize the archetype, the glorified image saints will share with Christ, and prophesy the marriage of the saint with a real, glorified human Christ at the end of time. The vertical system of Platonic symbolism is wrenched into a horizontal plane by a millennial theology predicated on the meeting of heaven and earth, divinity and humanity, in the Apocalypse.

Dickran and Ann Tashjian, in their *Memorials for Children of Change*, provide an alternative to Ludwig's approach by arguing that Puritan symbolism was rooted in Puritan funerary rituals and artistic genres rather than in a system of religious symbolism inherent in human nature.[22] The Tashjians contend that since funerary practices and art were in the civil domain, they could exist independently of, and with tacit approval from, the religious establishment. I suspect the Tashjians go too far in separating funerary art from religious restrictions. Though the placement of gravestones was not an act of worship, it was an act of deepest faith in doctrines of the last things, and there is no fundamental distinction between funerary symbolism in the civil domain and literary symbolism delivered from the pulpit. Nevertheless, the Tashjians' approach is fruitful, and I embrace the position that these symbols are rooted in Puritan culture, though I see that culture as primarily religious.

The Tashjians note that gravestones appeared during a period of crisis in the New England way, when sociological, political and economic forces threatened the continuation of the founders' errand in the wilderness:

Communal anxiety was not assuaged by warnings from the pulpit, as the ministers cast jeremiad after jeremiad upon their flock. Deserted by history and apparently corrupt from within, this transplanted culture heeded a reassertion of the religious values which had motivated the founding scarcely a generation before. Nathaniel Morton's *New Englands Memoriall* in 1669 was but one attempt to establish a provincial history of cultural ideals from which the community could derive a spiritual and historical identity. The gravestone was another—a tangible and enduring memorial which, as [Samuel] Mather implied, served "for the representation and remembrance of a person absent, for honour and Civil worship of any worthy person." The gravestone, then, not only commemorated the deceased individual but also confirmed the broad cultural goals and ideals of the New England settlement. In this respect, the gravestone was one mode of artistic expression which, along with literary forms, served to create a memorial of the past for this transplanted culture.[23]

This subject is pursued at length by David Stannard, but the cultural response I will examine deals less with the memorial of the past and more with prophecy of the future. Iconoclasm has long been viewed as an entirely antiaesthetic movement represented by the mindless destruction of art by fanatics. As such, it was a phenomenom that had to be put aside as an aberration before Puritan aesthetics could be discussed. But for the majority of Puritans, iconoclasm may well have been a positive aesthetic force intimately linked with their dearest hopes for future beauty as a spouse of Christ. Iconoclasm freed Puritans from the carnal trappings of human idols, allowing a purer appreciation of God's beauty. The famous remark in the preface to the *Bay Psalm Book* that "Gods altar needs not our polishings" is not antiaesthetic when recognized as an expression of the Puritan belief that any human art was anti-Christian if it distracted attention from God's truth. But art which reveals God's truth is not anti-Christian. It is my intent to demonstrate that the aesthetic of "bodilie eyes" transcends the destructive side of iconoclasm in the Puritan imagination. The Puritan saint who avoids idolatry in life would find suitable objects of worship in the Millennium. The *Bay Psalm Book* preface reasons that a plain style is best "soe we may sing in Sion the Lords songs of prayse according to his owne will; untill hee take us from hence, and wipe away all our teares, & bid us enter into our masters ioye to sing eternall Halleluiahs."[24] Earthly art is a prelude to heavenly art; it is useful in preparing the imagination for heavenly beauties. In the only known comment by a carver on gravestone art in the seventeenth century, the carver of the BW stone states the value of his craft is to be found "NOT ON THIS STONE / BUT ON THE REDERS MIND." The artifact is useful only as a vehicle to engrave ideas on the soul, a more permanent form of commemoration.

The eschatological literature and art of New England does less to memorialize than to transform the deceased into an avatar of future events which reveal the true nature of the saint's life. The deceased was seen as an example not only for imitation in life, but also as an image of what glorified saints will be in the Millennium. As the Festus Colton stone of 1768 states,

> This stone stands but to tell,
> Where his dust lies not what he was
> When Saints shall rise that day will show
> The part he acted here Below.

In the face of death, Puritan culture created an imaginative construct of a millennial future which, even when unfulfilled, provided an eschatological perspective on everyday life. The progress of the community and the lives of individuals within it came to be judged from the perspective of what "bodilie eyes" would see at the Judgment Day. The dead hovered in the very air above and slept in the earth below the community, ready to return in judgment and triumph. Eschatological literature and gravestone art reminded believers of the continuing presence of the dead with each new interment. Eschatological images stand as the centerpiece of millennial expectation, but more important to the life of the imagination in future periods of American culture, they stand as testimony to the ability of the Puritan imagination to transform the facts of death into images of personal and communal triumph.

1

Puritan Eschatology:
The Evidence of Things Not Seen

> What though he wanted the riches and pleasures of the world in his
> life, and pompious monuments at his funurall? Yet the memoriall of
> the just shall be blessed, when the name of the wicked shall rott (with
> their marble monuments). Pro. 10:7.

> —William Bradford,
> *Of Plymouth Plantation*

No part of the English church escaped the iconoclast's axe, hammer, or
torch during the periodic surges of destruction between 1540 and 1660.
Roodscreens, altars, icons, whole churches fell, and even graves within
and without the church were abused. English Puritan writers reveal the
vehemence with which the dreaded idols were attacked, if the evidence
of the defaced fabric of the Medieval church is not sufficient proof. The
rhetoric of the writings on idolatry goes beyond vehemence, however, to
betray a deep fear of the power of idols to pollute a people.[1] In particular,
it is a rhetoric of the fear of sexual pollution by gorging the senses with
idols, drawn from various biblical texts such as Ezekiel 16:17: "Thou hast
also taken thy fair jewels of my gold and of my silver, which I had given
thee, and madest to thyself images of men, and didst commit whoredom
with them." The Elizabethan homily which defined English protestant
attitudes towards idolatry for 100 years develops at length the association
of idolatry and whoredom, and it singles out icons as great offenders:

> Our Churches stand full of such great puppettes, wonderously decked and adourned. . . .
> You would beleve that the Images of our men Sainctes, were som P31nces of Persie
> lande, with theyr proude apparell, and the Idols of our women Sainctes, were nyce
> and well trimmed harlottes, temptying theyr paramours to wantonnesse: whereby the
> Sainctes of God are not honoured, but most dishonoured, and theyr godlynes, sob-
> ernes, chastitie, contempte of ryches, and of the vanitie of the worlde, defaced and
> brought in doubt, by such monstruous deckying, most differyng from their sober and
> godly lyues.[2]

As Henry Ainsworth wrote, "Idolatry is as sweet to the corrupted Conscience and mind of Man, as Lust and Fornication is to any wanton Body," and William Perkins reminded his congregation that God was a jealous bridegroom who would not have his spouse consort outside the marriage vows.[3]

The rhetoric of iconoclasm reflects both the millennial and the political concerns of Puritans who would keep the spouse, Christ's church, chaste on earth so that she would be fit for a heavenly marriage with the Lamb. For Daniel Featley, the mere presence at a service involving idolatrous rituals and images was enough to pollute even the pure in thought:

> To lift up the heart to God when they fall downe with their body before the Hoste or Image, will no more acquit them from Idolatry, than it will cleare a woman from adultery to thinke upon her husband when shee prostituteth her body to the impure soliciter of her chastity. . . . Is it not to bee feared that as the sheepe which conceived before the coloured roddes brought forth spotted lambes, so the prayers and meditations which are conceived before idols, will receive some impression from the image, and bee tainted with idolatry, or spotted with superstition?[4]

Featley's comments are charged with the politics of England in 1636, when reformation from within the Anglican church seemed increasingly remote, and the call for complete separation from and renewed destruction of idols fell on sympathetic ears. Featley's rhetoric points to the iconoclastic extremes of the New Model Army. A few years later, Samuel Chidley laments the incompleteness of the Army's work, and he proposes, in his *Thunder from the Throne of God Against the Temples of Idols*, that not a stone be left upon a stone in the Cathedrals. "These *grievous Idols Temples* were built for the service and support of *Idols*. And so long as the *Idols Temples* stand, The *Idols* are supported, *Superstition* nourished, *Idolatry* upheld and preserved: because their *Temples* are reserved. But take downe the *Idols Temples*. Then that means of preservation of those evils is taken away."[5]

Separation and Reformation are wed to millennialism in Chidley's mind. The carnal temples must be removed before the temple of the New Jerusalem can come down from heaven to earth. The vehemence of Chidley's rhetoric reflects a belief well established by the middle of the seventeenth century that the whore of Babylon in Revelation is the church of Rome. As William Guild argues:

> The summe of the mystery of this woman is this. 1. This woman as a woman, is a Church. 2. As a harlot, is a false and idolatrous Church. 3. As inebriating the Kings and inhabitants of the earth with the wine of her fornications, is a pretended Catholick

Church. 4. As a Mother of harlots is a mother Church. And, 5. As Mystical Babylon, which Ribera and other Romanists expound to be Rome, is the Roman Church, all which being put together makes up here by common consent the description of the Antichristian Church, which is therefore the Roman-mother-pretended Catholick Church.[6]

For Joseph Mede, Thomas Brightman, John Cotton, and other exegetes of the Apocalypse, the last times would be distinguished by the pollution of idolatry. Mede writes, "amongst all other Corruptions, only the Spiritual fornication of the Church and Spouse of Christ [*i.e.* with idols] will be found proper to these times."[7] The duty of every saint, then, was to keep pure in expectation of the millennial marriage and, in particular, to avoid those images which might seduce the believer into breaking the marriage vows with Christ. In the words of Richard Sibbes, "If a man hope for this comming of Christ, he will purifie himselfe for it, even as hee is pure. He will not appeare in his foule cloathes, but . . . will fit himselfe as the Bride for the comming of the Bridegroome."[8]

The Puritan fear of idolatry is intimately connected with their rejection of Catholic funeral rituals and traditions of commemoration of the dead. But the intensity of Puritan iconoclasm reveals the degree to which individuals invested personal hopes in the Millennium. Death is the event which inaugurates individual participation in the grand drama of the last things, and Puritans were understandably concerned that an idolatrous practice might damn them to everlasting punishment. Moreover, with the Calvinistic emphasis on the association of carnal sensuality, sin, and death, Puritans felt a need to destroy the idolatrous objects of the senses in order to remain chaste for a life after death. Calvin had rejected purgatory, one of the central doctrines of Catholic eschatology as well as one of the major justifications for such rituals as prayers and masses for the dead and prayers to icons for saintly intercession on behalf of the dead.[9] For Calvin, judgment came immediately at the moment of death, thus denying the need for or efficacy of rituals undertaken by the living to affect the state of the dead.[10] Judged souls awaited the Resurrection and the final judgment of the body and soul in a state of bliss or damnation, which Calvin called the "separate state." For Puritans, then, the moment of death gained an added sense of drama and finality, and improper activities, be they rituals or prayers, might endanger the souls of the dying and living alike. By examining the Puritan response to Catholic funerary ritual, we find the wellspring of feelings about idolatry and the use of images to commemorate the dead.

Puritans objected to two principles of Catholic funeral ritual. They rejected set forms of prayers or masses for the dead meant to affect the state of the dead. Particular fault was found with the last prayer at the grave, "That we with this our brother, and all other departed with true faith of thy holy Name, may have our perfect consummation, & bliss both in body and soule," which was seen to be too "confident, touching the salvation of the dead now buried."[11] Other Puritans objected to the word "brother" which could not be applied to all deceased, and the sectarian-spirited Puritans feared such pollution by association.[12] Second, Puritans objected to superstitions about the spirit world which seemed to be the basis of many Catholic rituals. Included was the hallowing of the air with psalm singing and bell tolling. Protestant revisions of the Catholic breviary strip away such prayers and practices and downgrade the ritualistic function of the priest to the point of suggesting that he not be present at the gravesite.

Since Puritan funeral services have little to do with the state of the deceased's soul, rituals and prayers retained from the breviary are used as warnings and encouragement for the living.[13] Thus the Catholic ritual is effectively transformed into a *memento mori* framework. The most Calvinist of all revisions in *The First Prayer-Book of Edward VI* gives a distinctly apocalyptic turn to the ceremony by placing the proof texts of Protestant belief in the Resurrection, Phillippians 3:21 and Revelation 13, to be read at the time of commendation at the graveside. Clearly Puritans understood this new focus of the funeral ritual, for long after English Protestants had moved or deleted these passages from the rite, they remained two of the most popular texts placed on New England gravestones.

Radical Puritans made the easy step from rejection of idolatry in Catholic burial ritual to the destruction of the trappings of that ritual, including sacred spaces in churches and holy ground and gravemarkers themselves. For one writer arguing that holy ground and burial rituals are idolatrous,

> the *Ceremonies* having place in *Gods worship*, and being mans device, must needes be *Idols*, or Idolatrous actions, *Quicquid praeter mandatum, est Idolum*, Whatsoever is placed in Gods worship, without the commandment *of God, is an Idol*. . . . The proofe of the former proposition, is from instance of *Abrahams grove*, Gen. 21:33 but being abused to Idolatry, as 2 *Kings* 12:10, *Jerem*. 51:2, *Esay*. 57:5, then God forbiddeth the usage of it, because it was an Idol, yea commanded to *destroy* it, *Deut*. 12:13.[14]

Puritans heeded this command, and John Weever's survey of the destruction of tombs by Puritans lists as defaced "Inscriptions or Epitaphs, especially if they began with an *orate pro anima*, or concluded with *cuius animae propitiatur Deus*."[15] Some sectaries were so anxious to follow

God's instructions on burial that they buried their dead with asses, as seemed to be required in Jeremiah 22.[16]

During the 1640s, antiritualism reached a peak, with no official prayers allowed at the funeral, with the body taken directly from home to the churchyard and buried with "neither Sermon, nor prayer, nor ringing of Bells, neither any kinde of other ceremony."[17] Parliament instituted one further reform, designed to appeal to the lower classes, requiring that all people must be buried in a winding sheet, rather than dumped naked into the grave. John Dunton's frivolous recollection of these times in a versified account of a funeral concludes: "*He's now box'd up*; (*the* Parliament *be thanked*) / *Whose Act has made my Rime in winding Blanket.*"[18] A more reasonable and telling remark on the attitudes of the time towards rituals and commemorative effigies is from William Perkins, who concluded, "words can doe no more but signifie, and figures can doe no more but represent."[19]

While the funeral service could be easily purged of idolatrous activities and the most obviously idolatrous commemorative effigies and icons could be destroyed, it was a more difficult task to define what forms of commemorative effigies were acceptable. Most Puritans felt commemoration could be entirely secular, in the form of portraits, biographies, and elegies, but the simple fact that gravestones were placed over the body of the deceased made Puritans suspicious even of portrait tomb sculpture. Was there not always the danger that commemoration of the dead with effigies could lead to the exaltation of human earthly, carnal nature rather than the workings of grace in the soul? Might not the images of famous people become idols as had the images of the saints?

Puritan concerns over the relationship of commemoration of the dead to idolatry surfaced at the very beginning of the Reformation in England. From the time of Aquinas, Catholics justified the use of images for their didactic function.[20] Images of Christ, Mary, and the saints were useful for instructing the ignorant, while the educated responded directly to the Word of God. In the belief that not all people were able to respond properly to the Word of God, Catholics distinguished between *latria* and *dulia*—*latria* being the worship of God, *dulia* the veneration of God in his angels and saints. John Phillips attributes the reformers' rejection of different classes of believers, who could or could not respond without the use of images, to the belief in a universal priesthood of believers. Believers did not need the authority of the church and its icons to understand the Word of God. Phillips concludes, "it was only when the control of religious images was taken from the teaching authority of the Church and when Scripture was considered the chief medium through which God could speak to man, that iconoclasm became essential to the Reformation.''[21] Many reformers also rejected the distinctions between *latria* and *dulia* because they distrusted the ability of fallen man to distinguish between the worship of God through images and the veneration of God's spirit in the saints whose lives were commemorated in images.

While rejecting the *latria* and the *dulia*, abused and unabused images, Cranmer, Hooper, Ridley, and other early advisors to Edward VI did not call for the destruction of all art. They wished to retain those images used for commemoration and remembrance, especially when found on the tombs of the nobility. In the 1548 order calling for the removal of images from the church, an important exception was made: "Provided that this act or any thing therein conteyned shall not extend to any Image or Picture sett or graven upon any tomb in any Church—only for a Monument of any King, Prince, or Nobleman or other dead person which hath not been commonly reputed and taken for a Saint."[22] The King's privy councilors recognized that Englishmen might be unable to distinguish between abused and unabused images, but they did not forsee difficulties in enforcing the preservation of tombs of the nobility. After all, the church stood as a concrete reminder of social order, and though it was to be reformed, the fundamental social hierarchy represented therein was not to be altered. Elaborate tombs were convenient reminders of the honor, if not the veneration, due one's social superiors.

The decrees from the early years of Elizabeth's reign indicate the confusion over commemorative images. In the 1559 Declaration of Certain Principle Articles of Religion, Article X omits the protection of commemorative images, and the destruction that followed forced Elizabeth to reassert the special status of monuments.[23] The tombs themselves were not attacked, but the effigies of the dead were. The homilies themselves were the source of confusion, for they seem to condemn any representational image:

> lest any woulde take occasion by the way of doutyng by wordes or names, it is thought good here to note fyrst of all, that although in common speache we use to call the likenesse or similitudes of men or other thynges Images, & not Idols: yet the Scriptures use the sayde two wordes (Idols and Images) indifferently for one thing always.[24]

The homily goes on to state it is simply impossible to make an image of the soul of any saint, so images can only represent the body as it rots in the grave. Another contributing factor to the confusion of portrait and icon may have been the medieval practice of depicting the deceased as he or she appeared in his or her early thirties, reflecting the belief that the resurrected body would be as old as was Christ at the time of His death.[25] Some iconoclasts were simply antiaesthetic. George Fox argued that artistic creation was fallen man's usurpation of God's right to creation, and Edmund Gurnay concluded, "better it were, that the art of painting, plaistering, carving, graving, and founding had never been found nor used, then one of them whose souls in the sight of God are so precious, should by occasion of Image or picture perish and be lost."[26] What is most likely, however, is that all of these objections, combined with a class-based resentment of social authority, allowed a wide range of discontents to unite in iconoclasm.

Commemoration of the good man did often become veneration of a saint when time erased the deceased's generation. Perkins admits, "Images serue to keepe in memorie friendes deceased, whom we reuerence," but these images became icons in the Roman church. In addition,

> Sundrie images in the church of Rome at the first, in all likelihood were inuented to represent, not the presence of persons of men, but mysteries after the manner of Emblems. The figure which is called Saint Margaret, destroying a dragon after she was deuored of it, in former times serued to represent, the calling of the Church of the Gentiles, being gathered by the preaching of the Gospel out of the bowels (as it were) of the deuill, of whom they were deuored. . . . Now these and like pictures of mysteries, were in processe of time reputed pictures of Saints; and are worshipped at this day of many, as they haue been heretofore, for the images of Saints indeed.[27]

Here in artistic terms we have Perkins's distrust of Catholic exegetical theory. Perkins argued in his immensely influential work, *The Arte of Prophecying*, that the Catholic fourfold method of analyzing Scripture could distort its literal truth; so also could human inventions in art lead to idolatry.[28] No manner of representation was safe, as the history of the Old Testament and Roman churches revealed.

Joseph Mede specifically relates Catholic idolatry to early pagan funerary rituals in an essay with profound implications for Puritan funerary art. After locating the origins of "the apostacy of the latter times" in idolatry, he invokes quasi-scientific research from Hermes Trismegistus to prove the similarity of the deifying and worshipping of saints and angels with the doctrine of daemons held by Old Testament Gentiles. "For the *Canonizing of the Souls of deceased Worthies* is not now first devised among Christians, but was an Idolatrous trick even from the days of the elder world; so that the Devil, when he brought in this *Apostolical* doctrine amongst Christians, swerved but little from his ancient method of seducing mankind."[29] Mede argues that this deification of deceased worthies led inexorably to idolatry, as the erection of pillars or columns to the memory of the dead, mentioned in Leviticus 26:1, was the root of superstition. "The summe of all this Mystery is, That Images were made as Bodies, to be informed with *Daemons* as with Souls. For an *Image* was as a Trap to catch *Daemons*, and a device to tie them to a place, and to keep them from flitting."[30] Hence arose the practices of worshipping daemons in shrines and sepulchres, the building of temples over burying places, and the erroneous beliefs in holy ground and relics.

Modern scholarship has shown Mede to be remarkably perceptive in his historical and anthropological assertions, and his contemporaries would have understood the applicability of his theory to ancient English traditions. Henriette s'Jacob attributes the development of the sepuchral effigy to a belief in "the desire of the soul to be re-incarnated into its former body. In this case the effigy is no longer a symbol, but intended as a vehicle for the soul to inhabit."[31] The pillars and columns mentioned by Mede and Perkins may be menhirs, which still dot English, Welsh, and Irish holy ground, and s'Jacob identifies the totemic powers associated with such monuments even in Puritan times. She writes, "Standing upright symbolizes the human posture. The menhir, the erect stone, is the lapidary double of the body and its permanent substitute. It was thought to contain the soul of the deceased, consequently endowed with magic qualities. Moreover, menhirs must be considered as abbreviated portraits of the dead."[32] The christianizing of these Celtic menhirs by early English missionaries has been described by Frederick Burgess.[33] Missionaries set up their staffs, wooden crosses, when preaching, and when the missionary died, his grave was marked by his cross and later by a stone pillar. The ground became holy ground, and persons converted by the missionary would be buried with him until a church was built on the site. Puritans knew these facts, and their rejection of holy ground extended to the pillars, images, and effigies associated with sepulchral monuments in both the church and the graveyard.

By the 1640s Puritans had nearly 100 years of iconoclasm behind them, and 100 years of preaching against Catholic ritual and art. While the rites and churches were purged of objectionable items, images had yet to be developed which expressed Puritan innovations in eschatology. The medieval repertory of tomb ornamentation in the *memento mori* and *danse macabre* traditions, such as skeletons, death's heads, and hourglasses, were revived in the late sixteenth century. Graves without the church, if marked at all, were often simply covered with stones, table tombs without decoration, or wooden and stone bedstead-like rails carved with epitaphs and emblems of mortality.[34] Before commemorative effigies or images describing the condition of the deceased's soul could appear in New England, safeguards would have to be developed to prevent them from becoming idols. Puritans would have to define precisely how such images were to be seen and used, so that the viewer would be sure to see the spiritual truth behind the image, the biblical text behind the emblem, and the power of grace which made the saint so commemorated fit for resurrection. Only then would effigies escape the iconoclast's hammer. Moreover, effigies could only develop in connection with a positive aesthetic theory which transcended what Perry Miller saw as the nonaesthetic of the Puritan Plain Style.[35]

Puritan advocates of the return of commemorative images framed their arguments carefully to avoid any taint of idolatry, while writers defending existing sepulchral art stressed its necessity as a visible reminder of class distinctions. One strategy was simply to assert the supremacy of the word and beg the question of the communicative value of images altogether. For Edmund Gurnay,

> There are other courses more apt to continue the remembrance of the dead, then those kind of Monuments; namely, Inscriptions & Epitaphs: For by such kind of expressions, the truest, and noblest, and most inward parts of the dead are apt to be far more lively and properly set forth; the tools of Carvers and Pensils of Painters being able to describe only their outsides, and so much of them as Fools and unworthy persons (yea, Stones or lumps of clay) may excell or resemble them in: whereas the pens of the Muses are able to flourish out their most hidden excellencies, and imprint their vertues. . . .[36]

But John Weever, a noted antiquarian who bewailed the loss of one thousand years of English sepulchral art, will not accept the dismissal of the visual arts. His *Ancient Fvneral Monvments* is clearly keyed to a Puritan, iconoclastic audience.[37] Before he will speak of the artistic and historical value of tombs, Weever defends their utility in preserving the body from violation and the living from disease. Next, he wholeheartedly agrees that burial should occur outside the city walls, on civil ground, thus circumventing objections to holy ground. He flavors his arguments with references to the practices of primitive Christians and Jews, culminating in an eschatological vision sure to appeal to embattled Puritans:

> Yet the true Christian, and such as by their liuely faith were adopted the children of God, had a further mysterie in this manner of their interments; for by the carriage and buriall of their dead corps without citie walls, they did publickly confirme, and witnesse, that the parties deceased were gone out of this world, to bee made free denizons of another citie, namely, Heauen, there to remaine with the blessed Saints in eternall happinesse.[38]

For Weever, the epitaph is the most important feature of the sepulchre, "a great motiue to bring us to repentance."[39] The cemetery itself can serve a didactic function as an emblem of the relationship of dead and living, the earthly city and the heavenly city. Though Puritan graves must not be in the church and the idea of holy ground is rejected, the placement of the graveyard reinforces the belief that death is the door between the church militant and the church triumphant.

The monument is defended as an emblem, and Weever here reveals Puritan attitudes towards both art and memorials:

> Funerall monuments then of costly workmanship, with curious engrauen Epitaphs, were called Sepulchra, id est, semipulchra, halfe faire and beautifull; the externall part or superficies thereof being gloriously beautified and adorned; and having nothing within, but dreadfull darkness, loathsome stinke, and rottenesse of bones, as it is in the Gospell, *Mat*. 23. And they are sometimes called memories, *a memoria vel a moriendo*, in that by them we are put in minde, and warned to consider our fragile condition; for they are externall helpes to excite, and stirre vp our inward thoughts, *habere memoriam mortis semper prae oculis*: to haue the remembrance of death enter before our eyes, and that our brethren defunct, may not be out of mind out of sight.[40]

The *memento mori* theme is endemic to the Puritan mind, yet its function is complex in Puritan aesthetics.[41] We must recall the context of Weever's argument, the fit memorializing of the dead while avoiding, on the one hand, the "pagan" tradition of extolling the virtuous man with the implication that immortality is achieved through fame rather than grace, and, on the other hand, the veneration of saints. Weever does invoke memory, but it is less the memory of the deceased than a reminder of one's own death to come. The process of elegizing is internalized, as the Puritan laments not just the death of an individual, but the death of that person within the living community. The deceased loses his or her individuality and becomes a personification of Death itself. Ezekiel Hopkins warns against the double death that occurs whenever one neglects an opportunity to apply death to one's own condition:

> 'Twill be no great mistake to account every Funeral we attend on, to be our own. Let us imagine our selves nailed up in the Coffin, laid in the Grave, covered over with Earth, and putrifying to wormes and dirt: this is only but a few dayes to anticipate what shall be. Not a Grave opens its mouth, but it plainly speaks thus much, that we are mortal and perishing; not a rotten bone, nor dead scull is scatered about it, but tells us we must shortly take up our abode with them in the same darknesse, and corruption. And if upon every such sad occasion we make not particular application of it to our selves, we not onely lose our friends lives but their very deaths too; yet herein are we generally faulty: When God snatcheth them from us, we usually reflect more upon the losse, than the example; and thereby as He deprives us of the comfort we had in their lives, so we deprive our selves of the instruction and benefit we might have by their deaths.[42]

For the Puritan, the death of an individual must be read as a means of receiving faith, the loss internalized, the virtues imitated, and finally the death placed in the context of the struggle of Death and eternal life in Christ. Aesthetically, meditation on death as a means of seeking faith has dramatic effects. The stasis, the finality, the stinking bones beneath the lively decoration that is life are transformed by a faith that can dramatize the life-giving grace behind the death's head. Perkins wrote:

> We must not iudge of our graues, as they appeare to the bodily eie, but we must looke vpon them by the eie of faith, & consider them as they are altered and chaunged by the death and buriall of Christ, who hauing vanquished death vpon the crosse, pursued him afterward to his oune denne, and foyled him there, and depriued him of this power. And by this meanes Christ in his oune death hath buried our death, and by the vertue of his buriall, as sweete incense hath sweetened and perfumed our graues, and made them of stinking and loathsome cabbins, to become princely palaces.[43]

Perkins sees through the tomb to the struggle of Christ against a personified Death re-enacted in the mind's eye of faith. From dramatic narrative, Perkins moves rapidly through a series of paradoxes, as Christ's death buries Death, the stink of death becomes sweet, and the cabin becomes a palace. This is a crucial transformation effected through the eyes of faith, when the Christian can rhetorically transform death into life by reliving biblical events.

The use of the imagination to effect similar transformations is found in a striking form in Puritan death-bed rituals. Nancy Lee Beaty has shown that Protestant *ars moriendi* placed great pressure on the *moriens* to act as the leading player in the drama of death.[44] What is remarkable about Protestant *ars moriendi* is the transference of Catholic prayers for the dead from the funeral rite to the death-bed scene. The dying person is coached to enact in his or her imagination those scenes which Catholics presented in funeral rituals and prayers. As the Catholic Mass for the Dead includes prayers that the deceased's soul might be accompanied by angels, might enter heaven, might see God, Thomas Becon prompts the dying person to imagine these events:

> Now God hath taken away the sight of your corporal eies, behold the Lord your God with the eies of your faith: doubt you not, but that shortly you shal see the glorious maiesty of god with the eyes of your soule, even as he is, face to face: which shall be unto you such ioy and so great comfort, that no tongue is able to expresse, nor heart able to thinke it.[45]

While denying prayers and masses Catholics direct to a soul in purgatory, Puritans expect the dying person to undergo a personal ritual in imagining the activities of heaven to be enjoyed by the soul:

> Now shall you see the glorious maiesty of God, face to face. Now shall you behold and perfectly know all the godly that have beene from the beginning of the World,

and be merry to reioyce with them. Now shal you see our Saviour and elder brother Christ as he is: Now shall you be cloathed with the white garments of immortality: Now shall you have a crowne of gold set upon your head. Now shall you eate of the Tree of Life, which is in the midst of the paradise of God, and drinke of the fountaine of living water. Now shall you be a pillar in the Temple of your God, and sit with him on his seat, and these your ioyes shall be everlasting, and never have end. Unto these ioyes shall you straight waies goe; and for evermore enioy them.[46]

If the dying person could be instructed to use the imagination to visualize eschatological scenes through a pastiche of biblical metaphors, why could not the living use such images to describe the experiences of the dead? In fact, Puritans did develop a variety of strategies for visualizing the experience of the deceased's soul from death to the Resurrection.

Barbara Lewalski, in her *Donne's Anniversaries and the Poetry of Praise*, offers several interesting avenues of approach to Puritan images of the soul.[47] The preacher of a funeral sermon and the carver of a gravestone faced a similar problem—how to describe the state of the soul separated from the body. In noting the compatibility of Protestant didacticism with certain features of the Fathers' funeral orations, Lewalski reveals the theological justifications for descriptions of the departed soul in bliss:

The Protestant denial of purgatory meant that the departed soul could be envisaged as enjoying heavenly glory at once, and the Protestant disavowal of the idea of personal merit meant that any praise of the deceased's good life redounded not to that individual but to God working in him. Moreover, the Protestant insistence upon the priesthood of believers made for an equalization of spiritual categories such as that all the elect (and not only designated saints or those exercising religious vocations) were understood to be called to and capable of the highest spiritual attainments. Given these premises, the charitable understanding must have it that the subject of any funeral sermon—however lowly or ordinary his life—was at the very time he lay in state a glorious saint of God.[48]

New England Puritans would have agreed with the rejection of purgatory and the judgment of charity outlined here. When they turned to make images of the state after death, however, they had two additional concerns which reached beyond the normal descriptions of the soul in its separate, glorious state. As we shall see below, Puritans in New England believed the glory achieved by the soul at death was an incomplete, intermediate glory that was anticipatory of full glory at the Resurrection. Though the soul was restored to the image of God at the death of a saint, its full glory would be realized only when it was joined to a resurrected body glorified in the likeness of Christ's body. Therefore New England descriptions of the soul in words and on stone are complicated by this two-stage process of glorification.

The images of the soul carved on gravestones often refer to both the present condition of the soul and the expected glory of the saint when soul and body are reunited. Second, Puritans were deeply concerned about the manner in which language and images describing the soul and the Resurrection World were to be apprehended and interpreted. Certainly at the Resurrection a real Resurrection body would be sensed with physical, though glorified senses, so sensual images and language were fit means to communicate something of the experience of the saints at that time. But how could such sensual terms be used to describe something that was by its very nature a spiritual mystery? Even if the soul had some thin envelope of perceptible substance, such as the Greek *eidolon*, how could carnal man perceive and describe such a substance? If Satan could become an angel of light, how was one to know whether the soul effigy carved in stone was not just an image invented in the mind of the carver by Satan to delude believers? These questions troubled Puritans, and it is a characteristic of their eschatological writings that the means of perceiving images of eschatological events and the meaning of the images themselves are discussed in the same breath. Since, under the doctrine of the means, descriptions of spiritual entities must be fitted to the capabilities of human senses, Puritan epistemology affects the range and type of symbols that are employed to depict eschatological events. Thus, before we can examine particular modes of visualizing the deceased, we must understand the development of a Puritan way of seeing.

The Eye of Faith

Throughout the seventeenth century, Puritans turned to the Bible to find guidance from God as to how Christians are to perceive spiritual beings and to understand spiritual truth. The Bible seemed to offer a variety of ways of seeing spiritual truths in the figurative language of Scripture as well as in the things of the world. God seemed to promise that grace would aid faithful Christians in seeing a restored soul in the image of God, and a restored world within the corruption of the fallen world. Puritans came to believe that God invites humans, in such texts as Hebrews 11 and 1 Corinthians 15, to imagine the world as God sees it. Where humans see failure and the effects of sin, God, through the imputation of Christ's holiness to the saints, sees His elect as justified saints beautifully reflecting His image. As Richard Sibbes writes, "Christians should have a double eye, one to set and fixe upon that which is ill in them, to humble them, and another upon that which is supernaturally gracious in them, to incourage themselves, they should looke upon themselves as Christ lookes upon them, and judge of themselves as he judgeth of them, by the better part."[49]

The eschatological force of Puritan theorizing on the power of such "spiritual eyes" derives from the fact that God's vision is prophetic. Since He sees from a position outside of time, from a perspective which is unaffected by the illusory nature of earthly experience, the saint who would see with God's eyes must use his imagination in a prophetic mode. Man would need eyes of faith even to approximate such a godly vision, and it was difficult to know just how these eyes functioned. Fortunately, the Bible provided guidance in this matter, especially through the Holy Spirit's habitual use of typology. In its simplest form, typology was the shadowing forth in "typical" people, places, objects, or events in the Old Testament "antitypical" truths revealed in the New Testament in Christ's life. One of the most significant developments of Puritan typology was the theory that some types were not fulfilled in Christ alone. Some types, called "perpetual" in a treatise by Samuel Mather, had moral efficacy relevant to all Christians.[50] Moreover, certain types such as the crossing of the River Jordan into the promised land and the building of Solomon's temple had fulfillment in such eschatological events as the entrance into heaven and the building of the New Jerusalem temple of the Millennium. The believer was instructed to see a person, place, or thing in the Old Testament in many different ways—as an actual historical presence, as a type or shadow of truths to be revealed in Christ, as correlative types providing guidance to Christians in all times, and finally as symbols of mysteries to be opened at the end of time.[51] From the perspective of a God who exists outside human time, all these images and states coexist, and at the end of time in the Resurrection World, believers would also be able to see how all types and all history worked to a single purpose. Puritans accepted the Resurrection world as the reality towards which the illusory images of this world pointed, and they tended to read the descriptions of the Resurrection world contained in the Book of Revelation as an allegorical and prophetic gloss of history. Revelation stands as the eye atop the pyramid of prophecy, and all historical events both support and are illumined by it. The aesthetics of Puritan eschatology and funerary art are predicated on a right viewing of biblical types and figures, for it was assumed the saint would "see" figurative language and art as shadows of future realities to be seen with "bodilie eyes."

As much as sin had shattered man's ability to apprehend divine truths, God held forth the promise that believers would receive eyes of faith which could transform decay, adversity, and death itself in a vision of hopefulness and purpose. Rhapsodizing on Christ as seen in the allegory of the bridegroom's invitation to his spouse to see him in the Song of Solomon, William Guild writes,

> A sight indeed needing a sharp-sighted eye to behold, and which is onely the eye of faith, whereby the wise men that came from the east saw him a king, though a new born infant, swaddled in clouts, and lying in a crib; and the theef on the crosse in like manner, though crowned with thorns, and hanging on a tree: by this eye likewise, the patriarks saw him in the Promises before the law; and all true beleeving Christians in his word, Sacraments, and gracious presence in his Chruch and their own hearts, under the Gospell. And therefore because the blind naturalist or worldling sees not these things, the daughters of *Sion* who have received the eye-salve of the spirit to discern spiritual things are like *Ezekiels* wheels, full of eyes, *Ezek.* 1. 18. They are called upon only to behold this spirituall sight, and to these only the promise is made, for Blessed are the pure in heart (sayes our saviour) for they shall see God.[52]

Through faith, even saints living under the law in the Old Testament could know, through shadowy types, Christ and salvation, and these blessings were anticipated through ceremonies, in places, and by people ordained as such types. These beliefs are so central to writers of the mid and late seventeenth century in England and New England that we must examine carefully the development of the notion of eyes of faith. William Perkins' commentary on the eleventh chapter of Hebrews, with its message of the ability of faith to provide sight, contains the earliest full-blown discussion of such sight as a determining factor in the knowledge of heaven, and his writings point to the aesthetic dimensions of Puritan epistemology.[53] In Hebrews 11:1, Paul had defined faith as "the substance of things hoped for, the evidence of things not seen," and Perkins agrees, making the faithful "seeing" of things not seen a crucial sign of the sanctified life. Perkins follows Calvin in noting that this vision must be implanted by Christ in the soul, but he goes beyond Calvin in emphasizing the powers the believer has to apprehend things that have as yet no substance in the physical sense of the term.[54] Faith has the power

> to take that thing in it selfe inuisible, and neuer yet seene, and so liuely to represent it to the heart of the beleeuer, and to the eye of his mind, as that after a sort hee presently seeth and inioyeth that inuisible thing. . . . [I]nuisible to the eyes of the bodie, it makes visible to the eye of the soule; the sight of which eye is both giuen and continued, and daily sharpened by *sauing faith*.[55]

Perkins draws some interesting conclusions from this principle. The saints of the Old Testament were thereby "truely Partakers of the bodie and blood of Christ," and they could hope for justification, sanctification, perfection of sanctification after death, resurrection and glorification even before these things had been revealed to man by Christ.[56] The intensity of Perkins' commitment to the eschatological implications of spiritual eyes is revealed in the very title of his treatise, *A Clovd of Faithfvll Witnesses, Leading to the Heavenly Canaan*. The faithful, under any affliction, darkness, or persecution, could identify their trials with those of Old Testament saints—a cloud of witnesses which would surely lead the hearts of believers to the heavenly Canaan. The community of Israel exists "substantially" in the imaginations of the saints, and the saints can live there by faith, despite the fact that Perkins' England in 1622 was anything but a promised land.

Perkins hesitantly explores the aesthetic power of his epistemology as he describes the sensuous attractions of heavenly visions which encourage the despairing saint. Significantly, he applauds the *artistry* of heaven:

> Here then we learne, that the third Heauen is like a piece of worke, wherein an excellent workeman hath spent his art, and shewed his skill; that is, that the highest heauen is a most glorious place, and surpaseth all other creatures of God in glorie and excellencie, so farre as therein shineth the glorie, skill, and wisdome of the Creator, more then in any other creature. . . . And this was figured in the *Temple* of Ierusalem, which was the mirrour and beautie of the world; for the building whereof, God hath both chose the skilfullest men, and indeed them also with extraordinarie gifts: namely *Bezaleel and Aholiab*.[57]

In encouraging saints to take comfort in the beauties of heaven, Perkins sidesteps the epistemological quagmire of the distinction between carnal imagination and truly spiritual sight. We have an exaltation of God's artistry and a reverence for the earthly artists who created the Temple, but we do not have a discussion of just how spiritual senses relate to man's human senses. Fortunately for Perkins, he wrote before Lockean epistemology would undermine the notion that any sense, even a spiritual eye of faith, can perceive something without substance. This would be a problem for such later writers as John Owen and Jonathan Edwards to tackle. Perkins also leaves unanswered several other questions with which the iconographer must reckon. Would the heavenly city in fact be visible at some future time, thus proving the literal validity of typical and figural descriptions? Would all need of imaginary or sensual apprehension of divine things cease with direct communication with the Godhead in heaven? Or would a physical *and* a spiritual heaven be experienced at the heights of sensual and intellectual joy?

After William Perkins, Richard Sibbes provides one of the earliest, and most comprehensive, discussions of man's capacity to enjoy spiritual beauty.[58] Sibbes recognized the need for a theoretical framework to support the connection of divine and earthly things, and he instinctively turned to the Puritan doctrine of the means. Essentially, Sibbes holds that all beings can be distinguished by the element in which they exist, and each being is fitted with the capacity to apprehend the nature of its element. In His wisdom, God fits the means of perception to the nature of things to be perceived. He also adapts spiritual truths to human understanding by clothing them in metaphors drawn from earthly experience. Man's element is distinguished by its inclusion of both earthly and divine things:

> Now when wee speake of the delights, and dainties, and excellencies of Gods house, wee speake to those that we wish, and wee hope haue spiritual sences answerable to these things. Every creature delights in its proper element: these things are the element of a Christian. Beetles delight in dirte, and swine in myre, the fish, in the sea, man hath his element here, and spirituall things are the element of a christian so farre as he is a christian, and that is his *ubi* the place that he delights in.[59]

The first duty of the Christian is to seek his element through spiritual senses. Flesh and spirit, earth and heaven, though separated by sin, are on a continuous hieratic scale within each individual and throughout the universe. In viewing the earthly and the sinful, man should see the possibilities of heaven and grace. Christian decorum calls for the highest sense to apprehend the highest beauty; thus sight seeks the element of light. Moreover, "Of sight comes love," so the Christian should imitate David who "had spiritual eyes, and hee desired to feed his spiritual eie sight with the best object that could be, (for therin is the happiness of man,) wherein stands a mans happiness? When ther is a concurrence of the most excellent obiect, with the most excellent power, and facultie of the soule, with delight and content in it."[60]

Of all Sibbes' writings on man's spiritual capacities, *A Glance of Heaven* provides the most detailed articulation of his sensational theories. He begins with a fairly scientific presentation of his epistemology, asserting that whatever enters the heart must come through the senses. Sibbes meets the objection that sinful physical senses cannot apprehend spiritual things by positing the existence of *new* senses in the converted saint. "If the naturall eye, and eare, and heart can never see nor heare, nor conceive the things of God, must there not be a supernaturall eare, and eye, and heart put into the soule? must not the heart and all be new molded againe?"[61] With these supernatural senses, the believer knows heaven "*by way of taste*: for the things of the life to come, there are few of them, but Gods children have some experimentall taste of them in this world: God reserves not all for the life to come, but he gives a grape of *Canaan* in this wilderness."[62]

There are three degrees of revelation, and the Christian acquires new senses at each stage. First, truths are revealed by God in the Word, by writing or by speech. Then there is a second revelation when the Spirit of God takes the veil off the soul and instills spiritual senses in the reader or hearer so that the truth of the Word can be known. Third, there is a higher discovery in heaven when eye, ear, and heart will know of mysteries not revealed on earth. Recalling Sibbes' insistence on the congruity of object and agent of perception, we can trace interesting stages in the parallel revelation of heavenly beauty and the saint's growing powers of perception. First, Sibbes cautions man to redefine beauty and eminence as the expression of inner, heavenly qualities and not as the result of external and sensory appeal, and here he anticipates Jonathan Edwards' distinction of primary and secondary beauty. "[T]he true reality of things, are in the things of another world, for eternity," he writes, "So if we talke of beauty, it is the Image of God that sets a beauty on the soule, that makes a man lovely in the eye of God. True beauty is to be like God."[63] Heavenly meditation encourages heavenly behaviour on earth, and this clothes man with the beauties of sanctification. Second, earthly beauty, if so inspired, contributes directly to heavenly beauty, for "heaven and earth differ but in degrees: therefore what is there in perfection, must be begun here."[64] Likewise, the glory of the church on earth leads to a beautiful church in heaven, for "*Ierusalem*, which is from above, must lead us to *Ierusalem* which is above."[65] Third, and most importantly for this study, Sibbes calls the desire for heaven a true sign of grace: "it is the disposition of a gracious heart, to desire the glorious comming of Christ Iesus."[66]

When Sibbes turns to discuss biblical histories and prophecies, he premises his understanding of God's progressive revelation of His plan for mankind on the progessive awakening of man's desire to participate in this plan. At each stage of history, from the deliverance of the Jews from Egypt, to the birth of Christ and the conversion of the Gentiles, to the Second Coming of Christ, mankind finds a concomitant desire that these events occur. Sibbes comes close to establishing a cause and effect relationship between man's desires and God's actions, as his evangelism brings him to the edge of Arminianism. Sibbes all but implies that human desires are necessary determinants of the time and place of the events which usher in the Millennium. In fact, the desires of the saints for the Chiliad and the glory of Christ at His Second Coming are intimately linked. "In regard of *Christ* himselfe," Sibbes writes, "Christ is in some sort imperfect till the latter day, till his second coming: for the mysticall body of Christ is his fulnesse; Christ is our fulnesse, and wee are his fulnesse; now Christs fulnesse is made up, when all the members of his mystical body are gathered and united together: the head and the members make but one naturall body; so Christ and the Church but one mysticall.''[67]

Sibbes is significant for his emphasis on the beauty of holiness and his description of the supernatural senses that are provided to permit perception of this beauty. What Sibbes does not do, however, is discuss a specific decorum for artistic realization and aesthetic appreciation of heavenly beauties seen with the new senses. Perhaps Sibbes' own nature, which tended toward an otherworldly spirituality, accounts for his hesitancy to describe sensuous means for realizing heaven and the image of God in meditation. It is also possible that the political climate of the 1630s demanded an otherworldly focus for Puritan expectations. Nevertheless, Sibbes defined man's capacity for spiritual perception, thereby providing subsequent writers with a foundation for more particular apprehension of divine things.

As Louis Martz has argued, Richard Baxter makes a significant contribution to the Puritan tradition of meditation by including the senses as a means of working up one's religious affections.[68] In the context of this study, Baxter's work is important for two reasons. First, he goes beyond Sibbes by locating the source of man's new senses in the Incarnation and Crucifixion of Christ. Baxter believed that Christ had authorized the visualization of heavenly things by clothing His divine nature in human flesh; His death and ascension to heaven not only opened heaven for the souls of believers, it also opened heaven as a subject of meditation. The Christian need not fear he will pollute heavenly things with "unclean lips," for

> the Lord is not now so terrible and inaccessible, not the Passage of Paradise so blocked up, as when the Law and curse reigned. . . . Wherefore finding, Beloved Christians, That the New and Living way is consecrated for us, through the veil, the flesh of Christ, by which we may with boldness enter into the Holiest, by the blood of Jesus; I shall draw near with fullest Assurance: And finding the flaming Sword removed, shall look again into the Paradise of our God: and because I know that this is no forbidden Fruit; and withal that it is good for food, and pleasant to the Spiritual Eyes, and a tree to be desired to make one truly wise and happy; I shall take (through the assistance of the Spirit) and eat thereof my self, and give to you (according to my power) that you may eat.[69]

Christ brought together heaven and earth for all believers, and Baxter encourages the Christian, like the High Priest, to see through the veil of Christ's flesh into the Holy of Holies, heaven. Baxter's work is also important because of its elevation of the Christian artist. Baxter feels the seer is also a sayer who should communicate the beauties of his vision. The imagery here is sacramental in the fullest sense. Not only has Christ's sacrifice worked salvation, it has also provided the means by which the

Christian who has partaken of the Sacrament may in turn offer his vision to others to take and eat.

The Saints Everlasting Rest does not contain an extended logical explanation of just how spiritual affections relate to human senses, but Baxter points to the Incarnation as a precedent for such a relationship. Moreover, incarnationalism is held up as a model for imaginative and artistic activity. Baxter's emphasis on Christ's human nature is contemporary with what E. Brooks Holifield has called a "revival of sacramental piety" in Puritanism, and both developments involve the use of the senses.[70] From the time of Baxter on, Puritan writers could turn to Christ's human nature for both a theological and an epistemological rationale for the compatability of man's spiritual and physical eyes, reaffirming the christological focus of Puritan eschatology and aesthetics.

From Spiritual Eyes to "Bodilie Eyes"

John Owen's *Meditations and Discourses Concerning the Glory of Christ* contains the most complete discussion of spiritual and "bodilie" eyes. He neatly avoids the epistemological debate over the knowledge of heavenly things by defining the *human, bodily* form of Christ as the conduit for man's apprehension of heavenly glory. He writes:

> That which at present I design to Demonstrate is, That the *Beholding of the Glory of Christ, is one of the greatest Priviledges and Advancements that Believers are capable of in this World, or that which is to come*. It is that whereby they are first gradually conformed unto it, and then fixed in the Eternal enjoyment of it. For here in this life, *beholding his Glory, they are changed or transformed into the likeness of it*, 2 Cor. 3:18, and hereafter, they shall be *for ever like unto him*, because *they shall see him as he is*, 1 John 3:1, 2. Hereon do our present Comforts, and future Blessedness depend. . . . THERE are therefore, two ways or degrees of *beholding the Glory of Christ*, which are constantly distinguished in the Scripture. The one is by *Faith* in this World, which is the Evidence of things not seen. The other is by *Sight*, or immediate vision in Eternity, 2 *Cor.* 5:7. . . . And it is the Lord Christ and his Glory, which are immediate objects both of this *Faith* and *Sight*.[71]

Owen is careful to distinguish spiritual vision from mere enthusiasm. Only a disturbed soul imagines heaven to be something different from what believers can foretaste, sense, and experience of heaven in biblically ordained images. Even in heaven there is no unmediated experience of God, for "All *Communications* from the Divine Being and infinite fulness in Heaven unto glorified Saints, are in, and through Christ Jesus."[72] Owen admits that the glory of Christ is not principally located in His human nature, but in the divine person which shines in the body. Nevertheless, glorified saints cannot have an intellectual view of Christ's divine person without physical senses trained on Christ's physical form. He writes,

> THERE will be use herein, of our bodily *eyes*, as shall be declared. For as *Job* says, *in our Flesh shall we see our Redeemer*, and our eyes shall behold him, Chap. 19:25, 26, 27. That our corporeal sence shall not be restored unto us, and that glorified above what we can conceive, but for this great use of the eternal beholding of Christ and his Glory. Unto whom is it not a matter of rejoycing, that with the *same eyes* wherewith they see the tokens and signs of him in the Sacrament of the Supper, they shall behold himself immediately, in his own person.[73]

Much of Owen's treatise delineates the distinctions between and similarities of the eye of faith and "bodilie eyes." The vision of Christ in heaven differs both in the object seen and in the visive power—the imperfection of both object (the incomplete descriptions of Christ in biblical language) and power (man's senses) in this world will be replaced by the real, substantial, glorious person of Christ as beheld by glorified eyes. The significance of Owen's treatise lies in its form of Christian humanism, for the highest communion possible with God is achieved with the aid of human senses. Moreover, unlike Sibbes, Perkins, and other proponents of man's supernatural senses, Owen believes that the supernatural senses work through rather than bypass human senses. A divine and supernatural light enters the saint and thereby distinguishes him from the unconverted sinner:

> God gives a superior, a supernatural Light, the Light of Faith and Grace, unto them whom he effectually calls unto the knowledge of himself by Jesus Christ. . . . Howbeit this new Light doth not abolish, blot out, or render useless the other Light of Nature, as the Sun when it riseth extinguisheth the Light of the Stars: But it directs it, and rectifies it, as unto its principle, object and end. Yet it is in its self, a Light quite of another Nature. But he who hath only the former Light, can understand nothing of it, because he hath no Taste or Experience of its Power and Operations. He may talk of it, and make Enquiries about it, but he knows it not.[74]

This light does more than reveal holy truth; the believer is attracted by the beauty of Christ in such things as the Word and the sacraments. Since the believer's appreciation of the beauty of holiness culminates in the person of Christ, there is an eschatological energy to Owen's aesthetics. The saint desires and anticipates the Chiliad as the climax of aesthetic as well as religious experience.

The saints of the Old Testament are especially fit models for Christian imitation in training spiritual eyes to anticipate "bodilie" sight, not only because they anticipated salvation through Christ in types and shadows, but because "*they* also *saw his Glory* through the obscurity of its Revelation."[75] The saints of the Old Testament used eyes of faith until Christ's first bodily appearance, as saints now must see by faith until His second. Therefore Owen directs us to texts of the Old Testament as well as of the New in which Christ's Incarnation and the beauties of his second coming are typed and prophesied. In particular, there are seven categories of texts by which we can meditate on Christ's glorious exaltation of human nature: Old Testament ceremonies, the whole book of the Song of Solomon ("A few days, a few hours spent in the frame characterised in it, is a Blessedness excelling all the treasure of the Earth"), Christ's personal appearances as an angel in the Old Testament, prophetic visions, the Gospels, the promises of Christ's coming in the Old Testament, and finally, various other metaphorical expressions of divine beauty which are specifically fit to our senses by God.[76]

While Puritans were prohibited from making physical images of Christ, they certainly were encouraged to meditate on mental pictures drawn from biblical language. At first glance, it is surprising that Puritans then used these mental pictures to fashion images of saints drawn from texts which seem to describe Christ. As we shall see below, Owen's list includes nearly all the forms and subject matter Puritan stonecarving takes. On closer examination, however, we find that Puritan strategies for visualizing restored souls and resurrected saints depend on theological assumptions about the union of divine and human nature in Christ which made for a restoration of fallen man in Christ's image. While no preacher would dare debase the deity by limiting Him to an anthropomorphic being, God Himself did create man in His likeness, and the Incarnation affirmed the compatibility of human and divine nature. Thus in some fashion man was "like" God, and it was up to the Puritan preacher and carver to determine just how to depict this likeness in words and stone.

2

Seeing is Believing: Puritan Strategies for Visualizing Divine Things

> Our flesh shall slumber in the ground,
> 'Til the last Trumpets' joyfull sound:
> Then burst the chains with sweet surprize
> And in our Saviour's image rise.
>
> —Betty Lane and Children stone, 1791

Seventeenth-century English writers recognized the radicalism of New Englanders. Their involvement in the millenarian movements of the 1650s culminated in the disastrous Fifth Monarchist uprising.[1] They also appeared on the left wing of reactions to Anglo-Catholic ritual and idolatry. While some Puritans argued to retain portions of Catholic liturgy, John Allin and Thomas Shepard called the whole Mass book idolatrous.[2] Indeed, when an anonymous author lamented the recent destruction of Cheapside Cross in 1641, the Cross testifies:

> I the foresaid Iasper Cross was assaulted and battered in the Kings high way, by many violent and insolent minded people, or rather ill-affected Brethren; and whether they were in their heighth of zeale, or else overcome with passion, or new wine lately come from *New-England*, I cannot be yet resolved. . . .[3]

Iconoclasm persisted in New England itself, as John Endecott cut the cross from the flag and William Bradford relished the thought of rotting "marble monuments."[4] Late into the eighteenth century in New England some gravestones have images chipped away (fig. 1). We can be certain that in this environment gravestone imagery would not be accepted unless it was free from any taint of idolatry and conformed with the eschatological and aesthetic theories of the Puritan left.

There are few records of Puritan attitudes towards grave markers in New England before the appearance of large numbers of stone markers in the 1670s. Funerals were generally simple, predominantly secular affairs, with ministerial participation often limited to the funeral sermon preached the Sunday after the interment. Puritans ensured no superstitions would center about holy ground by separating the meeting house and the graveyard, placing the latter under the control of civil authorities.[5] The gravestone itself fell somewhere between civil and religious use; despite the Tashjians and Robert Daly's contentions that gravestones were civil artifacts and thus escaped religious sanctions against images, the persistent defacing of effigies on stones indicates that some New Englanders were not so sure of the separation of civil and religious ceremonies.[6] Some wooden markers were undoubtedly used, and they may have been ornamented with *memento mori* images like those found in the borders of printed elegies and funeral sermons.

Nevertheless, the wholesale transition to stone markers during the 1670s seems to indicate changing cultural practices which may reflect contemporary events and shifting aesthetic theories. One can suggest that the great mortalities of King Philip's War and childhood disease, the loss of most of the first generation by 1670, uncertainty about the status of the colonies after the Restoration all contributed to a desire for more permanent commemoration of the dead. Whatever the social and psychological inspiration for New England stonecarving, the repertory of symbols developed reflects the prophetic theory of artistic expression discussed above. Whenever stone markers appear, in Boston, Essex County, Plymouth Colony or the Connecticut River Valley, the stone design recapitulates an evolutionary process from commemoration to prophecy.

This evolution can be seen in complete form in the Rumford, Rhode Island, cemetery on stones dating from the 1660s to the 1720s. The earliest stones simply commemorate the deceased by marking the place of the body, as one stone is marked simply "PC 1663." The desire to mark the particular location of the body is in keeping with literalist interpretations of the resurrection of the body. The second stage of gravestone development is marked by the inclusion of a text, most often drawn from the Bible, and usually with a prophetic message anticipating the Resurrection or the Millennium. One side of the IP stone of 1714 is carved with the initials of the deceased and his/her death date, but the other side proclaims "FOR OF SUCH IS THE KINGDOM OF GOD" (fig. 2). The final stage of early tombstone design comes with the inclusion of some design element, which either complements or supplants the text. When designs are first introduced, be they the fans of Massachusetts Bay, the rosettes of the Connecticut River Valley, or the death's head and spirit faces of Essex and Plymouth Counties, the overall structure of the stone design changes to reflect the importance of the prophetic design in relation to the commemorative epitaph. In Rumford, one carver places a heart-shaped winged death's head below the text, as if he is confused as to whether epitaph or image should dominate the viewer's attention (fig. 3). Finally, however, on Rumford stones, spirit faces and death's heads fill the tympani of the gravestones, as the prophetic message contained in New England stone design lords over the commemorative, verbal portion of the stone. New Englanders would come to understand that the final meaning of the gravestone design was that which could be perceived with their spiritual eyes in anticipation of views with "bodilie eyes" at the Resurrection. And by the time carving flowers in the 1690s, there are several clusters of images drawn from the Bible which could be easily presented on stones to help viewers visualize the last things.

Strategies of Visualization

The Image of God

The New Testament states repeatedly that people will be restored to the image of God in which they were created, and several texts promise that the Resurrection body would be made "like" Christ's body (2 Cor. 3:18; Phil. 3:21). In this life the image may be restored by God's gracious imputation of righteousness to the soul, and in the next life by the glorification of soul *and* resurrected body. The texts themselves, however, are the source of confusion over just what the image or likeness of God is and whether this image resides in the soul, in the faculties of the soul, or indeed in the whole person body and soul.

From the time of the Church Fathers, debate flourished on these questions, and Christian traditions of funerary art were profoundly affected depending on which camp was in the ascendancy.[7] Irenaeus and Tertullian held that Christ's human form was an image of God held up for all mankind to imitate. For their followers, the Incarnation justified attributing the image of God to both body and soul. St. Irenaeus, commenting on Genesis 1:26, could write, "In previous times [before the coming of Christ] man . . . was said to have been made according to the image of God, but he was not shown as such. For the Word according to Whose image man was made was still invisible. . . . But when the Word of God was made flesh . . . , He truly showed the image by becoming what His image was."[8] According to Tertullian, the image of God in Christ was the archetype for the creation of man, as "the divine image-likeness then received by Adam was a likeness to the future Christ Incarnate."[9] As Gerhart Ladner notes of this tradition, "incarnational thinking no doubt underlies the practice of a specifically Christian art since its beginnings in the late third century," since artists could present physical forms presumably capable of transmitting something of the glory of the image of God in the soul.[10] Tomb sculpture created in this "incarnational" tradition is generally realistic, emphasizing the resurrection of the very body within the tomb.

Ladner also traces the development of Christian art influenced by theologians locating the image of God exclusively in the soul. For Clement of Alexandria, the image of God is the Logos, with the image of the image in the mind of man—a view later shared by Origen, Augustine, Gregory of Nyssa, and Ambrose. Of especial interest to students of Puritan art and the poetry of Edward Taylor, as we shall see in chapters 5 and 6, is the metaphor of the soul of man being a clouded mirror in need of polishing by God so His image can be reflected.[11] Art created in this tradition is abstract and spiritualized, as best represented in Byzantine icons. Much of medieval funerary art can be viewed as a dialectic between spiritualized images and images reuniting body and soul in concretized effigies. In northern European art (represented by the Lindisfarne gospels, the Carolingian renaissance, and Anglo-Saxon art) incarnational models predominate. Nevertheless, spiritual tendencies merge with incarnational models at a deep level to create art "both strongly symbolic and strongly eschatological in character: it is both a visible language and a suggestion of things still to come."[12] In particular, we find spiritualistic tendencies in the gaze of the eyes in which an expression of awe and expectation signifies a soul awaiting the arrival of its Saviour, and this gaze is an artistic ancestor of the "bodilie eyes" we will find in Puritan stonecarving. While Puritans whole-heartedly adopted the metaphors the Greek Fathers used to describe the image of God in man, a crucial theological distinction distance was maintained. The Greek Fathers felt that the image could actually be restored during life, but Calvinists knew this to be impossible. The image might be refurbished to some extent as grace acted in a sanctified life, but perfection was only to be realized in heaven. When using the metaphors of the Greek Fathers to describe the transformation worked by grace on the soul, Puritans know that an inchoate state is described which will really exist only after death. It is in a spirit of anticipation, of eschatological expectation, that Puritans employ metaphors of perfection.

As we examine Puritan funerary art, we will find much the same tension between spiritual and incarnational models, as effigies effect a representation of the soul, the resurrected body, or a combination of the two. The issue for Puritans was complicated by a Calvinist decorum which demanded a radical separation of the spiritual and the earthly. As Barbara Lewalski has shown, when John Calvin set out to define the image, he wrote fully aware of the debate among the Church Fathers.[13] In his earliest treatise, *Psychopannychia*, Calvin writes:

> we will begin with man's creation, wherein we shall see of what nature he was made at first. The Sacred History tells us (Gen. i:26) of the purpose of God, before man was created, to make him "after his own image and likeness." These expressions cannot possibly be understood of his body, in which, though the wonderful work of God appears more than in all other creatures, his image nowhere shines forth. . . . For who is it that speaks thus, "Let us make man in our own image and likeness?" God himself, who is a Spirit, and cannot be represented by any bodily shape. But as a bodily image, which exhibits the external face, ought to express to the life all the traits and features, that thus the statue or picture may give us an idea of all that may be seen in the original, so this image of God must, by its likeness, implant some knowledge of God in our minds.[14]

In the *Institutes* Calvin blasts the Lutheran Osiander for holding that God's image was in both body and soul, thereby "mingling heaven and earth."[15] Calvin warns that "we are not left to conjecture what resemblance this image bears to its archetype," for all we can know is that certain spiritual qualities, wisdom, justice, and goodness are part and parcel of the image.[16] Even when forced to admit that the image of God may glow in the outward form, Calvin insists that the glow is an ineffable aura independent of the flesh.

Calvin's tendency to spiritualize biblical descriptions of the image is often at odds with his biblical literalism, as Heinrich Quistorp suggests.[17] Calvin calls the soul the temple of the spirit, rather than the body, and his spiritualized eschatology all but eliminates the physical beauties of both Christ's human form and the bodies of the resurrected saints. In fact, Christ's humanity dissolves into the Godhead at the end of time to prevent it from becoming a hindrance to the perception of God: "the humanity of Christ will no longer be the medium which prevented us from enjoying the ultimate vision of God."[18] While Puritans sympathized with Calvin's radical splitting of sinful humanity and heavenly grace, agreeing that grace alone could rescue man from the flesh, their intense focus on the person of Christ led to an eschatology which celebrated the glorification of man's flesh as well as his spirit. For example, Puritans developed the metaphor of a mirror reflecting God's image to describe both the soul and the body. As Thomas Pierce notes, risen saints are like Christ because they see him:

> the *Reflexion* of his Beauty shall be *imprinted* upon our persons, whilst we *behold* him. As for *Example* . . . when we look upon a Glass, which by being *Polite*, but not *transparent*, reflects the image of our persons, 'Tis called a '*Looking*-Glass" very fitly; because in our *looking* upon *It*, It seems to be *looking* upon *Us* too. . . . Now our

Persons in Heaven will be so polished, (*when this Corruptible shall have put on In-corruption,*) that we shall be in respect of *God*, what Looking-Glasses are in respect of *Us*; we receiving *his* likeness, as they do ours. . . . We shall be Mirrours exactly made; a kind of Looking-glasses with Eyes; whilst by *seeing* as we are *seen*, and *representing* the *Image* of what we *see*, we shall therefore be *like* unto God himself, because *we shall see him as he Is*.[19]

Several popular emblem books also show cherubs looking into a mirror or holding up hearts before it to see if it reflects God's image in the Law (fig. 4). While most writers understood this trope as merely an example, many Puritans in New England seem to have taken it quite literally, and countless gravestones for people of different ages and sex show identical images, and epitaphs claim that these images represent saints risen in Christ's image. The Betty Lane and Children stone, whose epitaph is quoted at the beginning of this chapter, is but one example, with the sun/Son image derived from Malachi 4:2 (fig. 5).

The Resurrection Body

The fervent desire among English Puritans for the Second Coming of Christ is nowhere more evident than in writings on the glories of the Resurrection. The resurrection of the body at the Last Judgment was an accepted part of Protestant dogma in England from the time of the Forty-Two Articles of Religion of 1553.[20] Puritans celebrating the miraculous union of humanity and divinity in Christ rhapsodize on the possibilities of human perfection after the Resurrection. Expositors held that Christ himself was the judge at the last day, and the return to earth of His human form from the highest heaven sparked the Resurrection, His body pulling the elect from the ground as if by a magnet. In fact, Puritans were so concerned with the physical resurrection that they made it a prime cause for Christ's Second Coming. As Richard Sibbes wrote, "He came to redeeme our soules, he must, and he will come to redeeme our bodies from corruption."[21]

Robert Bolton's treatise on the four last things, published posthumously in 1633 by Edward Bagshaw, epitomizes Puritan attitudes towards death, judgment, heaven, and hell. Of particular interest is Bolton's approach to the beatific vision in heaven and the resurrection world. Bolton stresses ravishment by divine beauty as a central element of meditation on death, and he defines a hyperbolic decorum appropriate to images of heaven's glory. Man should conceive of the most elaborate glories in full knowledge that these imaginations are inadequate to the task. It is with a certain playfulness that Bolton works up his descriptions only to fail;

it is as if he finds satisfaction in the fact that the greatest effort leads to the greatest failure. In a typical passage, the rhetoric builds and builds only to be let down suddenly, as language aspires to heaven only to fall back to earth:

> Mans heart can imagine miraculous admirabilities, rarest peeces, worlds of comforts and strange felicities. In conceipt it can convert all the stones upon earth into pearles, every grasse pile into an unvaluable jewell, the dust into silver, the sea into liquid gold, the aire into crystall. I can clothe the earth with farre more beauty and sweetnesse, than ever the Sun saw it. It can make every Starre a Sun, and all those Suns ten thousand times bigger and brighter then it is; &c.
>
> And yet the height and happiness of Evangelicall wisdome doth farre surpass the utmost which the eare, eye, or heart of man hath heard, seene, or can possible apprehend. And this so excellent light upon earth discovring the inestimable treasures of hidden wisdome in Christ, is but as a graine, to the riches golden mine, a drop to the Ocean, a little glimpse to the glory of the Sun; in respect of that fulness of joy hereafter, and everlasting pleasures above.[22]

Bolton is not discouraged by the inadequacy of the imagination. In fact, the imagination is an essential earthly feature, necessary to faith, which will not exist in heaven. When Christ is present, He is irresistible to everyone; faith and imagination can only exist when He is *not* personally visible on earth.

Armed with this hyperbolic method, Bolton leads us on a tour of the third heaven where Christ's body dwells as described in biblical metaphors. At his most rapturous, Bolton effuses that even the individual names, titles, and epithets attributed to heavenly joys will electrify the senses of the saints, as "Every word sounds a world of sweetnesse."[23] First, we have a general description of heaven, "the biggest and most beautifull Body of the whole creation, incorruptible, unmooveable, unalterable: wholly shining with the most exquisite glory and brightnesse of purest light."[24] The light is calculated to exceed that of 300 suns, but even this brightness is dull when compared to the lustre of Christ's body:

> Besides the superexcellency of its native lustre, that I may so speake, this blessed heaven wil yet be made infinitely more illustrious and resplendent by all the most admirable and amiable shining glory of that dearest ravishing object, to a glorified eye, the glorified Body of Iesvs Christ. In respect of the beauty and brightness whereof, all sydereal light is but a darksome mote, and blackest mid night. . . . Now, what a mighty and immeasureable masse of most glorious light will result and arise from that most admirable illustrious concurrence, and mutuall shining reflexions of the Empyrean Heaven more bright and beautifull than the Sun in his strength, the *Sun* of that sacred Pallace, and all the blessed Inhabitants? All which every glorified eye shall be supernaturally inlarged, enabled, and ennobl'd to behold in a kindly and comfortable manner with ineffable delight and everlastingnesse.[25]

Bolton next catalogs the qualities of the resurrection body. Freed from the defects of sin and nature, the body acquires several positive features—immortality, incorruptibility, potency, spirituality, glory, and the ability to move with great swiftness and agility. There was considerable debate about just how the saint moves, and Bolton duly notes previous arguments. Some writers felt that Christ and therefore saints had the power to resist gravity and rise at will, while others thought the saints would fly with wings as do angels. Even the number of wings was in doubt, since at least one extra pair was needed to shade the eyes from Christ's brightness, though no one explained how the saint could then see to fly.[26] Also, the speed of flight was of great concern, since the saints by their swiftness show their eagerness to do God's bidding. Increase Mather, for one, decided that the saint achieves speeds between that of an eagle and a beam of light.[27]

What appeals most to Bolton, however, is the beauty of the resurrection body, and here we have descriptions readily translatable into gravestone portraiture:

> The bodies of the Saints in heaven shall be passingly beautifull, shining, and amiable.
> . . . .
> 1. A due and comely proportion; an apt and congruent symmetry and mutual correspondency of all the parts of the body: or in a word, well favourednesse.
> 2. Amiableness of colour; a pleasing mixture of those two lively colours, of white and red. I add a third:
> 3. A cheerful, lively, lightsome aspect. When the two former materials (as it were) are pleasantly enliv'd and actuated by a lively quickness and modest merriness of countenance.[28]

As we shall see below, it is no coincidence that many of these features are to be found in the spouse in the Song of Solomon. These beauties are held up as patterns for imitation by all spouses of Christ in the church as the Gospel healthiness and cheerfulness appropriate to the saints on earth. The categories are susceptible to stylization, and in time this holy mein became a new sign of grace in Jonathan Edwards' eyes, and a subject of caricature in secular literature.

Bolton intersperses his descriptions with warnings against too much curiosity about divine mysteries, and he takes the Schoolmen to task for specifying the steps of glorification and the function of individual glorified senses. The quality of heavenly activities is more important than the individual incidents, and meditation on heaven should not lose its didactic value in a glowing mist of speculation.

Although subsequent writers adhere to many of Bolton's generalizations about the state of glory, there is a surprising amount of variation

of detail depending on the particular slant of the individual. Both theological and political motives determine which aspect of heavenly beauty
is emphasized. Fifth Monarchists focus on Christ and resurrected saints
reigning as kings and judges; writers concerned with church purity may
invoke the image of the spouse prepared for marriage with the Lamb; a
minister concerned with church polity and sacramentalism can present
the resurrected believer as the High Priest and heaven as the Holy of
Holies.

John Archer and Edward Bagshaw exemplify this variation. Writing
twenty years apart, both were influential chiliasts believing in Christ's
reign on earth, but the variations in England's political climate demanded
different rhetorical strategies. In the 1640s, John Archer exhorted saints
to fight for Christ's imminent kingdom, an approach impossible for Bagshaw in 1669. Nevertheless, the same language and the same descriptions
of Christ's kingdom were used by each man. By telling the saints what
they will see with "bodilie eyes" in this kingdom, Archer and Bagshaw
force their readers to refocus their spiritual eyes and to reinterpret biblical
metaphors and current events. This basic act of reinterpretation of current
events as foretastes of specific millennial events gives the language of
chiliasm much of its rhetorical force.

Previous writers have placed Archer in the Fifth Monarchy movement.[29] Archer's contribution to the Fifth Monarchist struggle to replace
earthly forms of government with a reign of the saints lies in his theorizing
on the nature of biblical monarchies. The personal reign of Christ is seen
as the natural conclusion of the earlier forms of Christ's government,
providential in the Old Testament and spiritual in the New. The saints
need go no further than the types of the kingdom of the Jewish Nation to
understand that Christ has always revealed himself as king to those who
would see the reality in the metaphor. Christ was present to Israel's
rulers:

> hee was an immediate and particular King to them, and was visible present amongst
> them in signes and tokens of presence, as the *Pillar of the Cloud and fire*, and after
> that in the *Tabernacle, Arke, Mercy-seate*, &c.
> Thus we se ever since Christ gathered a visible people and Kingdome, he fore-
> shewed his intent, to have a state *Monarchall* in the World, (for his spirituall Kingdome
> hee typified from the fall of *Adam*) by the Sacrifices, Altars, and the Priests, which
> were the Fathers and first borne of the Family; but this his *Monarchicall Government*
> hee began to typifie, when hee called a Nation to be his people; and as he typified it,
> so he fore-told and prophesid it.[30]

Archer transfers images from Revelation, Second Peter, and Old Testament types and figures, all of which are usually associated with heaven,

down to earth. A separate, heavenly state all but disappears in Archer's eschatology. This development serves to elevate the role of the senses, for images of the resurrection world are no longer carnal speculations and vain imaginings; rather, they are descriptions of real things to be seen with "bodilie eyes." The elaborate qualifications for membership in Christ's kingdom, the classes of martyrs and saints, the relationships of living and resurrected, sinner and saved, found in Archer's text are tedious to modern readers, but they do reveal the imaginative possibilities of biblical language in his mind.

Bagshaw elaborates on Archer's exegesis but abandons his tactics. Christ is shadowed forth by David, and the proof of the type comes, interestingly, from the fact that Christ was of the same flesh with David. Painfully aware of the debacle of the Fifth Monarchy movement, Bagshaw exhorts the saints to usher in the kingdom with prayer, not arms. Faith and fervency in prayer is a good indication that the kingdom is near. Bagshaw's work is a point of contact with New England traditions, since Increase Mather published in his *The Mystery of Israel's Salvation* of 1669 opinions similar to those voiced in the *Personall Reign*, and a copy of Bagshaw's treatise bearing Increase's autograph can be seen in the Mather collection at the Houghton Library. The following passage is scored in the margin of Mather's copy:

> As if he had said the desire of thy people are now more then ordinarily raised up and carried out, in hope of a sudden restauration, notwithstanding the present visible difficulties, which may hinder such an expectation, by seeing the Rubbish and Ruines of *Sion* and therefore I conclude, that the time of her deliverance is nigh: For this we must take for granted, that a *Spirit of Prayer*, which is the *Spirit of God in Believers* (*Rom*. 8:14, 26, 27.) is never given out but there is a willingness and propensity in the Heart of God at that time to grant the very thing, which he is prayed to for.[31]

Gravestones appear in New England at the time of this shift in tactics, and I suggest that one motive for their placement was to demonstrate faith and fervency in prayer, proof of the desire for the arrival of the resurrection world. Though markers were placed over the dead, the "Rubbish and Ruines of *Sion*," they bore prophetic images of reigning saints. As the 1727 Obadiah Smith stone, Norwichtown, Connecticut, proclaims: "NOW BETWEEN / THESE CARVED STONS / RICH TRESUER LIES / DEER SMITH HIS BONES."

The Canticles Tradition

The Song of Solomon, commonly called Canticles by Puritans, had long been a source of inspiration for Christian theologians and poets alike, and

Puritans proved no exception. From the time of the Church Fathers, Canticles was read primarily as a collection of allegories of Christ's love for his church and for the individual believer. As Karen E. Rowe notes in her study of Puritan writings on the text, "Sixteenth- and seventeenth-century exegesis of Canticles developed initially in reaction against earlier extravagant allegorizations of the Church Fathers and medieval expositors."[32] Despite the reformers' corrections of what they saw as Catholic excess, the Geneva Bible reaffirmed this interpretation with a simple headnote. There was a great deal of flexibility remaining in the allegorical tradition, and it is obvious that early English Protestant writers had little difficulty in fitting the Song of Solomon to their theology. One popular approach was to find Christ's workings in the conversion process presented metaphorically in Canticles. Thus John Dove's *The Conversion of Salomon* unfolds a paradigm of salvation, with certain verses revealing the depths of conviction and humiliation and others the heights of joyous assurance.[33]

Not only do Puritans find the text a rich storehouse of metaphorical and sensual langauge accommodating a variety of doctrinal stances, but they also relish the striking parallelism between the beauty of the spouse and her lover. Both have lily lips, dove eyes, pomegranate temples, and red cheeks. Thomas Beverly, in his poetic version of Canticles, attributes this coincidence to Christ's imputation of his righteousness to the soul. The spouse owns, "All Beauty I can own is Thine reflex'd, / As the worlds Light is Heaven Ray's convex'd."[34] Beverly's gloss on the beauty of the christian as a reflection of Christ's graciousness is thoroughly Protestant. What is tantalizing about reading Canticles in this fashion is that it holds out the possibility of systematizing a biblically ordained set of images to be used in saint's portraiture. If the images in Canticles are, in fact, related to the restoration of the image of God in man and may be read as particular signs of that restoration, then portraiture may become quite specific in revealing the qualities and beauties of righteousness.

The problem remains, however, of whether the beauty is a spiritual quality shining forth in the soul in this life and in heaven, or a physical beauty to be seen in the body itself on earth and in the Resurrection. In the first case, the images of Canticles would be metaphors and emblems alone, but in the second, a real physical beauty is described in admittedly hyperbolic fashion. Even in the second case complications arise—is the beauty of the spouse revealed only in the church of gospel times? Is it revealed in the Reformation? Or will it be revealed only at the Resurrection, when the church consummates her nuptials with Christ? Moreover, can Solomon's wedding song type forth a real marriage of each believer with Christ at the Resurrection, with the believer glorified physically in the image of the spouse? New England stonecarvers and ministers alike approach Canticles from a stance that combines several of these approaches, and it is this mixture of allegorical, typological, and prophetic exegesis which makes the New England tradition distinctive. That viewers of gravestones understood the complex mixing of modes represented here is apparent from the sophisticated epitaph of the Nathaniel Addams stone which adresses several audiences in a variety of personae, including the voice of the spouse in the last stanza (Canticles 3:1; 6:1):

> NOW HES GON TO ETERNALLY REST
> GOD WIL HIM SAFLY KEEP
> ALL THOUGH HES BURIED IN Ye DUST
> IN JESUS HE DOTH SLEEP
>
> O YOU HIS CHILDREN THAT ARE LEFT
> I PRAY LET SOME BE FOUND
> THAT DO ENDEAVOUR TO MAKE GOOD
> YOUR FOREGON LEADERS GROUND
>
> GRAVE SAINT BEHIND THAT CANNOT FIND
> THY OLD LOVE NIGHT NOR MORN
> PRAY LOOK ABOVE FOR THERS YOUR LOVE
> SINGING WITH Ye FIRST BORN

We must look to developments in early seventeenth-century English Canticles commentary to explain the New England use of the text to visualize the last things.

A significant break with the allegorical tradition is evident in such works as Thomas Brightman's *A Commentary on the Canticles* and John Cotton's two treatises on the text.[35] The preface to Brightman's work claims that his approach is unprecedented: "hee doth acknowledge a marriage between Christ and his Church; but in this he differs from the rest of Interpreters, that what they conclude to be always, he restrains to certain times."[36] Essentially, Brightman brings to Canticles an interpretation steeped in eschatology in order to shed some light on the progress of the church in history towards the apocalyptic marriage shadowed in the metaphors of Solomon. Bryan W. Ball discounts the effect of Brightman's approach since subsequent writers "failed to perpetuate the apocalyptic interpretation of Solomon. This approach to a book that contained little obvious apocalyptic imagery was perhaps too fanciful even for the mid-seventeenth century and remains as a caution against over-enthusiastic subjectivity in prophetic interpretation."[37] On closer examination, however, it is clear that however limited an impact Brightman's method had on doctrine, his apocalyptic focus profoundly affected the artistic use of Canticles metaphors.

Brightman finds the text loaded with types and prophecies of the church from David's time to the Second Coming of Christ, and he is pleasantly surprised that "This Prophesie following agreeth well neere in all things with that of Saint *Iohn* in the *Revelation*. They foreshew the same events in the like times."[38] He proceeds by matching the prophecies in Canticles to his scheme for the Book of Revelation. Chapters 1 to 4:6 are called "legal," describing the church from Solomon's time to the establishment of the primitive Christian church, with 3:6 to 4:6 chronicling the life of Christ. Chapters 4:6 through 8 contain "evangelical" types, culminating in the spouse's marriage to the Lamb.

While Brightman may have rescued Canticles from one kind of allegory and charged the text with historical immediacy, he did so at the expense of the personal and poetic power of the text. The dove eyes are a less affecting attribute of the spouse's beauty when they are seen as the preaching of "*Michael Cesena* and *Petrus de Carbaria* about the yeer 1277."[39] With Brightman we have fewer images of Christ and the saint's beauty, more of the progress of Christian doctrines, less of the beautiful effects of grace on the soul, and more of the history of an institution. Nevertheless, the imminence and certainty of Christ's physical return becomes the prophetic force of the whole book, for all the events described are preparatory to the marriage with Christ.

John Cotton accepted Brightman's typological scheme, but he was unwilling to abandon the personal relationship of the soul and Christ present in the earlier readings of the allegory of the lovers, and for this reason undertook to preach two series of sermons on Canticles. One is directed to the individual's relationship with Christ, and the other is a historical overview of the progress of the church. As Anthony Tuckney explained in the preface to Cotton's volume of 1655, the personal applications are wholly compatible with the prophetical-historical vision, standing as the "descant" to the "plaine-song."[40] The reader is advised to use Cotton's works both to understand his own spiritual condition and to find some meaning in the struggles of the church in the 1640s. A few years earlier, Nathaniel Homes had advised a similar strategy:

Touching the Book of *Canticles* in particular, that we take it to be a *Prophetical* History, or *Historical* Prophesie (after the manner of *Daniels* Prophesying) applying the several parts and passages thereof, to several times and states of the Church in succeeding Generations, from *Solomons* time, down to the second coming of Christ, though in the general, and abstracted Notion, all the whole book, we confess is *mystical*, signifying that *spiritual* love which is between Christ and his Church, and every true member, and their reciprocal love-carriage of one towards the other; let it be considered.[41]

Homes and Cotton's conjunction of the two readings should be kept in mind, for it is an example of the reader's need for exegetical bifocals, with one lens for reading God's will in current events and the other for anticipating a heavenly reward.

In a significant work by James Durham, *Clavis Cantici: or, an Exposition of the Song of Solomon*, a lengthy preface devoted to the tension between allegorical and typological readings bears directly on iconography in New England. This volume was in Edward Taylor's library, and Benjamin Keach advises the reader of his immensely influential *Tropologia* that his discussion of typology finds its theoretical foundation in Durham's work.[42] As a conservative typologist, Durham cannot accept Canticles as typical or prophetic, for literal events in this text are not fulfilled by literal events in the New Testament. He writes,

> We say, that this Song is not Typical, as being made up of two Histories, to wit, Solomon's Marriage, and Christ's nor doth it any way intend the comparing of these two together in the events, as to their facts or deeds: but it is allegorick, not respecting *Solomon*, or his Marriage, but aiming to set spiritual Mysteries in figurative expressions, in such a manner as may most effectuat that end, for inlightning the judgement, and moving of the affections, without any respect to that Story, or Fact of Solomon's.

More importantly, Durham objects to the prophetical reading because

> such an Interpretation would exceedingly spoil Believers of that Instruction and consolation, which the true scope giveth them; for then they were not to apply it to themselves, or to the Church, but at such a Time, and in such an Age: because if it shall be once fulfilled in others, or, if it be not applicable to them, because they not live in such a time, it will certainly marr their confidence in making any comfortable application of it to themselves. . . . [I]t was not intended to be Prophetical, but Doctrinal, Narrative, and Consolatory.[43]

Canticles not only provides an anatomy of spiritual states in the Christian life, it also explains gospel doctrines and the manner of Christ's workings in the human heart. Durham does warn his readers to pay close attention to the speaker of a given passage in order to determine whether it is the voice of the spouse or Christ. If Christ is speaking, the reader must decide whether He addresses the church militant, the church mystical, or the individual believer. Thus Durham does admit to one aspect of the prophetic readings by allowing application of some texts to the church militant.

Durham adds a significant dimension to Canticles exegesis in his comments on signs of Christ's favor to his church. Brightman had defined Christ's favor as the triumph of the church on earth, but Durham replaces this sign with the gift of heightened aesthetic abilities in the faithful. Believers are favored with an understanding of spiritual mysteries, and they are particularly distinguished by their love-sick apprehension of Christ's beauty. The saint sees the excellence of Christ shining through biblical metaphors and falls in love with Him. The clearer the sight, the stronger the love: "he manifests more of his loveliness to thse who have gotten a begun sight and esteem of it; . . . it's one of Christ's greatest favours to his Bride, and one of the special effects of his love, to set his loveliness upon her heart."[44] Through grace, the saint develops spiritual faculties which apprehend Christ's beauty in the sensual images of dove eyes, ruddy cheeks, and lily lips. The spouse is also transformed, as each physical feature is made beautiful as she reflects the restored image of God in the soul. "As the new or inner-man sets forth the new nature and habitual grace in the believer," Durham writes, "so the particular parts, eyes, lips, &c. signifie distinct parts of that new nature."[45] The eye is beautiful only if it sees Christ, the mouth only in its voicing of Christ's words.

As we shall see in chapters 6 and 7, stonecarvers adopted a similar aesthetic, using particular features of the spouse to depict the restored saint. New England's millennialism, however, worked a fundamental change in the perspective in which the spouse was seen. The saint's spiritual eyes saw the beauty of the spouse in holy behavior, but this beauty was also charged with millennial expectations of a glorified body in the image of the spouse resurrected to marry Christ. In the resurrection world, "bodilie eyes" would see a physically beautiful spouse as well as a spiritually beautiful one. Thus the carver can create a tension in the viewer of a gravestone effigy informed with images from Canticles, since each image is both an emblem of spiritual graces and a prophecy of resurrection graces. The gravestone image can provide consolation to the living in images of Christ's love for His beautiful saint, and it also can be a seal of Christ's promise to glorify the body at the Resurrection. It is thus in the Canticles tradition that we find the most provocative conjunction of images to be seen with both spiritual eyes and "bodilie eyes." In a text that contains so little specific reference to the last things, Puritans charged the metaphors with eschatological significance. This fact reveals the overwhelming degree to which the Puritan imagination was possessed by visions of the glorious end of the world. As we shall see in the poetry of Edward Taylor, prophecy is often at the root of Puritan conceptions of the nature of metaphor.

A Priest to the Temple

The Temple and the High Priest of the Old Testament held exciting typological possibilities for Puritan minister and carver alike. Besides the appeal the richness of the Temple and the garments of the High Priest held out to the imagination of any reader of the Old Testament, New Testament passages gave these objects special meanings as symbols of Christ and his doctrines. God ordained the creation of images of cherubs and rich objects for the Temple, and in Old Testament times the Temple with its glorious artistry was a visible sign of God's favor to his people. While Puritans knew that these objects alone could not please God, they felt that the New Testament had given spiritual meanings to the Temple and its furnishings which could now be useful in teaching Christians God's truths. For example, the veil separating the inner court from the Holy of Holies represented Christ's flesh which had to be rent before believers could enter heaven (Matt. 17:51; Heb. 10:19-20). Illustrations of the Temple were popular in many Bibles printed in the sixteenth and seventeenth centuries, and as late as 1720 exhibitions were held in London to display models and dioramas revealing to the public the latest archaeological/biblical knowledge about the Temple. In the version of the Geneva Bible printed in London in 1599, Puritans could see woodcuts of the Temple, the ark, mercy-seat, candlestick, pillars, garments of the High Priest, and so on.[46] While each aspect of the Temple and the High Priest's clothing was assigned a multitude of Christian meanings, Puritans agreed on their general significance. The Temple was seen as a foreshadowing of the spiritual beauties of Christ and his church. The Temple's tripartite division into outer court, inner court, and Holy of Holies represented the world, the gathered church, and heaven. Only the High Priest was permitted to enter the Holy of Holies, so Puritans saw him as a foreshadowing of Christ who would lead mankind into heaven.

New Englanders heard throughout the seventeenth century that they were High Priests elected to enter heaven, living stones or pillars in the church militant elected to be parts of the New Jerusalem Temple.[47] The rhetorical force of Temple imagery is demonstrated in Edward Taylor's sermon preached at the foundation of his church in Westfield in 1679. His church was a crude building that doubled as a fort, yet Taylor saw it as far more glorious than Solomon's Temple:

> Now here the foundation is a Pretious stone [Christ], & therefore the superstructure ought to be pretious stones. The foundation is a Pearl of great prise Mat. 13:48 & therefore the building must not be of pebles or paultry stones. Nay, but God saith they shall be with fair colours, of Agates, & Saphirs Isa 54:12. God will have a proportion attended in his building. Where the windows are of agats, the Gates shall be of carbuncles & all the borders of Pretious stones. Where one [dore?] is Saphires, an other shall be Jaspers, &tc, where each Gate is Smagardine or sparkling * * * the streets are pure gold. Rev 21:19-20, 22.[48]

The moment of death was naturally a focus for Temple imagery, for at death the saint underwent transformations from the state of flesh in the church militant to the state of spiritual life in the church triumphant. "Christ is the elect corner stone is Sion," wrote Increase Mather, and each saint was called a living stone placed on this cornerstone at the moment of death.[49] Edward Taylor conceived of the earthly church primarily as a vehicle for the transformation of believers from earthly clay to heavenly stones:

> Living stones in this Spiritual Building lie not in it as it is of this sort here below eternally. There is now one; & then another gathered hence as a choise Pearle to be sett in the Ring of glory. & hence in a little time the whole building will be translated hence, stone after stone: & so will disappeare if there be no addition made to it. The [which] that it may not disappeare, God is polishing some for it, as he is fetching some from it. & hence the building stands in need of those that are prepared for it.[50]

Samuel Mather's *The Figures or Types of the Old Testament* contains the classically conservative Puritan exegesis of the types of the Temple.[51] The three general significations of Temple types for Mather are Christ, the church, and every individual believer; the minutest detail bears significance to the intricate relationships among these three categories. Samuel Mather notes with care traditional exegesis of the Temple—the outer court as body and the inferior world open to the view and use of man, the inner court as soul and starry heavens, and the Holy of Holies as the spirit and third heaven where God dwells eternally. These interpretations are too static and allegorical for Mather, so he replaces them with the prophetic types of Christ and his church. The threefold division of the Temple is taken to signify the church visible, militant, and triumphant, and the believer trains his spiritual eyes on each detail of the furnishings of the temple to determine the symbolic unity of the church through these states. The utensils and furnishings of the Temple are important precisely because they contain this tripartite signification, and their superlative beauty derives from the glory of the church triumphant which they shadow forth. As the saint sees each utensil in its visible (Old Testament), militant (New Testament), and triumphant (heavenly) state, the utensil itself is endowed with meanings to draw the viewer towards its ultimate apocalyptic meaning.

Mather's most developed example of this process appears in his discussion of the trees of the Temple. We see the trees first as the actual timbers, then as representations of good things in nature, and finally as types of the qualities of righteousness that caused saints to be planted in the earthly and heavenly Temples.

The *Trees* that were placed in the Temple either for use, as Timber in the Building, or for Ornament in Sculptures and Ingravings, and the *Flowers*; I find them mystically applied in the Scripture to the Saints and People of God in the Church. The Trees themselves could not be planted in the Temple: but therefore the Sculptures of them were there, as representing the Trees themselves. *David* compares the Righteous to the Cedar and Palm-tree, *Psal*. 92:12, 13, 14. and himself unto the Olive-tree, which was used in and about the Doors of the House, Psal. 52:8. *But I am like a green Olive-tree in the House of God*. There were also Sculptures of Lillies [atop the pillars] in the Temple, 1 *Kings* 7:19, 22—and Saints are set forth by that Flower. . . . The Allusion seems to lie in the Gifts and Graces of the Spirit of God shadowed by the excellent Properties of those Trees and Flowers.[52]

Another architectural feature of the Temple of particular use to both Samuel and Increase Mather in setting out the types of the saint was the disposition of the pillars, Jachin and Boaz. These pillars were of great beauty and strength—we are to imagine them with luxuriant lily capitals—and they have a threefold meaning in accordance with that of the whole Temple. As types of God and Christ, they support the faith of the church, its safety, and most importantly, as types of particular saints and ministers, they are upright and strong. Simply put, the believer must be straight and strong to receive the crown of life promised in 2 Timothy 4:7-8. The saint who has these qualities both excells the pillars of the Temple in beauty and claims a place in the New Jerusalem. Individual fulfillment in heaven provides the spark which enlivens the type, making prophecy from metaphor. The Christian knows his or her superiority to the type in antitypical fulfillment, for

These Pillars were broken in pieces and carried away to *Babylon*, but living Pillars in the Spiritual Temple shall go out no more, Rev. 3:12. but abide in the House for ever, *John* 8:35. A true Believer is (as one saith) *Monumentum aere perennius*, more durable then Pillars of Brass. Would you be assured of the Crown of Glory? Is there in thee this rectitude and straitness, this Strength and Firmness in that House of God? Thou art then a Pillar in the House of God, and shalt go no more out.[53]

Where Samuel Mather personalizes these types to apply them to the individual saint, Increase Mather looks at the broader context of Revelation 3:12 to stress the millennial state of the Temple. In his "New Jerusalem" manuscript, Mather argues that Christians can, and indeed should, go beyond the limited construct of literal Old Testament type fulfilled by spiritual antitype. Though many Old Testament types of the Temple have been fulfilled in the gospel church and the literal Temple has long been destroyed, these facts do not rule out the reappearance of a new Temple in Sion. The realization of Old Testament types in the members of the gospel church was part of a process leading to the physical descent of New Jerusalem to the earth. Not only are believers promised a place as spiritual pillars in the church, but they also can expect this glory to be revealed on earth in the Millennium:

> There are in this verse [Rev. 3:12] two things prommised unto every such one. *1st.* The lord Jesus christ doth assure him that he will make him an everlasting pillar in the temple of his *god. As for him that overcomes, I will make him a pillar in the temple of my god and he shall go out no more.* There were Pillars in Sollomons temple. Two Pillars named Jachin and Boaz: but (saith christ) as for the faithfull christian, he shal be a Pillar in the spirituall temple and fixed there for ever. *2ly.* Christ doth heer Prommise the inscription of a glorious name. And under that there are three particulars Contain'd. *1st.* Saith the Lord *I will write upon him the name of my god*, that is he shall be knowne to be one that belongs to god. Such a glory shall be upon him as that all The world shall one day see and say, *That is a* child of god. *2ly* The name of the citty of god, The new Jerusalem that Comes downe out of heaven from god. *3ly* Christs new name shall be written uppon him.[54]

The multiplicity of meanings evoked by this image reveals to the viewer of Puritan gravestones the flexibility of the symbolic process for seventeenth-century Puritans. As we shall see below, pillars on a gravestone may commemorate the deceased's status in the church, emphasizing the spiritual qualities he or she made visible in life, or the pillars could be prophetic images of the imminent return of the resurrected saints as pillars of the New Jerusalem Temple.

The types of the Temple were useful to Puritans apart from commemorative and prophetic modes, for they could also be employed as means of private meditation and worship. In a literary analog, meditations on the Old Testament Temple by George Herbert and Edward Taylor provide a gloss on Temple images that will prove useful in our consideration of gravestone images. Herbert and Taylor shared the belief that man's purpose was to worship and praise God, as they shared the images of the Priest and the Temple to define their roles as minister and poet. But they disagreed on the meanings of the images themselves.[55]

In "Sion" Herbert defined the differences between Temple worship and church worship in terms of the failure of manmade objects to please God.[56] The "flowres and carvings," glory and pomp of Old Testament Temple worship, no longer affect God, for they have been abandoned by Him as fit means for man's worship of Him. The Christian temple is within: "now thy Architecture meets with sinne / For all thy frame and fabrick is within" (11. 11-12). The Temple the Christian poet builds will please God only if it is beautiful in its holiness. Herbert either internalizes the objects of the Temple, as in "The Altar," or he reads them as emblems of the holy life, as in "The Church-floore." Worship, then, for the Christian poet consists not in the creation of a beautiful thing, a prideful ele-

vation of the builder's skill, but rather in humble groanings in the temple
of the heart:

> All Solomons sea of Brasse and world of stone
> Is not so deare to thee, as one good grone.
> And truely brasse and stones are heavy things,
> Tombes for the dead, not Temples fitt for thee
> But grones are quick, and full of wings,
> And all their motions upward bee;
> And ever as they mount like larks, they sing,
> The note is sad, yet musique for a *King*.   (11. 17-24)

For Edward Taylor, worship and praise of the beauty of Christ called
for the use of things that had been ordained as types of His glory. In a
meditation on Hebrews 9:11, "By a Greater, and more Perfect Tabernacle," Taylor confronts sinful man's inability to worship God immediately. After the Fall, God gave man the medium of Christ through which
man could worship the Father. Taylor knows he cannot worship God
without a house, and he matches Herbert in the recognition that "An
house of Worship here will do no good, / Unless it type my Woe, in
which I douse, / And Remedy in deifyed Blood" (11. 14-16). But he
breaks with Herbert by presenting the type of the Temple rather than the
heart alone as a fit vehicle for praise. Where Herbert objects that the
human builders of the Temple received overmuch praise for their work,
Taylor knows God was their Creator, and all the things of the Temple
therefore "do Christs Shine hold." Moreover, though the type is nothing
compared with the antitype ("Their Glory's but a painted Sun on th'
Wall / Compared to thine"), the type is efficacious in working up holy
affections in poetic praises of God. For example, Taylor describes the oil
used in Temple services: "The flames whereof, enmixt with Grace as-
saile / With Grace the heart in th' Light that takes the Eye / To light us
in the way within the Vaile / Unto the Arke in which the Angells prie"
(11. 37-40). The Tabernacle, Temple, and Christ become one, a "Guide
of Temple Light / In to the Holy of Holies," his "Medium to God," his
"Medium of Worship." For Taylor, the poet's song of praise is not only
a groan; it is also an embracing of a glorious Christ in the medium of his
types. God invites Taylor to walk in the Old/New Testament tabernacle,
and his entrance brings both song and worship: "I will as I walke herein /
Thy Glory thee in *Temple* Musick bring" (11. 59-60, my italics). Taylor
believed the Christian equipped with spiritual eyes would see Christ's
beauty in the Temple, and this is precisely the use Puritans would make
of images of the Temple when carved on gravestones.

Spiritual eyes could also reveal the true glory of the church on earth.

Samuel Mather's treatise on the types is especially significant as it bears on the events surrounding its composition after the Restoration. Upon the downfall of the Puritan regime, Mather preached sermons in Dublin defining the dissenting response against the reintroduction of Anglican rituals.[58] Shortly thereafter he began his sermons on typology, no doubt intended as a conservative bulwark against Anglican repression of dissenting typology. His description of the Temple-church reveals an imaginative attempt to rally Puritans in the face of political decline:

> *See the Glory of the visible Church*, and of the Presence of God there. For all these glorious things are in the Temple, in the Holy of Holies there. And therefore you should see God himself there, and hear his Voice, though not visibly and audibly, but spiritually; yet really and powerfully and affectually speaking to the Heart. You should see these things by the Eye of Faith. When you come to a Meeting, though the World revile and call them Conventicles, you should see a guard of Angels and Cherubims round about you, &c.[59]

The cherubim protected God's people in the church, but they also were known to have hovered over the mercy-seat in the Holy of Holies. Only the High Priest entered the innermost court, the sanctuary of the Temple, but one of the fundamental assumptions of Protestant theology, the priesthood of all believers, provided an entrance for all believers into the Holy of Holies.

As a type of Christ, the High Priest passed through a veil into the Holy of Holies as Christ passed through death into heaven. As Increase Mather explains, "Particularly the *Veil* of the Temple typified the humane nature of Christ. . . . As there was no entring into the *Holy of Holies* but by the Veil; so there is no entring into Heaven but through that Sacrifice of the flesh, i.e. the humane nature of Christ."[60] Not only did Christ open heaven through his sacrifice, He also took possession of it and gave mankind a right to it. A member of the priesthood of all believers knew that his representative, Christ, was already in heaven, and faithful eyes would see each saint's conduct as proof of future residence there. As Thomas Goodwin wrote, "your Faith through this consideration, may see your selves as good as in Heaven already: For Christ in entred as a *Common Person* for you."[61]

For Samuel Mather, the type of the High Priest found its antitype in ministers and believers as well as in Christ. Given the privilege of the typical High Priest to pass into the Holy of Holies, his particular qualifications shadowed forth those graces which enabled the believer to enter heaven. In essence, Puritans could replace the objectionable veneration of the graces of particular Saints as practiced in the Catholic church with close study of the Old Testament type. In rejecting the *dulia* of the Catholic church, Puritans abandoned a portrait tradition replete with visual signs of the effects of grace—haloes, upraised eyes, gestures, and so on. The adornments of the High Priest were every bit as glorious as those of any saint, so they would appeal to the imaginations of believer, minister, and artist alike, but the High Priest would never be confused with any individual saint. Though adorned with the images of the High Priest, a portrait of a believer would be seen as sharing in the type, which finally glorified Christ and not the individual. The viewer would be constantly reminded that these types, though literal in nature, applied to the saint only because Christ had appeared as a "Common Person" in fulfillment of the type.

Mather informs us that the High Priest was typical in personal qualifications, apparel, consecration, and ministrations, but it is the rich apparel which sparks his imagination. Clearly the High Priest was not responsible to sumptuary laws requiring sobriety in dress. The beauty of the High Priest typifies the beauty of the saint clothed in righteousness:

> The general end and use of these Garments was to be *for Beauty and Glory*, Exod. 28:2. as betokening an higher Glory and Beauty of Holiness; as a Shadow of an higher Spiritual Clothing . . . the taking away of the guilt of Sin, and clothing the Soul with Christ's Righteousness.
> . . . .
> Believers therefore who are spiritual Priests, they should not clothe themselves with the filthy Rags of their own Righteousness, nor with the rotten Garments of counterfeit Graces, as Hypocrites and Justiciaries do; but get on this Priestly attire, seek it of Christ, Rev. 3:18.[62]

Images of the apparel of the High Priest are tailor-made to assuage the fear of death and corruption, for the imagination armed with these images could clothe the deceased in his passage into the temple of Death as the High Priest entering the Holy of Holies.

From Leviticus 8:7-9 Mather enumerates the nine garments of the Priest: the holy coat, girdle, robe, ephod, girdle of the ephod, breast plate, Urim and Thummin, mitre, and golden plate.[63] Some of these articles typify particular qualities shared by Christ and believer, but others typify Christ's representative righteousness. Thus the coat was imputed righteousness, while the girdle (truth, strength, readiness for action) and the Urim and Thummin (angelic reasoning, holiness, faith) would be worn by the saint personally during a holy life. The robe fringed with bells and pomegranates united in one image all evangelical acts—the voice of Christ in prayer and in the Gospels, the sweet fruits of Christ's prayers and preaching revealed in saints' holy lives. The mitre and breast plate were shadows of church polity, and the stones on the breast plate were en-

graved with the names of the twelve tribes of Israel. This garment symbolized the graces of the saints who were beautiful when set in gospel
order. The mitre was an ornament of authority and superiority, so the
saints' obedience to this authority ensured a beautiful gospel order.

The remaining apparel has eschatological significance. The ephod
held an onyx on each shoulder engraved with the names of the twelve
children of Israel. Thus when the Priest-Christ passed into the Temple-
heaven, God could see the believers as part of Christ's righteousness
when they, too, entered heaven at death. Christ also wears the golden
crown of holiness behind the veil, so believers may be assured that their
sins will be accepted by God because they are covered by Christ's crown.
The saint who must pass through the veil of flesh can gain comfort and
assurance through these types, and on gravestone after gravestone we
find images of triumph and splendor as the deceased clothed as the High
Priest enters the Temple (fig. 6).

Language

At first glance, most texts on New England make only the simplest comments on eschatological doctrines. Tombstones seldom claim more than
a presence as markers of the bodies of the deceased, and all we can know
of other conscious intention on the part of the makers is the often stated
warning to prepare for death. Puritans felt that language and art acted in
much the same manner to instruct the living; the Solomon Tracy stone,
1732, in Norwichtown, Connecticut, states, "THE DEAD IN SILENT /
LANGUAGE SAY / TO LIUING THINKING / READER HEARE /
O LOUING FRINDS / DOE NOT DELAY / BUT SPEDILY FOR /
DETH PREPARE." Puritans dreamed of the day when the often violent
debates over the meaning of Scripture would be over, and in the seventeenth century many Puritans believed harmony would only come when
people understood the universal language of heaven. For Richard Baxter
heavenly-mindedness was the key to religious and exegetical harmony:

> Surely, it we can get into the Holy of Holies, and bring thence the Name and Image
> of God, and get it closed up in our hearts, this would enable us to work wonders;
> every duty we performed would be a wonder; and they that heard, would be ready to
> say, Never man spake as this man speaketh. The spirit would possess us, as those
> flaming tongues, and make us every one to speak (not in the variety of the confounded
> Languages, but) in the Primitive pure Language of *Canaan*, the wonderful Works of
> God.[64]

Baxter expresses a sentiment that forms part of the mainstream of New
England attitudes towards eschatological language and art. If the saint is

heavenly-minded, he may discover the secret meaning of biblical metaphors. Indeed biblical language referred to spiritual truths, but it also
might reveal something of actual millennial events. In one of the most
interesting results of eschatological fervor, Puritans posited that the saint's
spiritual eyes allowed him to know through metaphorical language secrets
about the coming Millennium which are kept hidden from the unregener-
ate. Moreover, the Puritan fascination with the word explains the persist-
ance of gravestones which feature texts alone.

In the works of Thomas Parker we find an early example of New
Englanders' ability to appeal to eschatological metaphors to unite groups
of various doctrinal persuasions in a common millennial vision. He is an
interesting figure in early America, for his life is a fortuitious confluence
of theology, history, and artistry which reveals the dynamics of Essex
County society and theology at the time of the rise of gravestone carving.[65] Parker preached and published in England, was associated with
radical movements during the 1630s, and presented excellent credentials
when he arrived in Ipswich, Massachusetts, in 1634. His higher education
was conducted outside England for the most part because his dissenting
father was exiled in 1607. After studying with William Usher in Dublin,
he became a student of William Ames at Leyden, graduating in 1614, and
completing his education with a master's degree from the University of
Franeker in 1617. Parker's presbyterian leanings were apparent from the
start, as he was admonished by the Synod of Dort for his publications on
the subject.

Although he removed to New England and accepted a call to New-
bury, Massachusetts, on the New Hampshire frontier in 1635, his best
known work, *The Visions and Prophecies of Daniel Expounded*, appeared
in London in 1646. Parker's exegesis of the book of Daniel shows the
influence of Mede, Brightman, Eliot, Cotton, and others. His chronology
for the coming of the Millennium is derived from the image of the man
in Daniel 2:31-45, and each metal in the figure is read as a literal earthly
kingdom. The kingdom of stone is the kingdom of the saints, hewn from
the mountain of the Roman Empire to smash all anti-Christian powers.
Since Christ's gospel-kingdom has not destroyed all other kingdoms, Parker argues that the fulfillment of this prophecy will occur at the Second
Coming. The conquest of the world will take forty-five years, after which
Christ will appear. As John Eliot notes in his *Christian Commonwealth*,
Christ will not rule personally during the conquest; rather his spirit will
empower the saints to take up the fight.[66] Parker provides an ingenious
typological proof of the saints' knowledge of the imminence of these
events. The appearance of Gabriel in Daniel 8:15-16 typed the opening of
mysteries to saints at the last times:

for unto *Daniel* himself they were to be unknown . . . and to all others before the last time . . .; onely to Daniel, as in a Type, an explication is given, to be fully perfected in the Antitype, the later Saints who were alone to under the same. . . .
. . . .
[S]o in the last times the Saints shall understand, when none of the wicked shall understand.[67]

A secret understanding of the mysteries of the last times encouraged radicalism among Parker's readers, though Parker himself hedged on the exact date of the beginning of the forty-five years. His mathematical predictions pointed to 1649-50 or 1859-60 as climactic years, both fortuitous predictions as history has shown. Since Parker encourages saints to read types as a guide to their present actions, he is forced to discuss the nature of biblical language to support his arguments against an overly literal interpretation of Scripture which would tie one down to specific actions. It is in this discussion that we gain a valuable perspective on millennial aesthetics.

First, Parker rejects the literal, earthly reign of the saints: "As concerning the opinion of many Worthys, affirming, that the reign of the Saints a 1000 yeers, is to be expected in the glory of New-Jerusalem at the end of the yeers of Antichrist: I cannot possibly bring my judgement to incline unto it."[68] Rather, like John Cotton in his *Churches Resurrection*, Parker feels the thousand-year reign consists of the pouring out of the vials through the preaching and prayers of the ministry. As keeper of the Word, the ministry plays a crucial role in apocalyptic events, for ministers are the vital links between the types of biblical language and the workings of God's historical fulfillment of these types since they are secretly inspired by God concerning these mysteries. To answer critics who read biblical descriptions of the Millennium as foretelling literal events in an earthly kingdom, Parker makes a critical distinction between earthly and heavenly metaphors. He distinguishes between those which have an application to real events on earth that nonetheless have a spiritual significance on the one hand, and metaphors which describe the mysteries to be discovered in heaven after the Second Coming, on the other. Descriptions of temporal felicities in the New Jerusalem are to be understood of its state of "inchoation" on earth or of its state of heavenly perfection. In the latter case, the metaphors are to be understood in a spiritual, metaphorical sense instead of in a literal sense. There is, however, an intimate connection between the state of inchoation and the state of heavenly perfection. Parker writes,

in the state of inchoation the Ministers as Angels, letting the elect by conversion through the gates of particular Churches, into the community of the whole Church of

New-Jerusalem: shall hereby be instruments of bringing them into the heavenly perfection, and shall therein be glorified with their converts. And therefore in the state
of heavenly perfection, they are brought in under *such representations as will agree
to the foresaid relation* which they had unto their converts in the state of inchoation,
Apocalyps 12, 12. In like manner the Kings of the earth are said to bring their glory
to it . . . partly because in its state of inchoation they shall come unto it by conversion,
subjecting themselves, their Kingdoms and glory thereunto, in procuring the felicity
thereof: and partly because they shall stand in this frame of love unto Christ and his
Church, through all eternities in heavenly perfection. Rivers of water running, Hills
dropping new wine, Mountains flowing with milk, seven times increase of the light of
the Sun, abundance of Corn, and Feasts and Dancings, and joyfull Solemnities, to be
expected when Jerusalem shall be restored out of *Babylon*, are clearly Types and
mysticall Expressions of the spirituall glory of the Church in generall, which is the
New Jerusalem, when it shall be reduced out of the Babylon of Antichrist in the state
of inchoation, and principally when it shall ascend unto the height of heavenly felicity.[69]

It is the peculiar quality of biblical language that it can describe both
heaven and earth in the same word, and it is the peculiar ability of the
saint to know the spiritual and mystical senses of the images expressed
therein. The saints, especially the ministers, see a continuity between
heaven and earth, and the metaphoric descriptions of ministers and kings
are in fact prophecies of their activities in heaven. The liberating effect
of such language cannot be underestimated, for it transcends at once a
narrow, literal interpretation of metaphor and asserts a continuity of biblical metaphor and reality in the lives of saints from this world into the
next.

Hence the use of the word "angel" to describe a minister refers to
both the minister's office on earth and in heaven, and the earthly activity
takes on new status as preparatory to heavenly fulfillment. Parker implies
that the Millennium already permeates gospel order in the church, so
saints who are properly equipped with the power to read the types of the
last times take on the duties prescribed for the church in its state of
inchoation. Metaphor and types, then, become continuing means for pro-
jecting imaginatively one's identity into a millennial dimension. Parker is
an especially revealing exponent of millennial aesthetics—a believer in
the imminence of the Apocalypse, he was not tied to literal chiliasm; as
a Presbyterian, his scheme ensures ministerial authority in the last times
and in heaven. Though he does not answer the age-old question of whether
there is sex in heaven, we can be sure there will be sermons.

Parker's presbyterianism and his admission of the unconverted to the
Lord's Supper were anomalies in conservative congregational Essex County,
but church polity did not restrict ministers from sharing millennial aesthetics. No matter what the particular scheme for the Apocalypse, an
aesthetic including spiritual and "bodilie" eyes was flexible enough to

unify a multitude of doctrines under one imaginative system. When the question of shared acceptance of the idea of glorified senses in heaven arises, we can turn to Cotton Mather, a theologian of a far different color from Parker, and his description of Parker's telling response to the evidence of human frailty:

> The strains which his immoderate studies gave unto his organs of sight, brought a miserable defluxion of rheum upon his eyes; which proceeded so far, that one of them swelled until it came out of his head, and the other grew altogether dim some years before his death. Under this extreme loss he would, after a Christian and pleasant manner, give himself that consolation: "Well, they'll be restored shortly, at the resurrection."[70]

Parker's apocalyptic optimism is personal and communal, as the perfection of each saint is part and parcel of the glorification of the spouse of Christ. In New England, the essential appeal of the prophetic mode practised by Thomas Parker and, in its classic form, by Increase Mather, lies in this anticipation of individual perfection. For Increase Mather, personal fulfillment in the role of prophet is inseparable from the millennial glorification of New England's ecclesiology.

Figure 1. Anna Perkins, 1762, Newburyport, Massachusetts

Figure 2. The I P stone, 1714, Rumford, Rhode Island

Figure 3.   Bethiah Carpenter, ca. 1715, Rumford, Rhode Island

Figure 4. Emblem, Hermanus Hugo, *Pia Desideria: or Divine Adresses, in three books,* trans. Edmund Arwaker, 1686, p. 104, Brown University Library

Figure 5.   Betty Lane and Children, 1791, Rockingham, Vermont

Figure 6. Reverend Abraham Nott, 1756, Essex, Connecticut

3

Increase Mather and the
Prophecy of Perfection

Is there not a deep moral in the tale? Could the result of one, or all
our deeds, be shadowed forth and set before us, some would call it
Fate, and hurry onward, others be swept along by their passionate
desires, and none be turned aside by the PROPHETIC PICTURES.

—Nathaniel Hawthorne, "The Prophetic Pictures"

During the last quarter of the seventeenth century in New England, millennialism waxed strong in the sermons that poured from Boston presses.
Perhaps no man was more representative of the mood of the times than
Increase Mather who has been called the "foremost" Puritan by one
biographer.[1] In his jeremiads on New England's "errand into the wilderness," and in his treatises on the millennial conversion of the Jews and
on the events of the Apocalypse, Mather exhorted his readers to use the
remaining days of their lives, if not of the world itself, to prepare for these
great events. As Robert Middlekauff notes, "Increase Mather gained the
greatest intensity in his evangelical mood in his chiliasm, a belief that
predictions of Christ's Second Coming described a literal return in time
and space," and it is this literalism that characterizes all of his eschatological writings.[2]

Cotton Mather joined his father in these beliefs, so for fifty years
father and son dominated public utterances on the subject in New England; in the words of Perry Miller, "possessed by the true apocalyptic
spirit, they marched into the Age of Reason loudly crying the end of the
world was at hand."[3] Miller discredits the representative nature of the
Mathers' eschatology, but subsequent studies have shown the depth of
millennial belief in New England at the time.[4] During the period of the
Mather ascendancy, gravestone carving flourished in New England. It is
no coincidence that many of the themes sounded by the Mathers—the

Resurrection, the restoration of the New Jerusalem Temple, the return of Paradise—have counterparts in tombstone carving, for New England Puritans saw tombstone designs as affirmations of the most fundamental Christian doctrine of the resurrection of deceased saints. I suspect that we can never fully appreciate the religious fervor that gripped the common auditor in the Mathers' church during millennial pronouncements from the pulpit, just as we cannot fully recreate the impulse behind the carving of tombstones with eschatological themes. But we can reconstruct something of the imaginative context within which these personal responses occurred, a context in large part created by the Mathers.

At the foundation of New England eschatology was the belief that the prophecies of millennial perfection in the Bible would have a literal fulfillment on earth after the resurrection of saints with "bodilie eyes." Increase Mather produced an intensely personal vision of the individual saint's participation in cosmic millennial events. Through prayer and heavenly mediatation, at death and during the glorious events of the Resurrection, the saint could be intimately involved with the grandeur of God's providential scheme for human history. It is my contention that rhetorical strategies in preaching and stonecarving were developed to integrate the individual's imaginative needs, hopes, and expectations with the grand designs of God. To illustrate these strategies, I have chosen artifacts which have just such a mixture of personal and public meanings in order to demonstrate the imaginative medium which held together the Bible commonwealth: the Mathers' sermons, penned by the most prolific writers of the time, conveyed a form of prophecy which intimately involved individual acts of vision; and the gravestone, a communal monument placed on public ground, also made a statement on the importance of the individual saint. We shall see that Increase Mather's emphasis on the closeness of saints on earth with saints in the separate state and his focus on the personal nature of the Millennium explain the development of several New England stonecarving traditions.

In death as in life, Increase Mather's role as a prophet in the community was a subject of public debate. When he died on August 18, 1723, friend and foe alike realized that a man truly representative of the "New England way" was gone. The events surrounding Mather's funeral, the massive procession of ministers, the various elegies composed and the funeral sermons delivered, provide a rare insight into the attempt made by early eighteenth-century New Englanders to define their heritage. In the funeral sermons which tried to "place" Mather, argument centered on the definition of Mather as a prophet. At issue was whether the prophet is a divinely inspired seer in the tradition of Elijah or merely a teacher whose wisdom is the result of training and experience in the affairs of men.

The key documents treating Increase Mather both as man and symbol are Cotton Mather's *A Father Departing* and *Parentator* and Benjamin Colman's *The Prophet's Death Lamented and Improved*. Cotton Mather's funeral sermon, *A Father Departing*, set the symbolic context for subsequent sermons with its text (2 Kings 11:12) describing the remarkable translation of the prophet Elijah. Cotton Mather's purpose here is twofold: to define his father as another Elijah, and thereby to establish himself as Elisha, heir of the mantle of prophecy. The transportation of Elijah to heaven in a chariot was the work of "the Angels of GOD," dramatically proving that Elijah was a prophet to and a protector of his nation. God was not so obliging at the death of Increase Mather, but Cotton insisted that a like status as national prophet had been granted to his father:

> The Holy Spirit has used this Metaphor, to make us understand, what *Blessings* the World enjoys in *Good Men*, and which way they are so; Phil. II. 15. *Ye shine as Lights in the World*. GOD show'd the *Stars* of Heaven unto *Abraham*, and said, *So shall thy seed be*. Truly, The Children of *Abraham*, are like the *Stars of Heaven*, by performing the *Office*, as well as by answering the *Number*, of those *Lights in the World*. *Good Men* are *communicative* of their *Goodness;* They shed forth, and shoot out the Influences of *Light* unto the World about them.[5]

But the force of this metaphor goes further than just to extol the virtues of good men, for God uses the light of such men to deliver his land from spiritual and temporal evils, since they eventually lead their nation in the millennial kingdom.

Mather implies that God blesses the prophet's nation even after his death. Indeed, fit lamentation for a dead prophet may actually encourage God to bless the nation, and Mather concludes by observing that there is a continuing relationship between deceased and living saints, the cities of God in heaven and on earth:

> In the mean time, there is an Holy *Communion* with the *Departed Saints,* to be maintained by the *Surviving;* and this not only in *Remembring them who have spoken unto us the Word of GOD,* but also in *Considering the End of their Conversation,* and the *Sentiments* and *Enjoyments* of the Heavenly World, which they in the end arriv'd unto (p. 29).

Mather takes this communion literally, and in his new identity as Elisha, he claims to speak as a medium for his father to remind the congregation of heavenly rewards. Mather offers "such a view of him [Increase] as the Three *Apostles* once had of *Elias,* when they saw the *Excellent Glory* on the *Holy Mountain*" (p. 29). In his father's voice, Cotton describes the happiness of the saints in heaven and encourages the saints on earth to follow his lead in journeying to heaven. Mather's sermon provides a key insight into Puritan eschatology: he feels the community of saints both deceased and alive lead the church from earth to heaven. Certainly such emphasis on the authority of the dead would contribute to such acts of piety as placing gravestones for them.

Benjamin Colman, the Mathers' adversary in so many political struggles, delivered a highly commendatory sermon in the North Church one week after Cotton Mather's sermon.[6] Colman, however, framed a careful rebuttal to Mather's estimation of his father's prophetic role, using the language of prophecy itself to deny that modern prophets have a visionary power before or after death. Specifically, Colman's diction and imagery was that of the jeremiadic funeral sermon, as developed by Increase Mather, Samuel Willard, and others in the late seventeenth century, in which the deceased was described as a pillar or a "gap-man" in the wall of the church whose removal is a stern judgment on an apostate people.[7] The congregation must have been primed for standard jeremiadic fare when Colman invoked the biblical model for evangelical mourning at the death of a prophet: "WHERE should we look for the *Prophets* of the Lord but in *Judah* and *Jerusalem*? There God rais'd 'em up, for there was his visible Church and Kingdom. There then you must look for the Prophets death and graves, and for those that will lay their decease to heart."[8] The congregation would have expected Colman to complete the typological parallel by calling Boston/Israel to repentance, but Colman has invoked the biblical model for another purpose. Instead, he subtly encouraged the audience to transfer the typological and emotional trappings of mourning for a departed prophet from the dead minister to the office itself. The types are fulfilled not in the individual preacher but in the ministry of the gospel church. God

> sets [ministers] as strong and beautiful *Pillars* in his Church; and tho' he is often taking them down and removing them, yet he sets up others in their places; and so his Church yet stands and shall continue, tho' its Ministers cannot by reason of death; *being built upon the Prophets and Apostles, Jesus Christ himself being the Foundation, and the chief Corner Stone.*
>
> . . . .
>
> Put not your trust in Princes, nor in the Son of man in whom there is no help; his breath goeth forth, he returneth to his dust. God may justly break the *Creature* which we make our *stay* and *staff,* and cast that to the worms which we make our confidence and trust; make our *Idol.*[9]

Although Colman calls for repentance, faith in God, and the raising of children in the faith of their departed fathers as ways to ensure that the gap is filled and the pillar replaced, he has defused the traditional form of the jeremiad by denying typological significance to the ministers of the church. Here the implicit connection of the church militant and Israel, a connection established by the Covenant and made operative through the spirit of prophecy in the ministry, is broken. The typical priests and prophets of the Old Testament were fulfilled in Christ, and the gospel church will survive regardless of the death of ministers. The church is eternal, so living saints should look to the Bible for guidance, not to the prophecies of dead saints.

Besides depriving the church of its eschatological frame of reference, Colman goes on to deny that Increase Mather, or any minister, was a prophet in the biblical sense of the word. Colman notes that he has named Mather a prophet, explaining that "in a lax and improper sense, the word *Prophet* may sometimes stand for *all* the Ministers of Religion," but in the proper sense of the term,

> *Prophecy* was, That discovery of things secret, and prediction of things future, which it has pleased God to make unto his Church, by a particular Revelation of his Mind and Will, unto his Servants, at one time and another. . . . THUS a *Prophet* was an extraordinary Messenger and Inspired Man of God, favour'd with Visions and Revelations; a revealer of secrets and a Predicter of futurities; in which respect he was called a Seer, and was ordinarily sent with particular Messages of Gods favour or anger to Places or Persons; and was sometimes arm'd with a Miraculous power to do signs and mighty works, to evince his Mission from God.[10]

Since Mather was not a true seer, he should be remembered and revered as an "*Ordinary Teacher* in the Church of Christ," whose "Preaching may be called Prophecying."[11] Once this redefinition of a central New England metaphor, the minister as Old Testament prophet, had been effected, Colman could offer a new, more catholic vision of the errand in the wilderness. New Englanders need not feel responsible to divinely inspired seers, rather they should look to ministers for their guidance as men who are "sober, grave, wise, virtuous, tho'tful, solid and judicious Men; as well as devout and gracious."[12]

Cotton Mather, not one to take such a challenge lightly, penned *Parentator* the next year to surround his father's life with mythological, prophetic, and mystical incidents in an effort to place him squarely in the tradition of the inspired seers. He embarks on a curious, if not perverse, use of superstitious beliefs to describe Increase's birth; if one counts a late miscarriage, Increase is a seventh son, thereby likely to have the gift of prophecy.[13] We are told early in the text that "*Strange* things" occurred during his life, including rhapsodic visions at the Lord's Supper, and Cotton consistently quotes those diary passages that show Increase at mystical heights.

These examples are merely a prelude for the meat of *Parentator's* argument that Mather was prophetic in both his political and his ministerial career. In particular, close attention to scripture prophecies throughout his life led to a like inspiration in his writings, beginning with the *"Sober Chiliasm"* of *The Mystery of Israel's Salvation,* which, when preached in 1665, set Mather's lifelong pattern of inspired preaching on chiliastic themes:

> by Studying the *Prophecies,* he found, as many Holy Servants of GOD have done, a Communion with the *Lord GOD of the Holy Prophets* to be Sensibly Assisted & Advanced, And by *Meditations* on the *Paradisian State* of Things, he sailed so near to the *Land of Promise,* that he found the *Balsamic Breezes* of the Heavenly Country upon his mind, which, where they come, usually Refine and Sweeten, and Marvellously Purify the Souls that are Favoured with them.[14]

Increase also had illuminations about future events communicated to him by angels. In October of 1694, Increase had strange impressions of his going again to England in service of his country, while "there was among some in his Neighbourhood, a strange Descent of *Shining Spirits* that had upon them great marks of their being such *Angels* as they Declared themselves to be."[15] No matter that the journey was never made; the evidence was clear, and many years later some parishioners did suggest Mather's agency in England was needed. Though these incidents seem insignificant in retrospect, they do point to the larger purpose of Cotton Mather's text, the establishment of his father's life as *exemplum* with profound significance for the New England way. Cotton Mather would take his stand for his father's reputation upon Increase Mather's stature as a true seer and upon the fit reponse of the saints to such an inspired leader, and, indeed, to deceased saints in general.

Since the debacle of the Salem witchcraft trials, the disgrace of Sir William Phips, and his own resignation from the Harvard presidency, all occuring in the 1690s, Increase Mather had become increasingly otherworldly in his personal meditations and his preaching. In seeking coherence in the events of his father's life, Cotton used this otherworldliness after rejection in the political sphere as a final prophecy for New England. In his life, Increase Mather had suggested that if the church proved degenerate, the only way for God to preserve his people would be through divine, apocalyptic intervention. As we shall see below, Increase looked with increasing fervor for the descent of New Jerusalem to replace the corrupt, degenerate earthly city. Cotton agreed with his father on this point, and he could use the example of his father's life to prove the necessity of New England's turning to otherworldly faith and fervency in prayer for the acomplishment of apocalyptic prophesies. Increase Mather's translation to heaven, then, becomes a true recapitulation of Elijah's entrance into heaven if read in proper fashion. As Elijah's ascent had typified the resurrection of Christ, opening heaven to all believers, so Increase opened the vision of heaven to his church. The true seer rends the veil with prophecy, and Cotton Mather closes *Parentator* by quoting a funeral sermon charged with such eschatological expectations: " 'He [Increase] drew aside the Veil, and shewed you what is to be seen in *the most Holy place*; to be seen without Presumption or Profaneness; but with the greatest Advantage for a Progress towards *Perfection of Holiness in the Fear* of GOD. Thus he Invited you to accompany him in the *way to Zion, with your Faces thitherward.*' "[16]

What was the vision behind the veil which Mather opened to his congregation? From his first published treatise, *The Mystery of Israel's Salvation,* to his late meditations on death and the heavenly world, Mather explored the thickets of eschatology in painstaking detail. As James W. Davidson has shown, the minutiae of millennial events and signs were passionately debated by preachers and parishioners, for such seemingly arcane issues as the number of the beast, the pouring out of the vials, or the time of the death of the witnesses determined just where one stood in the flow of providential history.[17] With their eyes turned towards Europe and the Holy Land, New Englanders waited for signs of the fall of Mystical Babylon and the conversion of the Jews, the final events before the glorious advent of the millennial reign of the saints. Whatever differences developed over particulars, most ministers of Increase Mather's generation agreed that the earth was indeed approaching the last times, and the cataclysmic events described in Revelation could be no more than a generation or two away.

The generally tortuous, at times inconsistent, and always flexible interpretation of biblical language in such treatises leads modern readers, safe in a historical period which fears only man-made apocalypse, to view such speculations as arcane curiosities. Moreover, it is easy to point to the discrepancy between millennial hopes for New England and its apparent declension, the failure of the "errand into the wilderness."[18] In his study of the Mathers, Robert Middlekauff posits that Increase Mather responded to the declension first with jeremiads and finally with disappointment, as he turned his expectations from earthly to heavenly fulfillment of scripture prophecies. In cataloging Mather's political and ecclesiastical setbacks, Middlekauff writes, "These challenges and his defeats in meeting them stripped him of his confidence in New England as a redemptive force in history. To be sure, he admitted his disenchantment only occasionally, but the gradual evaporation of his corporate spirit is clear in the shift in his appeals from New England to the elect, to the mystical Israel of the types."[19] As Mather directed his eyes to the mystical church, he became obsessed with death and with the possibility of personal perfection in heaven instead of on earth, and finally with the idea of the saints on earth and in heaven awaiting the return of Christ. Though Middlekauff's observations go a long way towards explaining the personal and public pilgrimage of Increase Mather, there is another level of his eschatology which remained intact throughout his life, and in a great part explains the shift Middlekauff noted. His retreat from the expectation of a corporate fulfillment of New England's mission can, in fact, be seen as part of a larger strategy to preserve the more fundamental vision of a millennial reign of the church triumphant.

The qualities of Mather's preaching labelled "late" and "otherworldly" by Middlekauff, meditation on heaven, the belief that chiliasm is a sign of faith, the perfection of the millennial world of the mystical church, were in fact present in one of the earliest of Mather's writings, *The Mystery of Israel's Salvation.*[20] His "otherworldliness" must be redefined in terms of one of the marvelous paradoxes of Mather's millennialism, his belief that the other world will be realized on this world after the Apocalypse. As we shall see below, for Mather the passage through death to heaven is only part of a journey leading back to an earth rejuvenated by the descent of the New Jerusalem. Throughout his career Mather preached the reunion of mankind and Christ on the earth at the Resurrection. Herein lay the deepest appeal of his prophecies, for the world of the Millennium as he painted it before the eyes of his parishioners was a personal, human world which allowed for glorious perfection and the intimate reunion of the living saints, the saints in heaven, and Christ. Mather directed the saints to prepare for this reunion through the seemingly "otherworldly" activities of faith and fervency in prayer, heavenly meditation, and longing for death.

The effects of this chiliastic vision were two-fold. The union of God and man in Christ's form necessitates that the whole saint, both body and soul, be exalted and glorified when Christ returns. For a minister whose whole life was spent emphasizing the sacrifice of Christ in his flesh, and the depth of man's alienation from God through sinful flesh, the most glorious moment conceivable was the personal reunion in the flesh of man and Christ as brothers. Moreover, the appeal of Christ's humanity at the Resurrection is aesthetic, for his human form is the most beautiful object ever created, and it alone is capable of satisfying man's physical and spiritual senses perpetually. On these points Mather is repetitious and insistent:

God the Father cannot be seen with *bodily* eyes; He is *the invisible God*. The Divine Nature cannot be seen, but *Christ* by reason of his being Flesh, *may* be seen; and at *the latter day* every eye shall behold Him: Then shall *Job* (and every one else) in his Flesh see God.

. . . .

That body now fills the Third Heaven with glory. . . . When the souls which are now in Heaven shall come down from thence with Jesus Christ, and be reunited to their bodyes, and continue in this lower world as long as the Day of Judgement shall last, then does *New-Jerusalem* come down out of Heaven.

. . . . *

One Reason why Believers shall have Bodily Eyes restored to them at the Latter day, is, that so they may behold the Glory of the *God man* JESUS CHRIST.

. . . . :

For the *Covenant is made with the Person* consisting of Body & Soul, and not with the Soul only altho' principally.[21]

Not only will the saints enjoy a vision of Christ at the Resurrection, they will also be resurrected in glorified bodies which are "like unto" the glorious body of Christ.[22] The vision of the "bodilie eyes" is the moment which the saint anticipates on earth and in heaven. The saints in heaven now have an intellectual view, with spiritual eyes, of the glory of Christ's human form shining down from the third heaven into the separate state; while Mather would not have his congregation think of these saints entirely in earthly terms, he does assert that the saints have human senses "analogous" to human senses by which they see and hear.[23] Mather notes that the perfection of the human soul comes with the ravishment at the beatific vision which fills the soul's eyes with Christ's glory, so the saints on earth should direct their eyes of faith to Christ to prepare for heaven.[24] Moreover, he cites biblical proof that saints at the moment of death or during a special revelation granted by God (as to Moses on the mountain) pass into a special state in which the various powers of the eyes coalesce. Mather's favorite example was the vision of Saint Stephen:

Dying *Steven* saw Jesus at the Right hand of God: So a Believer is no sooner dead, but he has a soul-ravishing sight of the Man Christ Jesus at the Right hand of *GOD*. The Saints in heaven have an intellectual Vision of the Glory of Christ, such as the holy Angels have, and after the Resurrection they shall behold Christ with *bodily* eyes.[25]

Mather's sense of the glory of Christ is fundamentally visual, and his eschatological writings reverberate with the intensity of his descriptions of heavenly glories. The saint is assured continually that the eyes of faith can dwell on scripture similes depicting the realm of heaven and see in these similes something of what will be revealed in physical forms to "bodilie eyes" in the Millennium.

The second effect of Mather's chiliasm is a redefinition of the separate state, the heaven to which the souls of dead saints travel in anticipation of the Resurrection. Mather knew that he would be criticized for requiring saints in heaven to return to earth. Would not this diminish their enjoyment of heaven? In fact, Mather claims, the Millennium would allow a closer communion with Christ than was ever possible in heaven where saints only knew Christ intellectually.[26] The separate state is transitional, provided for the saints to develop their spiritual faculties. One effect of this revaluation was to reduce the emotional and doctrinal distance between saints on earth and the saints in the separate state, for saints in both conditions have the same yearnings for the vision of Christ with "bodilie eyes." Since the spiritual senses of the soul in heaven were outgrowths of the eyes of faith developed on earth, the differences between saints on earth and those in heaven were of degree rather than of kind. Mather's preaching on death and heaven spoke to those activities on earth which would affect one's condition in heaven, the exercise of the eyes of faith, the performance of good works, and the desire for the Chiliad. Thus death was less a cataclysmic break with friends and church on earth than like another stage on the saint's pilgrimage to the New Jerusalem.

Descriptions of the soul in its journey to heaven reveal Mather in one of his favorite rhetorical stances. He asks his congregation to focus their imaginations on the highly dramatic scenes of the souls, guarded by angels, fighting up through the agents of Satan who inhabit the air:

> The Souls of Believers, being separated from their Bodies, before they can get to Heaven, they must go thorow the Devils Country: the Air wherein we breath, is so: A Soul that is carried to Heaven, passeth thorow the midst of all the Pirates of Hell; but then there is no danger, since they have a glorious convoy of Angels. When the Devils see that Convoy, they dare not stir or come near the blessed Souls, which they behold environed with Angels, whom the Lord Christ has sent to be as a convoy, to bring them safe to be where he is, that they may behold his Glory.[27]

As we have seen earlier in the discussion of Protestant death-bed rituals, the imagination could create scenes which lend time and space to events which, with the rejection of purgatory, were in fact instantaneous. I suspect Mather fulfilled deep emotional needs with these descriptions, for the audience could participate in what is essentially a Christian comedy whose denouement is always known for the saint. The pleasure of imagining the passage of the soul to heaven is in the frustration of the devil who is driven from the air by angels protecting the soul (fig. 7). Moreover, Mather is quite specific about the location of the separate souls. He describes three heavens; the lowest heavens, essentially the earth's atmosphere, which is a changeable state of clouds, moving planets and stars, birds, and devils. Souls may occasionally visit this realm, but it is painful for them to do so. The separate souls inhabit the second heaven, fixed stars, from which they can see with spiritual eyes Christ's glowing body seated at the right hand of God in the third, eternal heaven. For Mather, the Resurrection is initiated by the movement of Christ down through the second heaven, from which the souls accompany Christ to rejoin their risen bodies in the first heaven. Mather here not only provides space for the imagination, he also provides a scenario for a return of ritualistic import to the Puritan funeral. There are indications that Puritans were encouraged to see the experience of the body as emblematic of the experiences of the soul:

> Men take care for the Bearers of the Body, when dead: God takes care for the Bearers of the Soul, when departed.
> Men are Bearers that carry the Body to the Grave: Angels are the Bearers that carry the Soul to Glory. Men mourning follow the Corpse to the House appointed for all the Living: Angels triumphing go along with the Soul to the Mansions prepared for all the Believing.[28]

Mather's eschatology of the separate state was popular with New England stonecarvers as well. Imps of death are often depicted lurking about the body, as on the William Dickson stone, Cambridge, Massachusetts (fig. 8). A great variety of forms develop depicting the soul in its separate state. The presentation can be more or less "realistic," depending on the date and the stonecarving tradition (fig. 9). And many stones use emblematic means to depict one, two or all three heavens (fig. 10).

Mather's chiliasm also led him to reformulate the corporate nature of the jeremiad.[29] For Increase Mather, the jeremiad was a useful tool for addressing New England's wrongs, and he often invoked the formula of spiritual decline provoking stern judgments to be met with reformation. Yet it would be a gross understatement to say the jeremiad did not always produce the desired results; to an impartial observer, the events from Mather's first publication in 1669 to his death in 1723 point to nothing more clearly than the failure of the New England mission, the spread of the true church in the American wilderness, and in particular, the failure of Mather's own church to retain preeminence in New England. In his funeral sermon for John and Abigail Foster, preached in 1711, Mather admits the decline of his church: "We in this Congregation have singular cause to be sensible of this Stroke upon us, for that it is on some accounts a finishing Stroke. Eighteen years ago, the Governour of the Province, and Four of the Council were Members belonging to this Church: Now there is none remaining; They are all *taken away* from us."[30] But in Mather's reaction to adversity we find him reaching deep into the symbolic resources of the language of eschatology which had served him well from his earliest writings. Mather holds out the possibility of maintaining God's favor to the church of true saints even if the colony as a whole refuses to follow suit. By slightly altering the formula of the jeremiad, Mather can hold up heavenly-mindedness and other-worldliness among saints patiently awaiting the divine intervention of the Apocalypse to reform the earth as a successful response to God's judgments.

Within the rhetoric of the jeremiad rests the implicit assumption that mankind can expect "visible" signs of God's will and of the great events of the last times prophesied in Daniel, Isaiah, Revelation, and elsewhere, so that the success of the church must be "visible" as well. In many of Mather's millennial texts, from *The Mystery of Israel's Salvation* (1669) to *Icabod* (1702), the visible glory of God's kingdom was seen in great leaders and great events, from the Reformation led by Luther and Calvin to the expected conversion of the Jews. But in other texts he found metaphors describing glories which would be visible only in the Millennium. Thus only five years after preaching *Ichabod,* which warned of the passing of a visible glory from New England, Mather claimed in *Meditations on Death* that the truly gracious usually lack this kind of visibility anyway. God's children are "like Princes in a Disguise in this world," and "their worth is not that which appears outwardly to a Carnal eye. It is the Grace which they are adorned with."[31] In fact, the present form of the world would soon be at an end, and it is only preserved for the sake of the few righteous people who are destined to live out their lives before the general conflagration of the earth. As with the individual, so with the church: "Considering the *Dark Aspect* which the Churches are at present under, I should be Ready to Conclude, that in less than one Generation, these *Bethels* will become *Bethavens;* were it not that the Happy Time draws near, when there will be a great Reformation of the Churches throughout the Earth," just prior to the Apocalypse.[32] It is in the preparation for these events that Mather finds an indication of New England's fruitfulness, and he is precise in defining activities the saints must undertake to please God. Spiritual vision will reveal to the saints the way to become the first fruits of God's kingdom: prayer, heavenly-mindedness, good works, and most important, fervent expectation of the Resurrection and the restitution of all things.

To accomplish this transformation of eschatological expectations, Mather first encouraged people to adopt a millennial frame of mind through meditations on heaven. Then he preached that millennial fervor was a sign of grace and a clear evidence of sanctification. As Robert Middlekauff notes, "If a man discovered that he believed in Christ's imminent return, he could take hope that he was one of the elect. Chiliasm was thereby added to one of the signs of assurance."[33] But this had been a feature of Mather's chiliasm from at least as early as his first publication, *The Mystery of Israel's Salvation,* and Mather puts this sign of assurance to a variety of uses throughout his career.

First, Mather argues that a right knowledge of millennial truths exercises new senses implanted by grace in the saint: "as for those whose understandings God hath opened to *conceive* and *receive* these truths they see a glory in them above the world, that eye hath not seen nor tongue can express."[34] Mather emphasizes the noetic quality of the eye of faith, since only through this eye can man know the highest mysteries concerning the resurrection of the dead and the glories of Christ and the angels. True saints have always had such visions, which represent the closest communion with God and angels possible on earth, a communion only shadowed forth and hinted at in the imperfect earthly church:

> The truth is, that whilst a man is dwelling upon these meditations, he is as it were in heaven upon earth, he hath fellowship with the Angels in heaven. . . . When men of God in former times have had their minds taken up with Divine Visions, Angels of God have been with them; verily so it is with the servants of God at this day, though the Ministry of the holy Angels be more secret, spiritual and invisible, than sometimes formerly. . . . But there is that which is better than fellowship with Angels, even communion with the blessed Holy God is to be seen and felt in these Meditations.
>
> And this I may affirm to you, that if there be any man which hath not had communion with the blessed holy God is to be seen and felt in these Meditations.
> either it is because he hath no grace in his soul, and these Mysteries are such things as an unregenerate heart can find no sap, nor savour in them.[35]

Mather forges a link between such meditations and the saint's behavior, since the saint is expected to imitate the behavior of the angels and the glorified saints in heaven. Thus the saint "orders his Conversation as one that thinks of and prepares for another world. . . . They don't see by Bodily Eyes what is in the other World, but by faith they see those Glorious things, and therefore they *Walk* and order their Conversation accordingly."[36] The primary heavenly activity on earth is the performance of good works. Although Mather repeatedly warned that mere works would not bring salvation, he knew his parishioners needed some tangible idea of the rewards in heaven that good works would bring. By claiming "The more Good we do on Earth, the more Glory shall we have when we come to Heaven,"[37] he appealed rhetorically to the commercial mentality that would use this doctrine as an occasion for Yankee bargaining with God. He asks,

> would our hearts chuse rather to be Holy than to be Rich and Great in the World? . . . What are our Lives and Conversations, are they holy and heavenly? Do we drive an heavenly Trade continually: Phil 3:20. *Our Conversation is in heaven.* Our trading

is there, says the Apostle. Every Saint of God has the Privilege of Trading there: He
sends Ventures to heaven, and has rich Returns. To be much in Prayers and Praises,
is to drive an Heavenly Trade.[38]

Mather also departs from traditional Calvinist eschatology by making
glorification a progressive rather than an instantaneous transformation.
Heaven is not a place of static joy, for as the saint is perfected in his
knowledge and experience of Christ in heaven, so his joys increase. Thus
from the inception of grace and growth of grace in the soul on earth, to
the separate state, to the Resurrection, and to the final glorification in the
third heaven, there is a continuous growth of joy. Moreover, Mather appeals to his congregation's sense of individual and class status by pro-
claiming that not all saints are equal in joy in heaven. Since some souls
are enlarged by gracious works on earth, they will be capable of more
joy: "Every One of them will be *Top-full of Glory*; yet will there be a
Difference, because some are more capacious Vessels than Others are.
. . . Can we think, that every Saint shall have as great a Crown of Glory
as *Paul* shall in that Day?"[39]

Second, Mather can also use millennial expectations to bolster the
authority of the ministry as a group of prophets. God sends premonitions
and revelations of upcoming millennial events to those He loves; *ergo* the
very writing of *The Mystery of Israel's Salvation* is proof positive of
Mather's status as chosen vessel. His church should be cognizant of this
privilege and prepare itself to join the heavenly body of saints. It is no
coincidence that John Davenport's preface to this volume attaches millennial significance to increased interest in the interpretation of prophecy,
since "when the time for the accomplishing of it [Israel's salvation] ap-
proacheth, many shall be stirred up to enquire with all diligence into the
meaning of it"(A2). Further, Davenport is sure that the Holy Spirit has
called Mather to the subject, and Mather himself adopts this position in
later writings.[40] Thus the words of the preacher both as prophet and
interpreter of prophecy are fused with the scripture prophecies themselves. In *Meditations on the Glory of the Heavenly World*, Mather imagines heavenly affirmation of the minister's success in putting into words
what tongue cannot express, for "the Saints in Glory say, It was a true
report which the Ministers of Christ brought unto us, when we were on
the Earth, concerning his Glory, but they never told us a Thousand part
of it: Now our Eyes have seen it, we see that it far exceedeth the same
which we heard" (p. 98). Heavenly-mindedness and the errand into the
wilderness were organically related in Mather's mind, since the wilderness
condition was especially conducive to special revelations from heaven.
Also, the first fruits grown in the wilderness contribute to the restitution
of all things soon to be accomplished. As Mather notes,

some of us are under special advantage to understand these mysterious truths *of God*; That is to say, such of us as are in an exiled condition in this wilderness. Indeed some came hither upon worldly accounts, but others there are that came into this wilderness purely upon spiritual accounts; . . .that so they might bear witness against the Name of the beast, and against his character, but also against all humane inventions in the worship of God. . . . *John's* being led into the wilderness to see *Romes* destruction, may signifie, that some faithful ones of God in a wilderness, shall have a wonderful discovery of those things made unto them. God hath led us into a wilderness, and surely it was not because the Lord hated us, but because he loved us, that he brought us hither into this Feshimon. Who knoweth but that he may send down his spirit upon us here, if we continue faithful before him?[41]

Mather's most heated discussion in *The Mystery of Israel's Salvation* concerns the purity of the millennial church, and here a strain of escha-tology links heavenly-mindedness to Mather's earliest statements on the church in the controversy over the Half-way Covenant. Again we should remember it was Davenport, conservative leader of forces opposed to the Half-way Covenant, who introduced Mather's first major publication, and Mather responded with jeremiadic fervor when he discussed God's pun-ishment of those that set up false ordinances and human inventions in worship and polity. Despite Mather's later about-face on the Half-way Covenant, he never retreated from the ideal of the purity of the millennial church:

And this will be not only here and there, even (as it is at this day amongst a few churches who in conscience to God endeavour that their building may be of living stones, which I look upon as first fruits of what shall be hereafter) in a particular church or *two*, but universally, Isa. 60:21. *thy people shall be all righteous.* There will not be a profane person tolerated in the Church in those days. . . . And what ever it is now, I am sure then, meer civility and morality, together with an outward profession will not be thought enough to qualifie for Church Member-ship, except there be ex-perience of the regenerating grace of God in the soul. . . . So that *circumcision in flesh,* baptism, and outward profession, will not be enough to give admittance into the Church of God, except there be the *Circumcision of the heart*; and what's that, but regeneration? (115-16)

The functional metaphors here are "first fruits" and "living stones," both with profound eschatological significance. "First fruits," be they pure churches, early conversions, assurance of salvation, or the resurrection of Christ, are real, earthly events that point to future fulfillment of God's promises. Following Jewish ritual as described in Leviticus, Mather uses "first fruits" to describe earthly events fraught with millennial signifi-cance precisely because they anticipate the literal fulfillment of God's promises: the coming down from heaven of New Jerusalem, built entirely of "living stones," the conversion of the Jews, the resurrection of the dead, the restitution of an earthly paradise, and the Second Coming of Christ. Christians then may become first fruits by participating in activities which are known to forecast the Millennium, including prayer, regeneration, obedience to prophecy delivered in pulpit and Bible, and, most importantly, joining pure churches as living stones.

The eyes of faith lead saints to these activities, and it is the visionary power of these eyes which, together with that of the soul's eyes in heaven and of the "bodilie eyes" of the resurrected saint, unites the living and the dead in anticipations of millennial glory. In Mather's writings about millennial fervor, about the relationship of the churches militant and triumphant, and about death, heaven, and the Resurrection, his strategy is to bring before the saints' eyes those visible continuities to be found in God's promises. His duty as minister in using prophetic language and images is to develop a rhetoric of millennial expectation which will encourage the saint to see the realization of prophecy through the veil of earthly events. This is not merely the reading of signs of the times, it is rather a personal preparation for the experience of the Millennium. The saint should strive for heavenly behavior and otherworldliness, but he must also live in and see his imperfect surroundings as if they were heavenly and perfect; he must see the potential, the inchoate perfection which the Bible describes. Thus Mather can reconcile a premillennial theology with its radical disjunction of heaven and earth, with an eschatological system which emphasizes the spiritual continuity between saints on earth, in heaven, and in the New Jerusalem. In this continuity rests the meaning of the imagery of eschatological literature and funerary art in late seventeenth and early eighteenth century New England.

Figure 7. Sarah Antram, 1732, Providence, Rhode Island

Figure 8.   William Dickson, 1692, Cambridge, Massachusetts

Figure 9.   Deacon Nathaniel Knowlton, 1726, Ipswich, Massachusetts

Figure 10. Captain Joseph Kingsbury, 1788, Pomfret, Connecticut

4

The Prophetic Design of
Early New England Carving

FRINDS SURE WOULD PROVE TO FAR UNKIND
IF OUT OF SIGHT THEY LEAVE HIM OUT OF MIND
—Captain Jonathan Poole, 1678
Wakefield, Massachusetts

By the early eighteenth century, stonecarvers in the Boston area developed a variety of forms which reveal the aesthetic and theological imprint of the Mathers' prophetic mode of expression. As might be expected from a culture so imbued with the Word, these artisans employed a sophisticated vocabulary of biblical images falling into the various categories of visualizing the last things. Gravestone design in the early period of carving before 1720 transcends its biblical base, however. Carvers were adept at borrowing images from other craft traditions, such as engraving and silversmithing, and from European and American oral and printed sources. In examining their incorporation of such images with the symbolic language of New England eschatology, we can trace the evolution of an American art. And in the works of three of the earliest carvers, the anonymous Charlestown carver, JN carver, and the Lamson family, the art of "bodilie eyes" begins.[1]

The Living Stones: The Charlestown Carver

As Increase Mather preached about the relationship between living and dead saints, stonecarvers in the last quarter of the seventeenth century laid the foundation for a decorative tradition based on temple images meant to link the earthly and heavenly churches.[2] Temple imagery drawn from the Old Testament, including pillars, arches, and cherubs, abounds by the 1690s. As the Old Testament Temple was seen in its architecture to signify the world, the church on earth and the church in heaven, so reference to these divisions defined the congregation's relationship to the church. Increase Mather repeatedly turned to the Temple to illustrate the peculiar conjunction of spirit and flesh, Christ and the believer, the church in heaven and the church on earth that was made by grace. The moment of death was naturally a focus for such imagery, for at death the saint exchanged the state of physical membership in the church militant for the state of spiritual life in the church triumphant. "Christ is the elect corner stone in Sion,"[3] Increase Mather wrote, and each saint becomes a "living stone" placed on this cornerstone in the heavenly temple at the moment of death. The saint is transformed into a living stone in several stages: the heart becomes a temple for the spirit of Christ through grace, the person becomes a living pillar in the church on earth, at death he or she is made a living stone in the heavenly temple, and finally, in the Resurrection he or she returns to earth as a living stone in the New Jerusalem.

For Increase Mather, interpretation of the Temple was determined by his christology. Not only was Christ the antitype of the Old Testament Temple and the High Priest, with his sacrifice opening the Holy of Holies, heaven, to all believers, but his union with human nature made possible the resurrection of the body in the New Jerusalem temple. The very connection between the churches militant and triumphant is made possible only by Christ's union of heaven and earth, spirit and flesh in his person. Thus Mather could write,

> The *Tabernacle* was a Type of Christ's humane nature, which is therefore called *the true Tabernacle.* . . . The Temple was the most costly, excellent, glorious, House in the world; thereby figureing the humane nature of Christ, which was adorned with graces and spiritual excellencies beyond any other man or creature. Particularly the *Veil* of the Temple typified the humane nature of Christ. . . . As there was no entring into the *Holy of Holies* but by the *Veil;* so there is no entring into the *Holy of Holies* but through that Sacrifice of the *flesh,* i.e. the *humane* nature of Christ. And this Truth is still mysteriously signified by that Ordinance of the *Lord's Supper.*[4]

The grave was the passageway from the earthly temple to the heavenly temple, and some of the earliest tombs in New England make reference to the paradoxical identity of the tomb and the temple for the saint. Puritans in England had adopted the conceit of the tomb as the house of death, and some early tombs in Windsor, Connecticut, are recreations of these English models. The best example of such house-tombs in New England is the Wolcott tomb of 1655, Windsor, Connecticut, which features a rectangular solid base with a barrel-vaulted "roof." The expense of such tombs and, perhaps, their association with the privileged class in England, vitiated their popularity in New England, but carvers adopted the basic themes of the tomb-temple relationship to a two-dimensional carving space. In fact, the earliest, and perhaps the most primitive surviving stones with decorative elements in Boston may have been seen by Puritans as symbolic of "living stones." The Samuel Bridge stone, 1672, and the Timothy Andrew stone, 1674, of Cambridge (figs. 11, 12) have an air of primitive simplicity, with the barest commemoration of the deceased within an arched flecked or incised border. The carver(s) may not have had the skill or inclination to shape the stone itself into an arched shape, but each uses the border to call the tomb-temple to mind. In fact, the primitive disregard for the stone itself evidenced by its lack of proper dressing and shaping may indicate that Puritans placed this marker less for commemoration and more for the symbolic purpose of indicating that here lies a living stone, a body which will rise to become part of the temple.

Certainly such an arched shape recalls the commonplace in Mather's time that death is "The Door of Eternity," but we must remember that this door was the entrance to a particular *place* in the Puritan imagination.[5] The essential transformation of the saint at death from physical being to spiritual being was accompanied by a no less important transformation from pillar of the earthly church to pillar in the mystical church.

Shortly after the appearance of the most primitive stones in the style of the Bridge and Andrew markers, a stonecutter known as the Charlestown carver codified the use of pillars as symbols of the translation of a deceased saint to a heavenly temple.[6] A remarkable example of his technique is found in the Neal Children stone, about 1678, in the Granary, Boston (fig. 13). While the heavily carved death's head in the vaulting of this low house reminds us of the tomb, in the individual vaults over the remains of the children the carver has incised another facade, which, as the Tashjians suggest, can be seen as "an ancillary metaphor for the temple of heaven."[7] Visually, the carver has "represented" the transformation that his faith tells him is already underway, as the children have become spiritual pillars in heaven.

The Charlestown carver cut pillars on several stones in Wakefield, Massachusetts, marking the graves of the seven "foundation men" of the Wakefield church, the original "pillars" on whom by custom the covenant of the church was built. On the John Person stone of 1679 (fig. 14), the pillars again start at ground level, move up to support an arch, and then give way to a deeply cut tympanum with emblems of mortality and a winged death's head. It is conceivable that these stones for the foundation men were meant to make a statement about the relationship of the deceased "pillars" to future generations of church members. This suggestion is borne out on a magnificently carved marker for Thomas Kendel, cut about 1676 (fig. 15), the epitaph of which reads: "Here in ye earth is layd on of ye 7 of this church foundation / So to Remain tl ye Powrful voice say Ris inherit a gloris Habitation / A patarn of piati & love & for peace / But now alas how short his race / Here we mourn and mourn we must / to see Zion stons lik Gold now layd in Dust." The first two lines of the epitaph present a complex conceit, as Kendel is depicted simultaneously as the inhabitant of the house of death, the church, and Zion; the viewer knows that these three houses define the saint's existence. The third line notes that Kendel is a fit pattern for hewing new living stones for the church, while the last line suggests that these living stones, though laid in dust, will rise to become pillars of gold in the New Jerusalem temple. The images on the stone brilliantly portray the saint's habitations. The pillar refers to Kendel as a founder of the church, but the placement of the death's head atop the pillar reminds us that Death has triumphed in removing this pillar from the church to his house. Nevertheless, a larger heavenly temple arches over Death's house, making death but a porter opening the way between the church and Zion. The cherubim call attention to both temples; their images on the veil separating the Holy of Holies from the inner court of the Old Testament Temple were held to be symbolic of their invisible ministry in guiding the saint's soul to heaven at death. Increase Mather affirms "there is a Communion between Angels in Heaven, and the Church on Earth, and that the Church is Surrounded with Angels, as the Temple was with Cherubims."[8] Kendel has joined the angels, and he may protect future generations of Wakefield church members until he rejoins the church physically at the Resurrection.

Some of the temple motifs on New England stones can be further illuminated by consulting Samuel Mather's *Figures or Types of the Old Testament.* Mather describes each aspect of the Old Testament Temple, its spiritual counterpart in the church, and its symbolic content as it reveals heavenly glories.[9] In discussing the pillars of the Temple, he writes,

> There were also Sculptures of Lillies /atop the pillars/ in the Temple, 1 *Kings* 7:19, 22.—and Saints are set forth by that flower. . . . The Allusion seems to lie in the Gifts and Graces of the Spirit of God shadowed by the excellent Properties of those Trees and Flowers.[10]

The two main pillars in the Temple were called Jachin and Boaz, and Samuel Mather singles them out as emblems of the spiritual qualities of those saints who are pillars of the Christian church. These pillars were of great beauty and strength, decked with lily capitals, and saints are beautiful and strong when they faithfully protect and support the church.

Moreover, the believer must be straight and strong to receive the crown of life promised in 2 Timothy 4:7-8. The saint who has these qualities, according to Mather, excels in beauty the pillars of the temple and gains a place in the New Jerusalem temple.[11]

Samuel Mather's analysis of the pillars illuminates the carvings on the Edmund Angier stone, 1692, Cambridge, Massachusetts (fig. 16). Replete with temple imagery, this stone communicates categorically Angier's importance as a saint in both the earthly and the heavenly temples. The epitaph, which tells us that Angier has "LEFT HIS EARTHLY & ENTRED INTO HIS HEAUENLY HOUSE," is flanked by the Jachin and Boaz pillars with flowered capitals. In the pilasters, however, stand the spiritual counterparts of Jachin and Boaz, which also support the temple. With an effigy of Angier at the "head" or capital of the pillar, the column itself is a profusion of fruits and leaves, which for Mather represent "the Gifts and Graces of the Spirit of God."

Gravestones emphasize the eschatological significance of temple imagery, reflecting the Puritan belief that images of the temple seen with spiritual eyes now prefigured actual temples to be seen with "bodilie eyes" when the New Jerusalem temple descended to earth. The transformation of believers from a physical to a spiritual condition at death is, in many sermons and poems, analogous to the transformation that occurs when people find faith while living.

Gravestones encouraged the living to transform themselves into temples commemorating the spirits of the dead, to reaffirm the continuity of the church. As the Jonathan Poole stone of 1678 reads,

> FRINDS SURE WOULD PROVE TO FAR UNKIND
> IF OUT OF SIGHT THEY LEAVE HIM OUT OF MIND
> & NOW HE LIES TRANSFORM'D TO NATIVE DUST
> IN EARTHS COLD WOMB AS OTHER MORTALS MUST
> It'S StRANGE HIS MAtCHLESSS WORTH INTOM'D SHOULD LY
> OR THAT HIS FAME SHOULD IN OBLIVION DY

The theological message is a simple one: believers are transformed into members of the mystical temple when converted and should therefore look to spiritual purity in the earthly temple. Moreover, they should never lose sight of the realization of the literal Zion in the final transformation of saints in the Resurrection. This doctrine finds imaginative applications in the ways in which the church and the saints are metaphorically described as spiritual beings. Increase Mather notes the fitness of literal descriptions of Old Testament types to both the gospel church and the heavenly Sion:

He [The Psalmist] asserts that Believers are *come to Mount Sion; the City of the Living God, the Heavenly Jerusalem.* By *Sion,* we are not to understand the Literal *Sion;* but the *Church of God,* of which *Sion* was a Figure. As for the Literal *Sion,* it had two heads; On one of which the Temple was Built, where the Priests did resort to Offer Sacrifice & Incense; which had a Typical respect to the *Priesthood* of our Lord Jesus Christ: On the Other head of *Sion, David* and the other Kings of *Judah* had their habitation, who were also Types of Christ. The *City of the Living God* and the *Heavenly Jerusalem,* intend the same thing with *Sion.* . . . The Church of GOD was typified thereby.
. . . .
The catholick mystical church is the mother of all true believers, There is no true believer but is a member of that church. The church is stil'd *The Heavenly Jerusalem.* Heb. 12:22. For that They that are truely belonging to the church of god Their names are written in heaven, and they are Borne from heaven, by the regenerating grace of *god* descending into theire *Soules.* Also Theire Conversations are In *heaven:* Jerusalem is sometimes taken for both the Litterall and Spirit Jerusalem.[12]

Thus the saints are allowed a certain imaginative freedom, a fluid movement between literal and spiritual significations of the language used to describe the church and the saints. Clearly this was an effective way to excite the congregation to see itself as a part of a glorious church which participates both in the earthly glory that was Solomon's Temple and in the heavenly glory that is being built in heaven through the death of saints, a glory to appear in the New Jerusalem. As Increase Mather notes, "a particular church which is a part of the catholicke church is a littel Jerusalem; and god and christ hath his throne there."[13] But it is the power to transform people in the earthly church into "living stones" in the New Jerusalem that this language would evoke, and Cotton Mather uses language to encourage this transformation through millennial fervor.

In a sermon preached at the founding of a church in Braintree, Massachusetts, in 1707, *The Temple Opening. A Particular Church Considered as a Temple of the Lord,* Mather invokes typology and sabbatism (the belief that the seventh age of the world is the Millennium) to place the founding of a particular church in a millennial context. Mather argues that the completion of the New Jerusalem temple is accomplished through the whole of human time:

And what? An *American Wilderness* be the Place, where the Glorious LORD shall *See Temples* Erected for Him! O Sovereign GRACE! O Wonderful GRACE! *It is even so, Lord, because it Pleases thee!* Indeed, the Whole CHURCH of GOD, collectively taken, is a TEMPLE, which our Magnificent Solomon is Building for Him. The Building is not yet Finished. The Period which answers to the *Seventh Year* wherein the Temple of *Solomon* was finished, is not yet arrived.[14]

But each converted sinner is a new stone in this building, and the ministers are the workmen of Solomon-Christ. One point Mather makes here is that the church should be built of the best materials, i.e. truly elect saints, but his most interesting imaginative leap links the literal and the figural levels of biblical description of the temple. Mather implies that the individual who sees biblical language with eyes of faith is able to live in and further the remarkable transformation of the spiritual temple:

> It is remarkable, That all the *Furniture* of the *Temple*, Seen by *John*, in the *Heavenly World*, is introduced, as *Living*. The very *Lamps*, are *Spirits;* the very *Horns* of the *Altar* have a *Voice:* The *Throne* it self *Speaks*. A *Church* is more like the *Temple* in the *Heavenly World*, than any *Inanimate Composition* that has been called a *Temple*. 'Tis *Living*, every part of it. But that it may have the more of a *Temple* is it, what was in the Temple of old, must be *Imitated* and *Spiritualized* in the Church of the LORD. A *Church* is to consider, what was to be *Seen*, and what was to be Done, in the Temple; and to take its Measures accordingly (pp. 10-11).

Thus one way to transform oneself into a living stone was through spiritual imitation of the ceremonies of the Old Testament Temple in gospel ordinances. This imitation would place the church in the cosmic history of God's church as it approached its completion in the millennial sabbath.

But there was another sort of transformation available to the saints which more particularly dealt with the death of church members. As we have seen with the epitaph of the Poole stone, the saints were encouraged to transform their memories into temples for the spirit of the dead, thus forging a link between the members of a church in the heavenly temple and those left behind in the church on earth. In Samuel Torrey's Epitaph for William Thompson, who died in 1666, we find a sophisticated literary example of the visual transformations effected on gravestones. Due to the verbal complexity of the poem, I print it in full.

> EPITAPH
> Here lies his corps, who, while he drew his breath,
> He lived the lively portraiture of Death,
> A walking tomb, a liveing sepulcher,
> In which blak meloncholy did interr
> A blessed soule, which god & nature have
> By Death delivered from yt liveing grave.
> By this thine epitaph, now thou art gon:
> Thy death it was thy resurection.
>
> Here lyes his Corps, whose spirit was divine,
> Too rich a relict for an earthly shrine,
> A secret temple closd, where in his god
> By solitudes of fellowship abode.

His gifts, his grace, his life, his light, retird,
He livd by life immediatly inspird.
Black darkness oft the Child of light befalls,
Yet hee had sumtimes lucid entervales.
Then let this epitaph to him be given:
Darkness dispelled by the light of heaven.

He did outlive his life; twas time to dye,
He shall out live his death eternally.
Wele not lament his timely Death, for why
Twas death to live, his life to dye;
But yet we cannot Chuse but sign to se
A Saint to make a Dark Catastrophe.
Then sleep, swete saint, & rest thy weary dust;
Sing requems to thy selfe among the just.
We hope ere long with ye to bear our part(s);
This epitaph to wright upon our hearts:
Sleep in this tomb till Christ ungrave thy dust,
Untill the resurection of the just.[15]

The poem is filled with paradoxical inversions of the powers of life and death, as expressed through the central metaphors of light, dark, the sepulchre, the temple, and the heart. These metaphors seem arbitrarily forced together until some facts of Thompson's life are known. Cotton Mather tells us in the *Magnalia Christi Americana* that Thompson "fell into that *Balneum diaboli,* a black *melancholy,*" which caused his derangement for years, including, Mather hints, suicide attempts.[16] Ministers often joined together to pray for his release from insanity and from life, and after one such session, Thompson became lucid and died in peace. In fact, the ministers acted as angels protecting him with prayers from the assaults of the devil. Mather ends the biography with a poem entitled "Remarks On The Bright and the Dark Side of that American Pillar," and its closing lines share the imagery of Torrey's epitaph: "Long had the churches begg'd the saint's release; / Releas'd at last, he dies in glorious *peace.* / The night is not so long, but *phosphor's* ray Approaching glories doth on high display. / Faith's *eye* in him discern'd the *morning star,* / His heart leap'd; sure the *sun* cannot be far."[17]

The title of Mather's poem shows the coherence of the light and dark imagery with temple images in the Torrey epitaph, for not only was Thompson, as minister, a pillar of the church, but his body itself was a temple for the spirit of God. Thompson's case struck the imaginations of his contemporaries precisely because his madness brought into question the relationship of the body-temple to the spirit. Could the body, and ultimately death, permanently damage the spirit?

In his treatment of these questions, Torrey reveals deeply seated symbolic structures in the Puritan mind. In Torrey's first stanza we have the conceit that the flesh, though the temple of the spirit, is still the cause for its corruption through sin. Paradoxically, the flesh causes a death which can only be remedied by the soul's dying into a new life of grace. In Thompson's case, this rebirth has been complicated by melancholy which has made the body literally a "walking tomb, a living sepulchre." Given the combined corruption of the flesh and mental illness, how is the soul to be released from the devil's tomb?

In the second stanza, Torrey suggests that the body is transformed from tomb to temple by the presence of the spirit of grace which survives intact in secret communion with God even when the soul is darkened. Thompson's fate therefore applies to all Christians since "Black darkness oft the Child of light befalls," and even the most gracious saints have times of black doubt, a momentary death in which gifts, grace, life, and light retire. When natural light retires, heavenly light will preserve the spirit. But natural light, even when aided by supernatural light, cannot outlive the darkness of death, so the saint must undergo the transformation of the tomb which frees the light of heaven to outlive even death. Nevertheless, the living lament this "Dark Catastrophe," literally a subversion of the order or system of things.

The last stanza calls for a final transformation of Thompson's tomb-temple into the hearts of the living. In the last three lines, Torrey asks that the epitaph be written upon the heart, and the ambiguous reference of "this tomb" implies that the saint sleeps both in the ground and in the hearts of the living until the Resurrection. Torrey would have the hearts of the saints in the church on earth be a temple for the memory of the dead saints of their church until the Resurrection reunites the saints of the earthly and the heavenly churches. The living saints must work this final transformation from the tomb and the page to the reader's heart, thus uniting tomb-temple-heart in a corporation of living readers and dead saints. For Cotton Mather, this union of the living and the spirit of the dead began even before Thompson's death, since it was the prayers of the ministry that protected and then aided in the release of his soul from darkness and the body's tomb.

Many New England tombstones refer to this expansion of the metaphor of the heart as the temple of the spirit to include the heart as a temple for the whole church in a community of love. Allan Ludwig has noted the conjunction of the heart, with an engraved epitaph, and eros figures lofting the heart towards heaven, signifying divine love. The heart alone appears on some of the earliest stones in New England, and he feels that in New England the heart "appears to have been associated most closely with symbols of the soul in bliss and always in symbolic opposition to the imagery of death."[18] On several early tombstones hearts are found issuing from the mouths of death's heads.

Although the heart was a common emblem of divine love in emblem books and on gravestones, the conceit of the heart as temple in Torrey's poem justifies particularizing some of these heart images as emblems of the love of the saints for those who have passed through the tomb into the temple of heaven. The triad of the heart as tomb, temple of spirit, and temple of memory is found on two stones in the Granary, Boston. On the Henry Messinger, Jr., stone, 1686 (fig. 17), possibly cut by the JN carver, the heart encloses a delicately cut fleur-de-lis, representing the spirit of Christ-lily indwelling in the Christian heart. The death's head atop the heart calls to mind the transformation of death that has killed the body without removing the spirit of love in the heart. On the Martha Waite stone of 1671 (fig. 18), the status of the deceased infant in the temple is articulated by the names of the parents carved on the borders on the heart. Not only is the spirit of Martha preserved in the hearts of her parents, it is also preserved in the temple of the church on earth and in heaven by the very membership of her parents in the church, a membership which includes Martha as child of the Covenant. The stark and plain nature of this stone reminds us that Puritans saw such artifacts as gravestones as means of communication rather than ends in themselves; once the memory of Martha was inscribed on the temple-hearts of the church, the image on the stone could dissolve into nothingness.

The JN Carver and the First Fruits

From about 1693 to 1710, a carver who signed his work "JN" placed stones in several graveyards in and around Boston.[19] While some of his designs present death's heads and flowers common to the *memento mori* tradition, JN's work is unique for a group of stones which include peacocks, dagons, and urns (figs.19-21). The dagon figure is of particular significance, for it is one of the first indications that Puritan New England would accept effigy-like figures in funerary art. While these designs were already common on silverware and in emblem books, when placed on gravestones they transcend the merely decorative use. JN's habit of adding a small death's head atop the urn suggests that the whole design has eschatological significance. Interpretations have been offered for the discrete elements of JN's designs, but when viewed in the context of contemporary comments on dagons, peacocks, and vegetation, these elements combine in a prophetic statement about the deceased.

Harriette Forbes first called attention to the virtuousity of JN's carving. She dubbed his most popular design the "Urn and Mermaid" style, but Ludwig and Tashjian rename the mermaids dagons.[20] Dagons were the half-human, half-fish or vegetable idols of the Philistines, and by the seventeenth century dagon was the generic term for any idol. But, as Allan Ludwig notes, "The use of dagons on Puritan gravestones is puzzling in the light of the fact that they were associated with paganism and the evil doings of Thomas Morton and his merrymen. . . . In any event it is not clear what pagan water deities were doing on Puritan gravestones."[21] Ludwig refers to William Bradford's account of Thomas Morton's carryings-on about the Maypole at Merrymount, including drunken friskings with Indian women. This episode concluded with the arrest of Morton and the renaming of Merrymount as Mount Dagon. Dickran and Ann Tashjian pursue Ludwig's suggestion in detail, noting contemporary uses of dagons in woodcuts, and establishing the seventeenth-century use of the dagon to represent humankind given over to base passions. They conclude: "Dagons thus indicated the fallen state of man, both in terms of his mortal sin and inevitable death, and so they appeared on New England gravestones in a visual context that nevertheless provided the affirmative possibilities of salvation."[22]

The image remains ambiguous, however, since JN has added wings to the dagons, and they seem to present the urn to the viewer as if to celebrate the deceased.[23] Perhaps JN added the wings to assert that fallen creatures could be transformed into angels, and that "bodilie eyes" might see such angels participate in the resurrection of the saint's body. The complexity of JN's design can be appreciated by surveying the visual sources JN seems to have drawn upon. One of the most popular seventeenth-century sources for information on heavenly beings was Thomas Heywood's *The Hierarchie of the Blessed Angells,* which codified in poetry and profuse illustration the orders of heaven.[24] One print depicts the fall of Dagon before the ark of the Lord as described in 1 Samuel 5 (fig. 22). The chapter heading on the opposite page not only has the urn, dagon, and vegetation motif common to many seventeenth-century books, it also includes peacocks lassoed by the dagons (fig. 23). Thus in one illustration we have all the elements unique to JN designs. While Harriette Forbes notes that peacocks often symbolized the Resurrection, it seems clear from Heywood's text and JN's designs that seventeenth-century Puritans assigned other meanings to peacocks. Heywood associates Adonis and Anamelech, idols bearing the form of a male peacock, with Dagon under the general heading of idolatry.

> *Adonis,* Adramelech the Idoll of the Sepharuaims, it bore the figure of a Peacock or a Mule: *Asdod* of the Philistines, which is likewise called *Dagon: Anamelech,* which

bore the semblance of a Horse or Pheasant Cocke, belonging to the inhabitants of Sepharuaim. . . . *Saturninus,* like a fish, but from the waste upward like a beautiful woman. . . .[25]

Thomas Wilson, in *A Complete Christian Dictionary,* notes the dual nature of the peacock, a strange combination of beauty and benevolence with vanity and hatred towards man: "it doth love man, reverence him and helpeth him when it seeth him hurt by other beasts," but "It's said to have the voyce of the Devill, (its voyce is terrible) the head of a Serpent (which being combed and weak, it resembleth) and the pace of a theef, being still and without noyse."[26] The peacock may be drawn displaying its tail to represent earthly vanity, or with tail down, to represent the overcoming of the flesh. In the Heywood illustration, the peacock with spread tail is lassoed by dagons, as if to indicate a connection between earthly vanity and pagan idolatry. This connection is confirmed by illustration from emblem literature. In a delightful emblem by the popular Otto Van Veen, whose designs were frequently reprinted in English Protestant emblem books, cherubs of divine love busily beat down the tail of a male peacock (fig. 24). The epigraph to the emblem reads, "divine love weighs down pride, / he who has more humility also has more humanity."[27] The peacock on the Cleverly stone (fig. 19) is a male peacock with tail down, and when seen in conjunction with the standard hourglass and death's head reminding the viewer of mortality, it seems appropriate to interpret the whole design as an emblem of the humiliation of the flesh in death which is sustained by divine love.

The emblem designs of cherubs of divine love may provide a final insight into JN's use of dagons. As Barbara Lewalski explains, emblem writers transform Eros and Anteros from secular love emblems into the figures of Anima and Divine love.[28] JN may have simply combined the figures of dagon and the cherub to signify the transformation from carnal, earthly love to divine love effected in the saints by grace. Another Van Veen emblem shows two cherubs carrying a silver salt urn to illustrate "The salt of the soul is love," meaning that divine love and salt preserve against spiritual and physical corruption (fig. 25). Puritan viewers of JN stones may have made a further connection between urns carrying salt and those containing the ashes of the dead, since it was a popular seventeenth-century belief that the salts in the ashes of the body may contain seeds of life which revivify the body at the Resurrection.[29] The urn and dagon design, then, may refer at once to idolatrous vanity and divine love, the humiliation of the flesh, and the Resurrection.

The final element of the JN design, the vegetation, is best understood in the context of late seventeenth-century commentary on the biblical account of the fall of Dagon. The miraculous disfiguring of Dagon follows close on the heels of the utter defeat of the Israelites at the hands of the Philistines, culminating in the deaths of Phineas, Eli, and Phineas's wife; the wife dies in childbirth. The newborn child is named Ichabod, "the glory departing," a name which held special significance for Increase Mather whose sermon by that title compares the defeat of the Israelites and the loss of the ark to the decline of grace in New England. This moment of death and defeat, the deepest humiliation of God's people, is followed by the miraculous triumph of the ark:

> 2 When the Philistines took the ark of God, they brought it into the house of Dagon, and set it by Dagon.
> 3 And when they of Ashdod arose early on the morrow, behold, Dagon was fallen upon his face to the earth before the ark of the Lord.

The Philistines are thereupon forced to return the ark to Israel in order to escape the Lord's judgments. The connection of this incident to the JN stones results from the typological reading of this text. In his *A Discourse Concerning Faith and Fervency in Prayer,* Mather reads the fall of Dagon before the ark as a type of the power of the gospel:

> *If it is our Duty to Pray that the Kingdom of Christ may be inlarged, then we ought to Pray that that may be done by means whereof the Lords Kingdom is inlarged.* Now this is accomplished by the Preaching of the Gospel. . . . As being the great Instrument by which the Kingdom of Christ is Propagated in the World. In places where the Gospel comes and is submitted to, Satan's Kingdom falls, as *Dagon* fell to the Ground before the Ark of the Lord, I Sam. 5:4. And Christs Holy Kingdom is built on the Ruines of it.[30]

Thus on one level, JN's designs can be read as calling for faith in fervency in prayer so that Christ's kingdom may be established in the wilderness. In this treatise, Mather encouraged prayer for the coming of the millennial kingdom and the resurrection of the saints, so the design also could refer to the resurrection of the particular saint buried beneath it. This aspect of the design is further confirmed by the fact that the ark of the Lord was also read as a type of Christ, whose resurrection holds out the promise of resurrection for all deceased saints. Thus the elevated urn is an appropriate image of this promise.

Within this context of prayer and resurrection, the other major element of the design, vegetation, takes on meanings also appropriate to the wilderness condition of the New England church. Vegetation, or fruitfulness, in the wilderness was a dominant symbolic concept in the late seventeenth century in New England since the actual fruitfulness of the land was linked in the jeremiad to the spiritual condition of the people. In such works as Wigglesworth's "God's Controversy with New England" or Mather's *Ichabod,* New Englanders were warned that their apostasy was responsible for the punishments God dealt the land through natural forces. Wigglesworth's poem was written at the time of the great drought of 1661, following the divisive Synod on the Half-way Covenant, "By a lover of New-England's Prosperity."[31] Wigglesworth's text ("Isaiah 5:4 What could have been done more to my vineyard, that I have not done in it? wherefore, when I looked that it should bring forth grapes, brought it forth wild grapes?") sets the theme for the poem's metaphoric structure: a rich land, planted, prospered by God, declined and so must be punished. God expected good fruits from his "seed," in particular those children of the godly whose lack of converting grace necessitated the Half-way Covenant. This failure of the seed, the barrenness of New England souls, is fittingly matched by the infertility of the land during the great drought. These pronouncements struck to the heart of New Englanders' anxieties about their physical and spiritual survival. For Wigglesworth, only one response was viable: a visible, social reformation of manners and a return to primitive piety. There was, however, another way for New Englanders to be fruitful, and if corporate New England failed in its reformation, the saints might still serve God by satisfying his demands in a more spiritual way. The gospel bears fruits as it is spread in the wilderness in several ways: by the conversion of individuals, the flourishing of the church, and finally by the restitution of the fruitfulness of Eden in the Resurrection world.

On the JN stones, fruitfulness is evoked on several levels. The figures on the Elizur Holyoke stone are nereids, female counterparts of dagons, (fig. 21). The figures themselves are sensuously entwined in sinuous vegetation, with the lower bodies all but indistinguishable from the vines. The urn, too, gives the impression of barely controlled movement and growth, with oversized handles creating a heartshape and bulbous gadrooning supported by tongue-like lilies. The design exudes fertility which is, indeed, the expected fruit of fervent prayer, providing a spiritual sap for growth in the barren strand:

> And we should therefore Pray that there may be a plentiful Effusion of the Holy Spirit on the world. Then will Converting work go forward among the Nations, and the Glorious Kingdom of Christ fill the earth. *When the Spirit is poured from an* (sic) *high, the Wilderness will be a fruitful Field,* Isa. 32:15. When the desolate Souls of sinners are Converted, *A Wilderness becomes a Fruitful Field.*[32]

Spiritually such fruitfulness is a metaphor for conversion-causing prayer. But Mather would not have seen this imagery as purely allegorical, for, as we have seen above, the establishment of God's literal kingdom was hastened by such conversions. Moreover, the saint knew that a literal restoration of a fruitful world would be part of the Millennium, so such images contained a prophetic force. In reference to biblical description of the restoration of paradise in Isaiah, Mather notes, "That text admits of an Allegorical interpretation, but it does not thence follow that a Literal one is wholly to be excluded, especially considering that the Apostle says, That God has by the Mouth of all his holy Prophets which have spoken since the World began, declared there shall be a Time of *the Restitution of all things,* Acts. 3:21."[33] Elsewhere, Mather explicitly compares conversion to the great change "which shall pass upon the World at the last and Great Day,"[34] and his understanding of biblical language allows the same language to describe these intimately related events.

Several biblical texts proved useful in symbolically relating prayer, the death of saints, and the Resurrection world through images of fruitfulness. From Leviticus 23, Christians had adopted the image of the "first fruits" in a complex of texts on heaven and the Resurrection. In the Old Testament the first fruits of harvest were offered by the priest to ensure the fruitfulness of the whole harvest. In Romans 8:23, Paul interpreted this offering as the first impression of spiritual assurance of heavenly salvation, and as Mather noted, "True saving Grace is eternal Life and Glory in the beginnings of it. It is called *the first fruits.*"[35] But Mather's millennialism lead him to specify the type of assurance involved as belief in the establishment of heavenly salvation on earth in the New Jerusalem, admonishing his congregation to "consider, That there will be a glorious inchoation and first fruits of that kingdom which the saints shall possess at the great day, even before Christ cometh to judge the earth."[36] Thus the living have the first fruits through their assurance, and this assurance grows until the moment of death. The lilies on the Holyoke stone can be seen as referring to this growth, since the saints were told "not [to] be like Stakes in an hedge which grow not, but rather like Lillies in a field which grow until they dye."[37] The hope of the Resurrection was also expressed through the image of the first fruits in 1 Corinthians 15:20, where Christ's resurrection is called the first fruits which ensures the resurrection of his servants. Joseph Sewall explained,

CHRIST by his Resurrection is become the First-Fruits of them that slept. 1 Cor. 15. 20. *But now is CHRIST* risen from *the dead, and become the first-fruits of them that slept.* As the First-Fruits being offer'd to GOD, under the Law, sanctified the whole, and were also an Earnest of the full Harvest: so in CHRIST's Resurrection, the People of GOD have an *Earnest, Pledge,* and *Assurance* of their *own* Resurrection to Glory and Immortality."[38]

On another level, the death of the individual saint could be seen as an offering of the first fruits of a congregation to God, and the acceptance of these fruits in heaven would insure the holiness of the lump, the saints left on earth. Death, then, can be celebrated on the JN stones as an offering of first fruits in the temple of heaven. In fact, Mather uses this idea of the gathering in of the first fruits by death in a particular millennial frame, as the sheaves are gathered before the earth is burned with fire on the day of judgment. As Mather notes in his etymology of the word used in Scripture to describe the death of the righteous, "nusaphim," "The word is a Metaphor taken from Husbandmen who when they see a Storm a coming, they *take away* their Corn out of the field and *gather it* into the barn. So does the Lord sometimes take his Wheat out of the World, and gather it into his heavenly barn, to Save it out of a Storm. When their bodies are lodged in the Grave, and their Souls are in Heaven no Storm in the World can hurt them."[39] Thus death can be seen as a sign of God's favor to the deceased, and indeed to the whole church for whom the individual saint has been offered as a first fruit. Symbolically, images of first fruits link prayer, conversion, death, and resurrection; in employing these images JN presented a profoundly optimistic prophecy for the preservation of saints in the wilderness of America. Increase Mather preached that biblical language had the particular quality of using the same metaphors to describe the state of inchoation on earth and the state of glory in the millennium. Similarly, JN's designs require the viewer to see a multitude of references to the condition of saints at the present time and in the Resurrection world. Like Mather, the JN carver established a symbolic mode for relating the individual to the corporate destiny of New England.

Glorified Saints and the Lamson Family

While the Charlestown carver and the JN carver developed images celebrating the progress and unity of the churches on earth and in heaven, it took the creativity of the Lamson family of Charlestown, Massachusetts,[40] to devise a symbolic system for the representation of glorified saints. From about 1685 to 1720, Joseph Lamson with his sons Nathaniel and Caleb develop an effigy portrait which reflects a belief in some form of contact between saints in heaven and on earth. Moreover, the distinctly corporal nature of the effigy and the close attention to the eyes emphasize the belief that glorified saints will see each other in the flesh with "bodilie eyes" at the Resurrection. The Lamsons further the use of vegetation imagery on gravestones by linking it to the effigy, implying that fertility and new life redound to the community by the influence of the deceased. And finally, we can examine in the Lamsons' work the process by which designs in the "bodilie eyes" tradition are integrated with *memento mori* images. While Joseph Lamson retained the standard death imagery in the tympani of his stones, he experimented in the pilasters which he widened to accommodate his prophetic images of saints. His sons then place the effigy in the tympanum itself, signaling a major departure in New England from the *memento mori* tradition.

Anthropomorphic figures such as dagons, imps, angels, and what may be crude soul effigies are present on stones cut before Joseph Lamson's time (active ca. 1685-ca. 1715), but there is little evidence of a conscious, shared set of images for depicting departed saints on these earlier stones. Carvers borrowed images from each other, experimenting freely with facial expression and hair style. On the George Hollard stone of 1688 in the Granary (fig. 26), the effigy in the pilaster is a crude copy of JN's dagon, yet a demonic face is cut well below what was once the ground line. Carvers often practiced new designs in this space, revealing the fancy of many Puritans. The stone was cut four years prior to the witchcraft hysteria in Salem, during which the belief in the power of the devil to take the shape of cats and dogs was frequently voiced. When the Hollard stone demon is seen in conjunction with the imps of death on the William Dickson stone of 1692, we are reminded that devils as well as angels populated the Puritan imagination (fig. 8).

In this context of experimentation, the subject matter of the Lamson effigies must be defined before conclusions can be drawn concerning the development of saint's portraiture from 1685 to 1715 and its relation to the "bodilie eyes" tradition. Dickran and Ann Tashjian take several positions on the derivation of effigies in the Lamson tradition.[41] At times they claim all winged figures are cherubs, at other times angels, and in one case, they assert an effigy is a combination of angel and saint's portraiture. The Tashjians cogently observe that cherubim were the only heavenly beings considered visible to earthly eyes, and they conclude on this evidence that only visible figures were permissible subjects of representation for Puritans. Yet the examples they give of cherub figures modeled after those on the veil in the Holy of Holies are on stones from the late eighteenth century with no design precedents on seventeenth-century stones.

For Allan Ludwig, the variety of effigies reveals confusion over the nature of the relationship between angels and glorified souls. He writes,

It can thus be assumed that glorified souls become angelic bodies but they are by no means the equals of the created angels. Sometimes the two can be distinguished from one another but more often than not the stones themselves are equivocal. . . . Were it not for the fact that the figure of the guardian angel was a commonly held belief in the literary tradition of colonial New England, I would not hesitate to cast most of the imagery on the side of the created angels.

. . . .

The problem is indeed a thorny one. I suspect that the imagery was in most cases a blend of angelic representation and that the stonecarvers and the patrons for whom they cut the stones did not often make any clear-cut distinctions between created angels and glorified souls and would have thought such distinctions quite academic.[42]

Ludwig may have hit the mark with his conclusion that such images were a blend, but for the wrong reasons. In the first place, one of the most appealing conceits of Puritan eschatology was that man would become more glorious than the angels in the Resurrection world, and this idea clearly fired many imaginations. Indeed, the angels were the highest "created nature," "Yet," as Mather tells us, "in respect of the *Word's* being made *flesh* the humane nature is exalted above the Angelical."[43] Because Christ took on human form, the resurrected saints would take on a glorified form more exalted than angelic nature. Secondly, the conflation of glorified saints and angels was no mere confusion or the result of disinterest in academic disputes. The Bible itself said the saints would be "equal" or "like unto" angels (Luke 20:36), and Mather dismisses those who say disputes over the nature of angels bring man's curiosity to forbidden ground: "Why hath God revealed so much in his Word concerning his Angels, but that he might have praise from us on that account: Because some have indulged themselves in vain and curious unscriptural speculations, others say it is dangerous to discourse and think of Angels. But if we keep to the Scripture, we may as safely discourse of Angels, as of the poorest worm on the Earth."[44]

When presented in abstract terms, the relationship between angels and saints did not hold a great imaginative appeal in and of itself, but once the abstractions were reduced to particulars by literal-minded Puritans, a passionate carving of effigies began. Mather, as we would expect, outlined behavior on earth and glories in heaven which would make the saints like angels. He devoted a complete sermon in his *Meditations on the GLORY of Heaven* to the doctrine "In the Resurrection World, the Children of God shall be as the Angels of Heaven." He claims, "White Robes are an Ensign of Glory. The glorious Angels of Heaven, would sometimes appear in *White Robes*; and the Spirits of Just men made perfect are like Angels; and therefore they must be represented as having *white Robes* on them" (p. 87). Elsewhere he writes, to be "zealous in good works: This is to be like an Angel. If we are like the Angels in respect of Holiness, after the Resurrection we shall be like them (and that not only as to our Souls, but our Bodies too) in respect of Glory and Immortality."[45] We should be careful not to underestimate the power of these suggestions to the Puritan imagination. For a mind beset with the knowledge of man's sinful imperfection, here was a promise of personal perfection and glory even greater than that of the angels. As Edward Taylor exults,

> You Holy Angells, Morning-Stars, bright Sparks,
>   Give place: and lower your top gallants. Shew
> Your top-saile Conjues to our slender barkes:
>   The highest honour to our nature's due.
>   Its neerer Godhead by the Godhead made
>   Than yours in you that never from God stray'd.[46]

The challenge to minister and carver alike was to create a symbolic mode both personal and transcendental, capable of representing inexpressible glories and abstract doctrines in forms emotionally and visually appealing. Such forms must appeal sensually without debasing the spirituality of heaven, they must motivate the living to struggle to gain the heavenly state, and finally they must present the dead in a condition comforting to the friends and relations touched by the loss of a saint.

Of the precursors of the Lamson effigy style, the Deacon Thomas Parker stone (fig. 27) of Wakefield, Massachusetts, is one of the first to employ the formula of a vegetation-filled pilaster topped by an effigy in the capital. The stone has little emotive power because the effigies lack animation. They float in space separated from the pilaster by a heavy line, and the blank eyes and thick face are a cold and expressionless death mask. The similarity of these effigies to those on the Kendel stone (fig. 15) suggests these are guardian angels or angels of death.

The first "humanized" effigies appear on the Mary Briant stone of 1688 (fig. 28A). The effigy surmounts a delicately fashioned torso made of leaves falling over gourds and grapes atop a grouping of leaves which suggest hips. The carver has removed the band previously set between the effigy and the pilaster, and the resulting visual impression is that the fruits are the "body" of the effigy. The eyes are still blank, but they seem to shine, and the expression of the face is softened. Despite the increased visual coherence of the design, there remains an ambiguity of reference. Are the fruits the rewards granted the soul in heaven, do they reflect the life of the saint, or do they represent the bounty which will come to the church when such first fruits are sent to heaven? It seems certain that the carver understood the eschatology of "bodilie eyes," since the shining eyes point to the shining glories saints see in heaven. On the Elizabeth

Mountfort stone (fig. 29), the carver makes a visual pun on the idea that saints shine like Christ by seeing Him with "bodilie eyes," since the eyes are carved in the shape of a fish, the ancient symbol for Christ.

Joseph Lamson takes the lead in developing sophisticated designs with alert effigies and elaborate pilasters. In a symbolic system analogous to that of the Mathers, he further humanizes portrait effigies and more precisely defines the relationships between saints in the separate state and saints on earth.

By comparing the Mary Briant stone of 1688 (fig. 28A) with the Elizabeth Bunker marker of 1710 (fig. 28B), we detect Joseph Lamson's alteration of the earlier design to stress the relationship of the deceased saint to the living. The same basic design structure is preserved, with an effigy placed atop a triangular-shaped neck followed by gourds, but Lamson makes some key substitutions within these areas. The eyes on the Briant stone are luminous and blank, but the Bunker eyes have pupils and gaze downwards. Next, Lamson replaces the leaves at the neck with rays of light, adds a Geneva collar, and transformes the gourds into breasts. These substitutions remove the possibility that the designs in the pilaster are only the rewards of heaven, for the elements Lamson has chosen were traditional symbols of the spiritual gifts a saint, through grace, can pass along to other saints. The rays of light and the Geneva collar recall the saint's inclusion in the priesthood of all believers, and the example of the saint's life provides spiritual illumination of the Christian life for other saints. As Allan Ludwig has noted, breasts were a common sign of the spiritual milk each saint offers as food to the children of the church, and the image in appearing on a gravestone carries the implication that such nourishment continues even in death through the memories of the living who meditate on the departed saint's life.[47] The epitaph on the Hannah Hubert stone of Cambridge notes the dual role of the Christian parent as dispenser of spiritual as well as physical nourishment. She was "A TENDER & LOUING MOTHER TO HIS CHILDREN CAREFUL OF THEIR SOULS & BODIES LOUING & FAITHFULL DILIGENT & PRUDENT WHO DEPARTED THIS LIFE IN SWEET PEACE." The effigies in the pilasters on this stone rest on fig leaves, followed by clusters of breasts, and both images recall various biblical texts extolling the fruitfulness of Christian life.

The priesthood of each saint is communicated by the presence of breasts even when the Geneva collar, found on the Bunker stone, is absent. Canticles 8, describing the breasts of the spouse, was interpreted by Puritans as a description of the growth of Christ's spouse, the gospel Church, as the Word of God was dispensed through the breasts of the ministry. Cotton Mather notes the strangeness of describing ministers with breasts, but he feels such androgynous imagery has biblical precedence and reveals a symbolic truth. He wrote of his father, "such *Ministers* are your *Mothers* too. Have they not *Travailed in Birth* for you, that a CHRIST may be seen *formed in you*? Are not their *Lips* the *Breasts* thro' which the *sincere Milk of the Word* has pass'd unto you, for your Nourishment?"[48] There was a millennial significance to such breast imagery as well, and here the relevance of this imagery to death is made explicit. The fulness of the spouse's breasts in Canticles 8 was commonly interpreted as a sign of the fulness of the Gentile church. When the Gentile church was complete, Christ's return as bridegroom for the apocalyptic marriage of the Lamb was imminent. Thus, the harvesting of the saints at death, in their ministerial fulness as members of the Gentile church, is a clear warning to living saints to drink from the breasts of the Word before it is too late. The communication of grace through the breasts of departed priest-saints was made even more explicit on the Mary Gould stone of 1709 in Wakefield (fig. 30A) and the Sibyll Wigglesworth marker of 1708 in Cambridge (fig. 30B). On the Gould stone, conduits are cut on the breasts which spill onto fig leaves, while on the Wigglesworth stone, Lamson has eliminated rays and leaves entirely, connecting the breasts with their pipes of grace directly to the effigy.

Lamson frequently included grapes in the pilasters as well, and this fruit also held an iconic significance relating the rewards of heaven to God's people on earth. Of course the blood of the grapes, wine, was used sacramentally to signify the believer's union to Christ, who promised heaven to the saints, but a rich aura of meaning for the symbol also arises from biblical texts on the wilderness condition of God's people. In Numbers 13 the Israelites in the wilderness send spies into the promised land to report on its richness. They return with sweet clusters of grapes from Eschol, and for Christians, this incident promised in an allegory the glories to be found in Canaan-heaven. The New England Puritans saw themselves as just such a wilderness people, so grapes carved on a gravestone imaged the salvation of the whole people as well as the individual saint. Moreover, given the formula of the jeremiad, with God threatening to cut off vines which bear wild grapes in his vineyard, the grapes cut on gravestones provided reassurance that the dead saint was the sweet grape of a fruitful vineyard who was called home after his labors.

While these stones imply a relationship between dead and living saints, it is in a remarkable series of stones executed in 1709 by Joseph and Nathaniel Lamson that we find the specific forms the relationship takes. The best-known example of this period, the Jonathan Pierpont stone of Wakefield, Massachusetts (figs. 31, 32), contains the full repertoire of symbols we have come to associate with the classic Lamson stone—

death's head in tympanum, imps of death carrying a pall and hourglass in the frieze, and finely carved portrait effigies in the pilasters. The Pierpont stone is strikingly unusual in that the pilasters are widened to allow larger effigies, drawing the viewer's attention from the death's head to the pilasters. The tension created between the central figure of the design, with all the trappings of death, and the pilasters, with the signs of rejuvenation, embodies the very idea of the saint's triumph over death and his continuing presence in the living church. The epitaph on this stone reveals some of the dynamics behind this development:

> A Fruitful Christian And a pastor Who
> Did good to all, and lov'd all good to do:
> A tender Husband; and a parent Kind:
> A Faithful Friend, Which Who, oh! Who can find
> A preacher, that a bright Example gave
> Of Rules he preach'd, the Souls of Men to save
> A PIERPONT All of this, here leves his dust,
> And Waits the Resurrection of the Just

Here the fruitfulness of the Christian life is verbally and visually cataloged, and Pierpont now waits as a soul hovering over his dust for the resurrection due a good man. Yet the effigy makes a statement about the form of waiting that Pierpont experiences, since the minister is seen reading from his Bible, with eyes turned down towards his congregation as if to see that his message is still received. On the Captain and Mrs. Pyam Blower stone of Cambridge, and the John Russell stone of Copp's Hill, the effigy is shown in prayer as he/she looks down from the separate state. Visually, these effigies are recreations of the traditional orant figure of early Christian art. Such orants prayed over the tomb, and they were highly humanized figures seemingly conscious of events both in heaven and on earth. Similarly, the epitaph on the Blower stone asserts "In Ther Death They Ware Not Divided," with the implication that the separate state was one in which departed saints were endowed with recognizable personalities and reunited with their loved ones. Moreover, the viewer of the stone is invited to imagine that Pierpont will soon be seen with "bodilie eyes" in the glorified Resurrection body that the idealized effigy suggests.

While we have seen that Increase and Cotton Mather modified Calvin's ideas on the separate state, it seems that the Lamsons have gone farther and are dangerously close to the heretical doctrine of the intercession of the saints. Of the Mathers, Increase is much more circumspect about the consciousness of the saints in heaven about earthly events, and he never encourages attempts to make contact with the dead through prayers. In 1708 Mather penned his *A Dissertation Wherein the Strange Doctrine . . .*, one of his many attacks on Solomon Stoddard's granting of full church membership to the unconverted.[49] While the bulk of this treatise concerns Stoddard's innovations, Mather adds two appendices concerning the imminence of the Millennium. These appendices seem out of place unless one recalls that Mather had always insisted on church purity as a sign of millennial fervor, and Mather implies that the very saints in heaven are concerned with Stoddard's relaxation of church rules. Increase Mather leaves direct intervention in human affairs to the angels, but the saints may be imagined as conscious of earthly events:

> Undoubtedly, the Glorified Spirits in the *Heavenly Jerusalem*, altho' they are not concerned in our Particular Affairs, nevertheless, are not Ignorant of the Great Things done on the Earth, wherein the Church in General is concerned. And the Tidings of the Downfal of *Mystical Babylon*, when they shall hear of it, will cause them to Rejoyce. (p. 110)

The saint in heaven has more than a dilettant's interest in the fall of Babylon, since this event initiates his or her return to earth with Christ. Nevertheless, there is no direct communication to be received from or sent to these saints. The only communication from beings in the separate state came from angels, and at the moment of death, a truly blessed saint might have a vision of the angels coming to transport his soul to heaven.

Cotton Mather, however, had few of his father's scruples about contact between the living and the dead. What were suggestions and metaphors in Increase's work become literal facts framed with half-hearted caveats in Cotton's writings. In a manuscript treatise composed about 1725, the "Triparadisus," the younger Mather blithely asserts that appearances by the dead are common in his neighborhood, and he spends many pages recounting incidents of recently departed saints returning as ghosts to deliver messages to the living. He also explicitly encourages fervent prayers to the dead to grant visionary powers to saints on earth:

> There is an *Intercourse* with *paradise*, and communion with the *Departed Spirits* of the Faithful there, which is indeed So far from un-Lawful to be ask'd for, and Sought for, that our Sanctity, & our *Conversation with Heaven* Live very much in the study of it. It is indeed said, They have *no more a portion forever in anything that is done under the Sun*. But if they have *Nothing* to do with *us*, We have *something* to Do with *Them*; and we should as far as we can affect ourselves, & inflame our *zeal* and confirm our *peace*, and strengthen our *Hope*, from what we know concerning *them*. This will be no criminal *Necromancy*! The *Saints*, whose *Bodies* are *Laid in* the Earth, are the *Excellent ones* in whom we are to have a singular *Delight*, and are the Nobler members of the *Family*, which we in a *Lower State* belong unto. And they may be thus convers'd

withal. To bring some warmth into us, & make our *Hearts burn within* us, Lett us thus bring down the Rayes of *Paradise* upon our souls.[50]

Certainly the effigies on the Bunker and Wigglesworth stones, with rays and pipes streaming down, would encourage saints to pray for this warmth from heaven.

The willingness of Cotton Mather to expand on the details of the Millennium his father left unexplored sheds light on other iconic features of the Lamsons' art. Increase Mather felt it was finally beyond human ken to conceive of the particular events and conditions of heaven. Although he insisted on the literal nature of the conversion of the Jews, the first and second resurrections, Armageddon, and the descent of the New Jerusalem, he chose not to speculate on God's exact methods in bringing these events to pass. While many biblical descriptions of the church would be realized before "bodilie eyes" in perceptible form on earth during the Millennium, some were only "to receive their full and everlasting accomplishment In *heaven* above forever."[51] On one point in particular father and son parted company, with Cotton opting for a doctrine which opened a new arena of contact between living and resurrected saints. Millennialists had long quibbled over the nature and chronology of the first and second resurrections prophecied in Revelations 20. For some exegetes, the first was spiritual, with the advent of grace in the soul, while the second was general at the Day of Judgment. For others, the first resurrection was a literal rising of the martyrs, who ruled in vengeance with living saints until the general, second resurrection. This interpretation presented a problem, for it mingled glorified saints and living humans on the earth in a fashion beyond the credence of all but the most fanatical millennialists.

Increase Mather chose a solution which, to his mind, compromised neither the literal interpretation of scripture nor common sense. At the appearance of Christ, all the saints rise, and the saints living on earth at this time are instantly transformed into glorified beings without experiencing death. For the duration of the Judgment Day, which coincides with the 1000 years of the Millennium, the wicked rise and are judged by Christ and his saints. With this scheme, Mather avoids the problem of contact between resurrected, luminous saints and saints still living in the flesh.[52]

Cotton Mather agreed that the events described in Revelation 20 are "the most free from *Allegory*, and from the Involution of prophetical Figures; (how agreeably!) as describing indeed that that Age and State, wherein all things relating to the *Kingdome of God*, will be most *clearly understood*."[53] But Cotton does not conflate the Judgment Day and the Millennium, so when the New Jerusalem appears and the dead saints are resurrected, the living saints are *not* transformed instantly, and they continue to live out the natural course of their lives on earth. Unlike his father, Cotton believed that the New Jerusalem would not come down to earth, rather it would hover, 1,500 miles square, in the clouds above Jerusalem. Winged saints could fly back and forth between the New Jerusalem and the millennial state on earth, enjoying pleasant communion with the saints on earth.

Cotton Mather's decision that a heavenly New Jerusalem in the sky and a millennial kingdom on earth were compatible made for some remarkable imaginative leaps in accommodating the glories of heaven and doggedly earthbound metaphors. The reasons for such theological and imaginative gymnastics may have lain in Mather's frustrated drive for earthly power, since the main business of the resurrected and earthly saints is iron-fisted governance of peaceable kingdoms on earth.[54] While Increase Mather noted in the *Angelographia* that the resurrected saints would perform visibly what the angels before the Millennium do invisibly, he never encouraged fabulations of the sort created by Cotton.

Cotton Mather held the dream of the worldly power of resurrected saints too dearly to avoid exulting over the change that was to come, and his "Triparadisus" and the earlier "Problema Theologicum" give full treatment to the saints' power. Cotton notes in the "Problema Theologicum" that the saints in this life are "shutt out generally from any share in the government of *this present world*," but

> There will be in the *New Jerusalem* the *Raised Saints*, who will be *aequal to the Angels*, and will indeed be the *Angels*, the *Teachers*, and the *Rulers* of the *New World*.
> . . . .
> The *Raised Saints*, who when they shall *Renew their Youth*, (at the Redemption) Shall be *like the Eagles*, and mount up *with Eagles wings*, (which the Jewes take to be the prophetic phrase for the *Bodyes of the Resurrection*:) These will be the *Angels* of the *New World*. . . . What the Angels now do more *Invisibly*, while the *Wheels* of *this World* are turning, the *Raised Saints, Receiving a Kingdome that cannot be moved*, will more *Visibly* do in that *World to Come*.[55]

The ultimate silent partners, the resurrected saints will fly down with instructions from Christ to consult with the earthly administrators of the millennial bureaucracy. Mather promises that even women will have the privilege of being involved in the workings of state.

The saints on earth live out their natural lives under these conditions and are translated to heaven without experiencing death. Mather begins a passage describing the saints in the New Jerusalem looking down from the clouds at old saints, ready to swoop down and carry them away, but he crosses this out and substitutes a slightly more restrained conceit:

> And as the Faithful when they Dy, have their *Spirits* transported by *Angels*, into the *Rest*, wherein they are to wait for the coming of the *Kingdome*, so when the Time comes for any to be Translated from the *New Earth* into the *New Heavens*, the *Raised Saints* may have something to do about the Transportation.[56]

Cotton Mather's insistence on intimate, personal contact between dying and resurrected saints at the moment of death/translation in the Millennium adds another layer of meaning to the portrait effigies cut by the Lamsons. After 1720, many stones cut by Nathaniel and Caleb Lamson depict a winged effigy in the typanum, either alone or hovering over a skull, surrounded with vegetation. Such images can be interpreted as the transformation of the saint into a spirit at the moment of death, but Mather's vision allows us to particularize the process as Puritans understood it. Perhaps the very moment of death is shown here, with a saint from one's own congregation arriving with death to transport the saint to the New Jerusalem. Also, the vegetation may signify the restitution of all things that is another feature of the Millennium, and would be a prime feature of the saints' experience.

In his various discussions of the contact between living saints and departed spirits, risen and living saints, Cotton Mather wipes away epistemological conundrums over the contact between and perception of spiritual and physical beings, essentially conflating the power of "spiritual" and "bodilie eyes." He believed souls could take on a sensible substance at will to make themselves seen and felt by the living, and in a characteristic display of scholarship, he presents biblical, Jewish, and Chaldean authority for his contention that the soul has two clothings. One clothing is invisible, but the other is a sensible fire or light:

> May not that agree somewhat, with the fulgent *glory*, which came upon the *Body* of our Lord, at His *Transfiguration*?—And with what we read in the Old Testament Of the Just *Rising* from their Graves, and then *Shining as the Brightness of the firmament & the Stars forever & ever*: And in the Kingdom of the Father? We have shewed [shrewd?] reasons to think, That our *First Parents* while they continued in their Sinless Integrity, had something of this *Luminous garments* upon them, and had, in it, both their *Shelter* and their *Beauty*. Tis called *Wstis Onychine* in the Jewish Tradition of it; from the Resemblance to an *onyx* in the Colour of it; and unto the *Nails* on our fingers, in some other circumstances.[57]

Mather here touches the very roots of Puritan speculations on death, for he reveals the blurring of distinctions between the ineffable and the effable, the spirit and the flesh that surround discussions of death and resurrection. The Resurrection body itself is paradoxically called a "spiritual body," and one is lead to conclude that Mather and other Puritans believed the soul in the separate state and the resurrected saint could move between spiritual and material existence almost at will. Yet we have been prepared for such a realization in the conflation of spiritual and bodily powers of perceptions in much of Puritan eschatology. As Cotton Mather insisted, "the *Faculty*, and the *Object* must be agreeable to one another," and in the Resurrection world, both spiritual and physical beings must be known by spiritual and physical senses.[58]

Cotton Mather's descriptions of the Resurrection body provide us with one more insight concerning gravestone effigies. For Increase Mather, the substance of the Resurrection body had always presented a problem. At times, he felt it was the original body reconstituted; when evidence from natural science indicated the difficulty of this task, or when he suspected the new heavens and earth would be created *ex nihilo* as was the original universe, he declared the Resurrection body would be made from new materials. Cotton Mather presents a unique solution to this problem, in a remarkable mix of theology, science, and sheer imagination, and in the process reveals the reason for the peculiarly androgynous nature of portrait effigies of resurrected saints. Mather begins with a standard list of the qualities of the Resurrection body ("admirably fitt for the Business of the *Heavenly places*")—luminosity, immortality, the strength of a lion, freedom from the force of gravity, wings covered with silver and gold. But his explanation of just how these bodies are created in the image of Christ's human nature is unique. First, Mather argues that the bodies of the Resurrection will be created out of Christ's human substance as was Eve's from Adam. The "sleep" Adam experienced when Eve was created was actually a return of his flesh into a prenatal protoplasmic state in which the embryo was no more developed than a mass of tissues with a spine. Eve's body was made from a template of this spine, called a "rib" in Genesis.

This first creation resulted in two sexes, a development which contributed to the Fall of mankind, and there was no place for such a difference in heaven. Mather is insistent on this point, writing "But The *Different Sexes*!—NO—There will be no *Different Sexes*, in the *Holy City*. . . . They will So *putt on Christ* that there will be *neither male nor female*, nor any more Difference between them. . . ."[59] To create an androgynous, or at least asexual, Resurrection body, Christ himself returns to a protoplasmic state, and from his substance makes new bodies. Thus "there will be no more Differrence of Sexes, but both sexes will be again united in *one Body* as they were before this *Deep Sleep* upon the *protoplast*; and all shall be *perfect men*."[60] Here Mather flirts with Gnostic views on the androgynous nature of the flesh, but he quickly reasserts the principle of male dominance.[61] Mather defended himself against those who called these remarks chauvinistic by emphasizing the great honor of being made like Christ, a man. Indeed women's rights are restricted in this world, but once women become like men, they will be able to exercise the powers of priests and governors in the New Jerusalem:

> The *Female Sex* may think they have some cause to complain of us, that we stint them so much in their *Education*, and abridge them of many points wherein they might be serviceable. But, *ye Handmaids of the Lord*, A REDEEMER who was *Born of a Woman*, intends unknown *Dignities* for you, and will make an use of you beyond what we yett know, to serve His *Kingdome*, when it shall *cease to be with* you as now it is, and your *Subjection* to *Men*, shall with your *Distinction* from them, no longer be considered. . . . The Name, Woman, is to be heard no more.[62]

Despite the oddity of these remarks to the modern ear, Mather was sure he had the latest in scientific opinion behind him, and his assertions about the sexless nature of the body created from the substance of Christ seem to have been widely held in the culture judging from the effigies of the glorified saint. These effigies are generally indistinguishable as males or females, and carvers seemed equally at ease in adorning women's stones with masculine effigies and carving breasts on effigies for men. The body was androgynous, and biblical metaphors drawn from female or male sexual attributes could be freely applied to the resurrected saints. Moreover, Mather believed that resurrected saints would be restored to their youth, and he knowingly or unknowingly affirmed medieval tradition which held that the saint rose as a thirty-three-year-old, the age of Christ at his resurrection. From our perspective, once several hundred stones have been viewed cut with the same effigy, the effects of these doctrines seem depersonalizing, deadening the creativity of the carver. Yet we must remember that for the Puritan, the most personal and creative union possible was that with Christ and the family of God at the Resurrection, and each image reaffirmed symbolically the biblical prophecy. Driven by eschatological expectation, New Englanders created a personal vision of perfection. In the works of Edward Taylor and the carving tradition of the Collins family in central New England, we shall see how deeply prophecy informed the use of all biblical metaphors.

Figure 11.   Samuel Bridge, 1672, Cambridge, Massachusetts

Figure 12.   Timothy Andrew, 1674, Cambridge, Massachusetts

Figure 13. The Neal Children, ca. 1671, the Granary, Boston, Massachusetts

Figure 14.   John Person, 1679, Wakefield, Massachusetts

Figure 15. Thomas Kendel, ca. 1676, Wakefield, Massachusetts

Figure 16.   Edmund Angier, 1692, Cambridge, Massachusetts

Figure 17. Henry Messinger, Jr., 1686, the Granary, Boston, Massachusetts

Figure 18.   Martha Waite, 1681, the Granary, Boston,
              Massachusetts

Figure 19. Lieutenant John Cleverly, 1703, Quincy,
Massachusetts

Figure 20. William Button, 1693, Portsmouth, New Hampshire

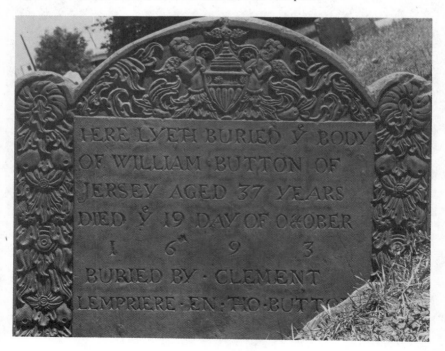

Figure 21. Elizur Holyoke, 1710, the Granary, Boston, Massachusetts

Figure 22. "The Thrones," Thomas Heywood, *The Hierarchie of the Blessed Angells,* 1635, p. 110, Brown University Library

Figure 23. Headpiece, chapter three, "The Thrones," Thomas Heywood, *The Hierarchie of the Blessed Angells*, 1635, p. 111, Brown University Library

Figure 25. "Animae sal est amor," emblem, Otto Van Veen, *Amoris Divini Emblemata*, 1615, p. 104, Brown University Library

Figure 24. "Svperbiam Odit," emblem, Otto Van Veen, *Amoris Divini Emblemata*, 1615, p. 112, Brown University Library

Figure 26.   George Hollard, 1688, the Granary, Boston,
            Massachusetts

Figure 27.   Deacon Thomas Parker, 1680, Wakefield,
Massachusetts

Figure 28A. Mary Briant, 1688, Wakefield, Massachusetts

Figure 28B. Elizabeth Bunker, 1710, Cambridge, Massachusetts

Figure 29. Elizabeth Mountfort, 1703, Wakefield, Massachusetts

Figure 30A. Mary Gould, 1709,
Wakefield, Massachusetts

Figure 30B. Sybill Wigglesworth, 1708,
Cambridge, Massachusetts

Figure 31. Reverend Jonathan Pierpont, 1709, Wakefield,
            Massachusetts

Figure 32. Reverend Jonathan Pierpont, 1709, Wakefield,
            Massachusetts

5

Edward Taylor and the
Metaphors of Perfection

Oh! Glorious Body! Pull my eye lids ope:
  Make my quick Eye, Lord, thy brisk Glory greet,
Whose rapid flames when they my heart revoke
  From other Beauties, make't for thee more sweet.

—Edward Taylor, Meditation 2:74

Edward Taylor's life as a poet and minister in the frontier town of West-field, Massachusetts, where he served from 1671 until his death in 1729, presents many paradoxes. He was at once the private writer unpublished until 1939 and the public figure who married into two of the most prominent families of Connecticut. He was the pastor to a small congregation while keeping abreast of colonial affairs through correspondence and visits with such worthies as Increase Mather and Samuel Sewall. And he engaged in a life-long battle with Solomon Stoddard's liberalization of church membership requirements in Northampton. Many writers see a fundamental conservatism in his public and private lives, as he defended the purity of the church and wrote in a metaphysical style which was out of fashion even when Taylor left England in 1668. Karl Keller finds in Taylor a "primitive" resistance to stylistic change:

> The art of living was to the meditative Taylor a matter of preserving identity inward against the grain of civilization. In his poems time stands still, he is not tied to time, really free of time by virtue of his faith. In the privacy of his mediation, renunciation gave him victory over meaninglessness.[1]

Despite the conservative cast to much of Taylor's thought, his imaginative response to Puritan eschatology was in many ways ahead of his time. He anticipates the wholesale substitution of images of heavenly glory for images of death which characterizes eighteenth century stone-carving. One of Taylor's artistic accomplishments is his manipulation of biblical metaphors of perfection to present the glories to which sinful but saved humans are entitled. Taylor's faith leads him to explore the language of the Bible which describes the saint's personal participation in heavenly glories, and gravestone carvers repeat this process by applying biblical metaphors of perfection to the individual deceased saint.

Taylor's aesthetics and his theology are inseparable, so in his theology we can find his justification for concentrating on the glories as well as the miseries of fallen humanity. His religious and artistic lives shared a common focus in the celebration of the Lord's Supper. Believing that the sacrament of the Lord's Supper signified the union of human and divine nature in Christ, Taylor felt that only redeemed people had a right to participate in the Supper and thus celebrate their union with Christ. His meditations were written as preparations for and reflections on his celebration of the Lord's Supper.[2] Despite the great variety of the *Preparatory Meditations,* they all reflect his sense of unworthiness, his aspirations for holiness, and his wonder at the sacramental union of deformed human nature and divine nature. As Taylor's doctrinal life was dominated by his understanding of the Lord's Supper, so his eschatology is enlivened by the promised reunion of Christ and humanity, divine and human nature at the Resurrection. Praising Christ's glory and beauty in the Sacrament and at the Resurrection is Taylor's primary aesthetic and religious goal. Taylor uses the aesthetics of "bodilie eyes" to argue that the saints will be physically glorified in the image of Christ at the Resurrection; therefore he feels free to imagine himself in the biblical metaphors and types describing Christ's perfection. In his poetry as well as in the stonecarving of his region, biblical images are thus personalized to give the imagination some inkling of what "bodilie eyes" will see.[3]

While Taylor's eschatology is identical to that of Increase Mather, his fervent attention to the aesthetic dimensions of the Apocalypse reveal the poet in the preacher.[4] In his notes on the Day of Judgment transcribed under the doctrinal headings from the "Profession of Faith" delivered at the founding of the Westfield church, Taylor combines doctrine with an appreciation of the joys of the Resurrection. Thomas M. and Virginia L. Davis note the "characteristic literalness of Taylor's imagination" in this text, as well as the fact that "the extended conceits which he employs to make especially vivid the Last Great Day look forward to the 'Preparatory Meditations' and 'Gods Determinations touching his Elect.' "[5] Taylor agrees with Increase Mather that the Day of Judgment begins with Christ's personal appearance, an appearance which sparks the Resurrection:

first there is the Collection of the outward man all together, the flesh, & bones that are rotted to dust, & all dispersed is gathered together again, dust to its dust, & each bit of it to its proper place & bone to bone to constitute the humane body of the very matterialls that lay down, Job 19:26. Which probably may be the work of the holy Angels, Mat. 13:39. & then the Soule shall be brought out of that Mansion, where it hath been gloriously welcomed ever Since its departure, probably by the holy Angels, who carried it there from the bodie, Luk. 16:22, into its own proper body again. & oh! that Joy that the bodie shall now be wrapt up in at their meeting, whereby it shall as it were leap out of [the] grave at the Resurrection.[6]

The saints are judged in the "morning" of the 1000-year-long day, and then they join Christ to judge the damned in the "afternoon." Taylor's rhetoric approaches white heat when he discusses the beauty of Christ: "Oh! the glory of the Humane Nature of [Christ] Oh! the glory of that unconceivable union of [Hu]mane Nature & Divine in the person of the Son."[7] Taylor goes into great detail about the "absolute Perfection" of the Resurrection body, and some of his speculations have iconographic significance for the depiction of saints on gravestones. "He that dies a Child shall rise in a full Stature," he writes, and "he that at his death wanted a finger, hand, arm, toe, foot, leg, eye, or the like, shall at his Resurrection meet with the want of none of these." There will be no "frowns or freckles," and the body which was a prison to the soul at death "at the Resurrection it shall be as golden wings to the Soule for the Soule to fly about Gods Service withall. Here it is the pinion of the Soule, but then it shall be the Souls wing, & with the Soule shall mount up to heaven, I Thes. 4:19."[8] Thus Taylor explains an iconographic motif, the wings, by which carvers could represent the "spiritualized" Resurrection body. Taylor repeatedly describes the powers of the "bodilie eyes," which "shall not weary in beholding all the glory in heaven." Finally, Taylor is concerned as a sacred singer about the powers of the fancy and the poetic voice in heaven. He writes,

Oh how will the Influence of heavens Glorie upon the Fancy, that nimbly & heart-inflaming faculty make it set its Soule inamouring & felicitating Pauses, & Quavers overall Gods work & wayes. & to make the golden Strings of the Soule to tryumph for joy.
. . . .

The Ultimate Influence of heavenlie Glory upon the Soule. & that is this it sets the Soule a Singing forth the Praises of the Lord. God having made the Soule Such a glorious Musicall Instrument of his praises, & the holy Ghost having so gloriously Strung it with the golden wyer of grace, & heavenly Glory having Shored up the Strings to Sound forth the Songs of Zions King, the pouring forth of the Influence of glory play upon the Soule Eternall praises unto God.[9]

Taylor knows that true art and acceptable praise can only occur in this glorified state in heaven, and he hopes Christ will accept "this Lisp till I am glorifide."[10]

But Taylor also implies in this sermon that through biblical metaphors saints can at least anticipate something of heavenly glory. Taylor as a poet of praise is particularly concerned with the beauty of Christ's human form, not only because it is the highest object of praise, but also because as a saint he will share in Christ's glorification of human nature. Thus biblical descriptions of Christ reveal man's future perfection:

> He shall come to be admired at, 2 Thes. 1:10. Then he shall come in his glory, Mat. 25:31. If the bodies of the Saints shall at the Resurrection Shine like the body of the Sun, what shall the body of Christ the Son of God Shine like. It is called a body of glory now, Phi. 3:21. If he appeared so glorious in the Vision among his churches, Rev. 1:12.—what shall his glory be now he comes to appear in his glory? If his description, Cant. 5:10—shows his glory to be so transcendent: what shall he show himselfe to be when he shall appeare in a more transcendent Glory then there is in that? If in the government of the world, Eze. 1:26, 17, he appeare so glorious what will the glory of his appearance in his judging of the world be? Surely if he appeared in a vision to Daniel having his body like unto byrill, his arms & feet in Colour like unto polisht brass, his eyes like Lumps of fire, his face like a slash of Lightening, & his voice like a clap of thunder, as Dan. 10:6 & 9, oh then what glory shall he now appeare in?[11]

By analogy, Taylor explains that the glory of the resurrected saint is a pale image of Christ's glory, just as the metaphoric description of Christ is a pale image of his personal beauty. The effect of this analogy would not have been lost on his congregation, and we shall see Taylor developing at length the analogy between theanthropy, by which human nature participates in Christ's glory, and the ability of language to express divine beauty. Moreover, as mankind will reflect the glory of Christ's human nature, so also can humans imagine themselves in heaven participating in the glories described by scripture metaphors.

Taylor does not forget the *memento mori* theme; he is all too aware of the leprous deformity of sin everpresent in human life. But he does feel that union with Christ elevates man to the highest beauty in heaven that language is capable of expressing. Throughout his writings, Taylor searches for confirmation of his identity as a saint who would undergo this transformation. With each new voice, with each metaphor drawn from scripture to describe the beauty of sainthood, Taylor achieves in imagination what his faith would have him hope concerning Christ's love for him. Through the imagination Taylor finds release from death, sinful corruption, and deformity.

In Taylor's eschatology, then, the union of human and divine nature is of primary importance, and his comments on theanthropy also reveal several elements of his aesthetic theory. Taylor believed that the Incarnation had elevated human nature above that of the angels, and by becoming part of Christ's mystical body, the church, mankind partook of this glorious "theandricall" elevation.[12] Taylor's devotion to theanthropy has frequently invited comment, and one critic establishes this interest as the foundation of a brand of Calvinistic Christian humanism in Taylor. Karl Keller argues that this "is a concept which is one of the primary sources of Taylor's delight in Calvinism and a considerable stimulus behind his writing his meditative poetry. In the two series of his Meditations he is the rather flamboyant artist of a doctrine which, he feels, throws light into the dark corners of man's condition. Taylor feels that as he concentrates on the physical Christ, he is concentrating on man: the Incarnation is a form of humanism."[13] In fact, the presence of Christ's personality in the Trinity gives saints the right to claim a personal relationship with God. Taylor indeed reminds us that "A Physicall Union of God and Man, is absolutely impossible," that "Two Natures distance-standing, infinite," are "In Essence two, in Properties each are / Unlike, as unlike can be." Nevertheless, Christ's incarnation has made his human nature part of the Trinity as well, for "The Godhead personated in Gods Son / Assum'd the Manhood to its Person . . . Naming one Godhead person, in our Creed, / The Word-made-Flesh" (2:44). Taylor makes it absolutely clear to his congregation that their only hope for a personal union with God, for the Resurrection, for the glories of assuming personally Christ's splendor, lies in becoming part of the church.

The church is a mystical corporation, the body of Christ, in which each believer is by synecdoche taken for the whole.[14] This union is eternal, "For the Humanity is necessary to the Headship," and Taylor envisions an harmonious growth of Christian behavior which fulfills both Christ and the individual. Taylor claims that in the *imitatio Christi* Christ's life and personality accrue to a saint who is otherwise a non-person dead in sin:

> Strive to hold forth the Glory of the Person of Christ in your Christian life, and Conversation. The Person of Christ is most Glorious. He is the King of Glory Psa: 24. *ult*. Now all the glory of his Person is derived to his Manhood by the way of this personall Union. And by the Mysticall Union to every Child of God. Hence then as the personall Union, gives the Manhood propriety in the Glory, and Efficiency of his person: So the Mysticall Union unto the person entitles every Member to the Same Glory, and the Influences thereof, and the duty of Every member to improove all the talents thus derived unto it, calls upon all to se to this: and the attendance upon this call will make the Shine of this Glory breake forth in an holy Life to the glory of the Unions, both Mysticall, and personall. Oh! then mentain the Glory of Christ by a Christ like life. (*C*, p. 104)

Taylor's application of this analogy informs his eschatology, typology, and his use of metaphor. By imitating Christ, the believer can become a crystal through which Christ's light shines. Taylor repeatedly invokes the example of the *teleioi*, the "perfect" in 1 Corinthians 2:6, to describe saints who have accepted Christ's wisdom. Revealing his fondness for one of the favorite metaphors of the Greek Fathers, Taylor sees this perfection as the attainment of the goal or end of Christian life in obedience to the indwelling spirit of Christ which endows the saint with spiritual senses and wisdom above carnal nature in preparation for heavenly life.[15] While Taylor knows that this perfection cannot be achieved during life, one of the most interesting aspects of his poetry is his use of metaphors which imply that Christ will accept his own as if this perfection were indeed already accomplished. Taylor delights in expressing his disbelief that one so sinful as himself can be described by the Holy Spirit in biblical metaphors as a glorious being. Only after death will humans undergo the transformation which will make them glorious, so Taylor can use metaphors to contrast his knowledge of his sinful ugliness with God's promise to clothe him in righteousness.

Taylor insists death cannot break the union between Christ and the human body and soul: "The body of a Saint abides united to Christ in the Grave, and by this argument Christ prooves the Resurrection out of Moses, Mar. 12:26, 27, saying I am the God of Abraham, etc. so that Abraham, Isaak, and Jakob being in a Mysticall Union with God (i,e, United in the Covenant of Grace) tho' their bodies were in the grave, their Union to God was not dissolved. God still Stiles himselfe their God. Hence tho' their bodies were dead they were so but for a time, they must live again."[16] In his elegy on Samuel Hooker, Taylor makes it clear that the saint's glory is progressively revealed as he is conformed to Christ. He puns on the name of Christ when he describes death as a process whereby the flesh is refined to reveal His shine. The epitaph for Hooker reads,

> A turffe of Glory, Rich Celestiall Dust,
> Bit of Christ here in Death's Cradle husht.
> An Orb of Heavenly Sunshine: a bright Star
> That never glimmerd: ever shining faire,
> A Paradise bespangled all with Grace:
> A Curious Web o'relaid with holy lace
> A Magazeen of Prudence: Golden Pot
> Of Gracious Flowers never to be forgot
> Farmingtons Glory, and its Pulpits Grace
> Lies here a Chrystallizing till the trace

Of Time is at an end and all out run.
Then shall arise and quite outshine the Sun.
(*Works*, p. 486)

There is nothing unorthodox in Taylor's hyperbolic praise of Hooker as "An Orb of Heavenly Sunshine," since such language would have been understood in its metaphorical context—it is grace that makes Hooker bright, grace that makes a "paradise" in a fallen world. Such extravagance is to be expected when Taylor brings together his favorite metaphors. The turf of Paradise, the child of Christ born into new life ready to be born again at the Resurrection, shining within the robes of righteousness, waits for the Second Coming. But the force of Taylor's metaphors is in the implication that the saints have Christ's image shining in them even on earth. Taylor uses the common pun of sun/Son when he describes Hooker, and he also puns on the relationship of Christ and Hooker who is "*christ*alized" by transmitting the light of the sun/Son. Moreover, since this punning is used in the early lines of the epitaph, it would be natural for a reader to see a pun in the last line, when Taylor notes that Hooker will outshine the sun at the Resurrection. Taylor also uses his metaphors of glory to work an artful transformation of a common emblem of death, the hourglass. The hourglass is normally associated with the pulpit as well as with death, since it was set to time the minister's sermon. Hooker's time of preaching and his life have indeed "out run," but paradoxically, when eternity has run out through the crystal of his body, he shall outrun death itself.

Given that the saints are mystically united to Christ, to what extent can they use biblical metaphors and types describing Christ to understand something of their own souls? As Norman Grabo argues, Taylor's *Christographia* presents a picture of Christ which the saint copies in his life. Grabo writes, "What we must conclude is that, in its participation in the second person of the trinity, human nature partakes of those properties and qualifications of the Godhead treated in Sermons VI through XIII: life, power, grace, truth, ecclesiastical headship, and authority" (*C*, p. xxvii). Each of these properties and qualifications was shadowed forth by Old Testament types, and by union with Christ saints fulfill these types as well. Through Christ, the richness of Old Testament typological descriptions of persons, places, and things can be applied to the experiences of the individual believer.[17]

In arguing for the typological nature of Old Testament passages which do not find specific fulfillment in Christ's life, Taylor explains, "Tho' they may Speake out particular things that are not to be founde in Christ personally considered, yet they are in Christ Mystically Considered. Tho' they belong not to the proper body Personall, yet they belong to his Body Mysticall, and so their accomplishment falls upon Christ in this Sense, that are not under the other: and in this Sense their Truth ariseth from Christ: and so is in Christ" (*C*, p. 277). This assertion underlies much of Taylor's use of biblical language, since it broadens and personalizes the application of symbolic language to the life of each saint. Every saint not only can forge an imaginative unity with Christ and participate in his glory, shadowed in the multitude of exemplary people, events, and things of the Old Testament, but the saint can also see himself as an essential part of Christ's mystical body bringing to fulfillment the promises and prophecies of the Old Testament. The first thirty meditations of Taylor's second series shows Taylor imagining himself in just this way. In the sermon that accompanied Taylor's first meditation in this series, he indicates the emotional and aesthetic response appropriate to the types:

> Suppose a picture of a thorowly accomplisht Person was drawn to the Life of the most Exquisit art in most Sparkling Colours in all the World, adorned with richest orient Gems that are to be found in all the Creation of God. What should wee think of this draught? Oh! the Vivid beautiousness of this Piece! But now this being presented to you, you should have it thus flowerisht over: Well tho this is so glorious, yet its but a dull Shadow, & Smutty Lineament of the person it represents. Would not this be an high Encomium of the Beauty of that person whose Portraiture it is? But all this is to be found & more abundantly before us in the present case. Oh then the Beauty of this glorious Object! What a Lovely one then is Christ Jesus, that is here presented you for you to set your love upon![18]

Taylor uses this extension of the types in two ways. First, he "spiritualizes," to use his term, types that are not wholly fulfilled in Christ so that they may be applied to each believer. In a meditation on Israel's escape from the bondage of Egypt, he writes,

> But Isra'ls coming out of Egypt thus,
>   I such a Coppy that doth well Descry
> Not onely Christ in person unto us.
>   But Spirituall Christ, and Egypt Spiritually.
>   Egyptian bondage whence gates Israel shows
>   The Spirituall bondage whence Christ's children goe.
> (2:58)

Second, Taylor personalizes biblical types so that Christ, foreshadowed in the Old Testament type, prepares both for His own coming and His coming through grace into the hearts of the Elect. The type not only reveals Christ but is also a vehicle by which Christ remakes each saint as a member of His mystical body. The relationship of Christ and believer cannot be known directly, for it is indeed a "mystical" union, but through the types the saint can come to know Christ indirectly:

> Eternall Love burnisht in Glory thick,
>   Doth butt, and Center in thee, Lord, my joy.
> Thou portrai'd art in Colours bright, that stick
>   Their Glory on the Choicest Saints, Whereby
> They are thy Pictures made. Samson Exceld
> Herein thy Type, as he thy foes once queld.
> ....
> Be thou my Samson, Lord, a Rising Sun,
>   Of Righteousness unto my Soule, I pray.
> Conquour my Foes. Let Graces Spouts all run
>   Upon my Soule O're which thy sunshine lay.
> And set me in thy Sunshine, make each flower
>   Of Grace in me thy Praise perfum'd out poure.
> (2:11)

As the mystical body is the fulness of Christ, Taylor fully expects man to participate in the "shine" of Christ's glory which imbues typology with its special position as the acme of biblical symbology. While Taylor is still aware of the total depravity of man, by personalizing typology, he allows imaginative flights of meditation on the possibilities of human glory through Christ's human nature.

Taylor's concentration on the union of man and Christ is at its most intense in his discussion of the symbol of that union in the Sacrament. In his *Treatise Concerning the Lord's Supper*, written in rebuttal to Solomon Stoddard who had opened participation in the Lord's Supper to all adults, even those who had not professed themselves members of the mystical body of Christ, Taylor's arguments on sacramental theory and theanthropy are inseparable.[19] Stoddard rejected the use of the parable of the "wedden feast" in Matthew 11 as an argument for the purity of the Lord's Supper because he felt this parable referred to the presence of the Elect at the Last Judgment when Christ the King would be present.[20] Since one could not know with total assurance who would be present at that feast, it was permissible to admit all professed Christians to the Sacrament.

For Taylor, the parable limned Christ's spiritual presence. While he admits that God will judge those that come to the Judgment Day without the "wedden garment" of Christ's righteousness, he insists that this parable does not refer to the last things:

Thus we see by these instances that Christ opened His mouth in parables illustrating all things in general heads of the whole of Christian doctrine; from the persons of the Trinity to eternal glory conferred on the righteous at the day of judgment. And you

> see our text falls in with that tier of parables which respect God's carrying on of His gospel grace and dispensation by the hands of His faithful servants. (*TCLS*, pp. 3-4)

Nevertheless, Taylor finds participation in the sacramental feast such a spiritual delight that he repeatedly conflates heavenly glory and the glory of earthly sainthood in the *Treatise*. He explains,

> Truly the excellency of this wedden garment is so great that it doth not only accomplish the soul for this wedden feast, but also for eternal glory itself. For it is the white raiment that Christ promiseth that such shall walk in with Him, that overcome (Rev. 3:5). Well then it hath an excellency answerable to the glory of heaven, answerable to the society of heaven, and therefore answerable to the glory of glorified saints and glorious angels, yea, unto Christ in glory and the Godhead, through divine grace, who requires no more excellency than what lies in this embroidered garment in order to the enjoyment thereof. . . .[21] (*TCLS*, p. 173)

In a meditation on the Lord's Supper, Taylor provides a heavenly context from Revelation for the Lord's Supper: "The Palace where thou this dost Celebrate / Is New Jerusalem . . ." (2:109). When Taylor describes the dressing of believers in the wedding garment, he emphasizes the recapitulative nature of conversion which installs each saint in a process of revivification stretching from the beginning to the end of time:

> this is the best robe . . . , the chief or prime noble robe, Adam's first glorious array that covered the whole man now renewed in Christ. It is the most profitable work as being the soul's espousal to Christ, implantation in Christ, the imbedding of it into God's love, the embossing of it into Christ's heart, the imbellishing of it with graces of God's Spirit, the imbibing of it with the waters of life, the acquitting of it of all its sin, the accomplishing of it with all glorious qualifications, the investing of it in Christ's righteousness, the infrenchizing of it a free denizen of the city of the saints, the inaugurizing of it a child of adoption, the inrolling of its name in the records of glory, the intailing upon it the kingdom of heaven, and the obtaining of an inheritance with the saints in light. (*TCLS*, pp. 23-24)

This robe cannot be rent by death. Taylor is careful to explain that the robe is woven on the loom of theanthropy, a loom of unbreakable human and divine parts. If Christ's theanthropy were not eternal, then it would be fraudulent to dress man with metaphors of holiness.

When Taylor considers Christ's promises in his sacramental meditations, he speaks as a church member who has a reasonable assurance that these promises apply to him. He celebrates their fulfillment in poetry as he celebrates his communion with Christ in the Lord's Supper. Although Taylor never reaches the level of assurance of the mystic, not even in his meditations on Canticles, his use of metaphorical language celebrates the perfect union which will be seen with "bodilie eyes." As we shall see below, the imagination of human glorification is the motivating force behind the transition in gravestone art from the *memento mori* theme to themes of heavenly glory. Moreover, Taylor not only provides a rationale for the repertory of eschatological symbolism, he also provides, in his theorizing on the powers of "spiritual eyes," the epistemological basis for viewing these images. Where Increase Mather concentrates on the union of God and man at the Resurrection, when saints gain glorified "bodilie eyes," Taylor celebrates the spiritual eyes that come with membership in Christ's mystical body. One of the catch phrases in the debate over who was fit for participation in the Lord's Supper was "the ability to discern the Lord's body" in the Sacrament, and for Taylor such discernment was only possible in saints who were part of this body. Saints need

> A discerning eye to discern spiritual things. It is the fault of the unworthy not to discern the body of Christ herein. The body of Christ here is to be taken synechdochically, *pars pro toto*, for whole Christ, as crucified in His human body. For otherwise this body profits not. . . . The body of Christ may also be discerned in its mystical relation, as giving influences nutritive to its members. (*TCLS*, p. 75)

The Supper was such a profoundly aesthetic experience for Taylor precisely because it celebrated the union which gave believers spiritual senses to perceive the glory of Christ. Further, Taylor's focus on the personal union of Christ and believer led to a humanized and personalized eschatological vision.

Spiritual Eyes and the Collins Tradition

Taylor's understanding of the metaphors that describe the glories of saints united to Christ in life and at the Resurrection led him to transform traditional symbols of death into symbols of life. As we have seen above, he strips the hourglass of its signification as an emblem of death, and in his most explicit comment on the commonest emblem of death, the skull, he rejects its meaning outright:

> The Painter lies who pensills death's Face grim
> > With White bare butter Teeth, bare staring bones,
> With Empty Eyeholes, Ghostly lookes which fling
> > Such Dread to see as raiseth Deadly groans,
> > For thou has farely Washt Deaths grim grim face
> > And made his Chilly finger-Ends drip grace.
> (1:34)

Carvers working in Essex County, Massachusetts, and eastern Connecticut at the time Taylor works these changes in his poetry display a similar transformation in the treatment of death imagery. Indeed, the most startling development in funerary art in the period from 1690 to 1735 is the humanization of the effigies cut on gravestones. Blank-eyed faces with primitive marks for nose, mouth, and eyes developed by John Hartshorn in Essex County become rapidly transformed by his followers in New London County, Connecticut, Obadiah Wheeler and the Collins family, after Hartshorn moved there in 1720.[22] By 1735 stones cut by Benjamin and Julius Collins display delicately carved and molded faces of saints in glory with double-outlined almond shaped eyes alertly gazing from the stones, and the effigies are surrounded by other images of the Resurrection drawn from Revelation. While it is not possible to argue for any direct influence of preacher on carver or vice-versa, a shared artistic tradition as well as a web of theological and personal relationships can be established in the region. When the closeness of both Taylor and his congregation's personal contacts with eastern Connecticut becomes clear, the analogies between Taylor's poetry and the stonecarving in the Collins tradition can be seen as the natural product of shared aesthetic and eschatological values.

The Dewey family was the pillar of the Westfield community, and it was Thomas Dewey who led the delegation to Boston which convinced Taylor to travel to Westfield on November 27, 1671. Dewey was also a landowner in eastern Connecticut, and while we do not know how Taylor first met Reverend James Fitch of Norwichtown whose daughter Taylor would wed, it is possible that Dewey provided the introduction.[23] The connection with the Norwichtown community continued after the death of Elizabeth Fitch Taylor in 1689, for Taylor's daughter Anne married Fitch's successor, Benjamin Lord. When Anne died in 1748 after years of paralysis with rheumatoid arthritis, Lord speaks of Taylor in a note in her funeral sermon, and the epitaph on her tombstone also mentions Taylor's ministry in Westfield.[24] Both of these notices imply that Taylor's memory was still cherished in family-conscious Norwichtown some twenty years after his death. Finally, after the disruptions of the Great Awakening, parishioners from a nearby church in Newent, together with other separating individuals from the area, joined in forming at Bennington, Vermont, the state's first church. In 1748 Jedediah Dewey founded a Separate church in Westfield, and when he led his parishioners to Bennington in 1763, he became the pastor of all there.[25] Among the emigrants to Vermont was Zerubbabel Collins, perhaps the greatest stonecarver of eighteenth-century New England, whose presence capped over 100 years of theological and artistic cross-fertilization between Westfield and eastern Connecticut.

Taylor's acquaintance with the *memento mori* symbols of death in the Connecticut River valley makes his rejection of those symbols in interments he supervised all the more significant. From the Westfield cemetery itself and from graveyards in towns Taylor visited we can assemble stones representative of carving styles Taylor saw. Decorative traditions came late to the Connecticut River valley, but the winged death's head design was in Westfield during the last decades of Taylor's life. He would have known that Thomas Johnson's work was an imitation in sandstone of the Boston winged death's head (fig. 33), and primitive versions of the effigy appeared from a variety of hands by the 1720s (figs. 34, 35).[26] While these designs are rather abstract and crude in comparison to Boston styles, we can detect stylistic patterns. Images of life and resurrection are restricted to the pilasters, while the death's head at best can be seen as a representation of the soul in the separate state, an image devoid of reference to the Resurrection. Only one early Connecticut valley carver seems aware of the "bodilie eyes" tradition; the Aron Cooke stone with its humanized effigy represents a design which may have been seen by Taylor in the last years of his life (fig. 36).

The gravestones in the Taylor family plot recapitulate much of the history of New England stonecarving, but there are no stones with death's heads. For his wife he chose a stone without decoration, possibly carved by George Griswold or William Stanclift, reflecting the simplest style of the commemorative impulse (fig. 37).[27] For his son Samuel (d. 1709), however, there is a "table" stone, a rectangular slab on four posts, reminiscent of the markers reserved for the English gentry. This style was rare in New England with its antiaristocratic bias, so Taylor here makes a statement about the social status of his family. Similar stones mark the tombs of Thomas Hooker and Samuel Stone in Hartford, Connecticut. As was usual during the seventeenth century, stones were not placed for the numerous dead Taylor infants, although he commemorated them in poetry. But Taylor's own stone reveals the dramatic shift in Connecticut valley aesthetics, as an alert effigy in the "bodilie eyes" tradition, with crown of life, uplifted wings, and flanked by vegetation prophesies the Resurrection (fig. 38). Through Taylor's writings, we can understand the sophisticated aesthetic and religious values represented by such stones.

As we have seen in the work of the Lamson family, the tell-tale sign of the prophetic or "bodilie eyes" tradition is the articulation of alive, seeing eyes. Such attention to the eyes in the Hartshorn-Wheeler-Collins tradition is analogous to the Lamson style, but as with Edward Taylor's poetry, there is a distinct emphasis on images of light. For Taylor it is the shine of Christ's body and soul that gives humans the power to "see" Christ.[28] In a meditation entitled "That wee may look upon thee," Taylor confesses that Christ alone can equip human eyes to see his beauty:

> The bodies Eyes are blind, no sight therein
>   Is Cleare enough to take a sight of this.
> Its the internall Eye Sight takes this thing
>   This glorious light the Sin blind Eye doth miss.
>   Th'Internall Eye with Christ's Eye Salve annointed
>   Is on this beauteous face alone well pointed.
> (2:147)

In a crucial series of meditations on the relationship of Christ and man's human natures, the power of man's spiritual senses and the imagination (2:72-76), Taylor locates the source of man's imaginative powers in the discerning of Christ's body with spiritual eyes. Taylor's doctrinal argument in this series concerns Christ's glorification of human nature which ensures the resurrection and glorification of the bodies of saints. In the first meditation (2:72), Taylor places the body of Christ at the right hand of God and comments that he, too, will sit there "As Species in their Genus do combine." Then he discusses human nature thus "Received into Glory" (2:73), sings a paean to "His Glorious Body" (2:74), bewails "Our Vile Bodie" (2:75) uncleansed by grace, and ends with the affirmation that Christ "shall change our vile body, that it may be fashioned like his Glorious body" (2:76). Within this doctrinal structure, Taylor presents an artistic argument for the enlivening of the spiritual senses which will permit him to understand the transformation of human nature. He begins the series with the plea, "Enoculate into my mentall Eye / The Visive Spirits of the Holy Ghost," and "Enrich my Phansy with Seraphick Life" so that his art can adequately express the glory of Christ. This inoculation is crucial to Taylor's theological and artistic life, for without it he can neither understand nor praise God.

The climax of this drama comes at the end of the third act of this five part series, when Taylor explicitly connects his aesthetic powers with the perception of Christ's humanity:

> Oh! Glorious Body! Pull my eye lids ope:
>   Make my quick Eye, Lord, thy brisk Glory greet,
> Whose rapid flames when they my heart revoke
>   From other Beauties, make't for thee more sweet.
>   If such blest Sight shall twist my heart with thine,
>   Thy Glory make the Web, thy Praise the Twine.
> (2:74)

For Taylor, the eyes are a sign of the whole relationship of divine and human nature, spiritual beauty and aesthetic perception. When Christ's body sends out rays, Taylor concludes, "My Tunes shall dance then on these Rayes and Caper / Unto thy Praise" (2:76). The eyes are understandably prominent on gravestones which commemorate the body of a saint awaiting resurrection, when the rays of Christ's body will open the eyes and make the saint's body shine in praise.

In Norwichtown, Connecticut, Obadiah Wheeler joins Taylor in this eschatological connection between the eye and the Resurrection body by carving a footstone for Abigail Lothrop in the shape of an eye (fig. 39). This footstone and its headstone reveal in their placement ancient assumptions about the events of the Resurrection. Folk tradition assumed that the millennial day would start in the east with the rising of the sun/Son, so bodies were buried with their feet to the east allowing the saint to sit up and greet Christ.[29] Most headstones in New England face west, and the viewer of the stone thus looks to the east, seeing in the image on the stone an anticipation of what the saint will see when rising from the grave. The viewer is reminded that he, too, will be judged, and since the risen saints judge the rest of mankind with Christ, the image on the stone represents both the coming of Christ and the coming of his saints risen in his image. A possible explanation for the unusual emphasis on the eye on the Lothrop footstone lies in the supposed presence of another eye at the Resurrection, the eye of God which supervises the reassembling of the dust of the deceased. As Taylor writes,

> When the last Cock shall Crow the last day in
> And the Arch Angells Trumpets sound shall ring
> Then th'Eye Omniscient seek shall all there round
> Each dust death's mill had very finely ground,
> Which in death's smoky furnace will refinde
> And Each to'ts fellow hath exactly joyn't,
> Is raised up anew and made all bright
> And Christalized; all top full of delight.
> (*Works*, "A Fig for thee Oh! Death," p. 487)

Taylor laments that death's "Slowness me detains from Christ's bright face," and Wheeler's stones present a complex image of the eyes gathered at the Resurrection.

The strongest evidence of a gravestone tradition which parallels Taylor's linking of theanthropy and the senses is in the progression of imagery on Hartshorn, Wheeler, and Collins stones in the Norwichtown region. On the Alice Hart stone (fig. 40), we have an advanced example of Hartshorn's craft in Essex County, Massachusetts, prior to his removal to

Connecticut. A humanized face, though with hollow, unarticulated eyes, is set upon shoulders between bird-shaped banded figures. This presentation suggests the resurrection of the body more than the flight of the soul, since the shoulders seem to push their way up out of the ground. Further, the bird-shapes resemble serpents sufficiently to suggest the wages of sin in the Garden of Eden which caused death to take this saint. But Christ transformed sin and death into life, so here the serpents become birds, traditional symbols of the Resurrection. The eyes of the birds are penetrating, duplicating those of the effigy. Above the head is the folk symbol for the tree of life, formed by the outline of the bird figures, and the tree surmounts the effigy as a crown of life. The mixing of symbols on this stone proved unstable in Essex County, Massachusetts, and within a few years of the development of this style, the conceit splits in two, with Essex County carving calcifying in cold ghost effigies in the work of the Worster family, and the Connecticut tradition developing a repertoire of resurrection imagery.

One of the clearest examples of this split occurs on the Sara Leffingwell stone of Norwichtown (fig. 41), cut about 1735 by Obadiah Wheeler. There are two sets of eyes, above and within the effigy, and several significant alterations of Hartshorn's design are apparent. First, the carver has emphasized the separation of the image clusters by carving a thick band above the effigy and adding a nub above the tympanum. The banding becomes a set of wings, and a frieze with spirals and a heart runs below the tympanum. Moreover, the eyes of each effigy are now double-outlined, further humanizing their stare by suggesting pupils. The eyes at the top of the stone are joined into a face as the tree of life from the Hart stone becomes a furrowed brow, and a crown appears atop the effigy. This image is confusing in itself. Perhaps it is an illustration of the believer's sets of spiritual and physical eyes. A similar image is presented in Taylor's poem on Canticles 5:10, which in his Day of Judgment sermon was read as a foreshadowing of Christ's millennial beauty:

> When thou, my Lord, mee mad'st, thou madst my heart
> a Seate for love, and love enthronedst there.
> Thou also madst an object by thy Art
> For Love to be laid out upon most Cleare.
> The ruling Stamp of this Choice object shows
> God's Beauty, beautifuller than the rose.
>
> I sent mine Eye, love's Pursevant, to seek
> This Object out, the which to naturall
> I found it mixt with White and Red most sweet.
> On which love naturall doth sweetly fall.
> But if its spirituall, then Orient Grace
> Imbellisht th'object in this Case.
> (2:116)

In Canticles, Taylor finds descriptions of Christ fit for exciting physical and spiritual eyes and affections. Metaphor provides sensual objects for exciting spiritual affections, and on this gravestone both sets of eyes rise over the heart. The use of an ancillary carving space above the tympanum is popular with the Collins family, and the work of Benjamin and Julius refines the hearts and eyes of Wheeler's work. If for Taylor Christ's wisdom is a shine which enlightens the believer's intellect so that he may see in biblical metaphors the beauty of grace which stirs his affections to love Christ, Collins localizes the epitome of this love at the Resurrection. On the Abigail Huntington stone of Norwichtown, 1734 (fig. 42), the rays of light from the face of the effigy shine down into the heart on the frieze. Moreover, the Collinses conflate the powers of spiritual and Resurrection "bodilie eyes" by carving the eyes closed, as if the body sleeps blissfully awaiting the moment when its eyes will be activated by the soul's eyes and pulled open to see Christ. The area in which "spiritual eyes" appear on the Leffingwell stone now contains a tree of life, and the double sets of eyes have melded in a single design.

Julius and Benjamin Collins' work increases in complexity after 1735 when a large repertoire of symbols and facial expressions appear. The variety of these symbols will be discussed later in conjunction with Taylor's use of tableaux and allegory, but the facial expressions can be examined most fruitfully in terms of the eschatological moment commemorated on the stones. Both Benjamin and Julius Collins take the facial expression articulated by Wheeler on the Abigail Huntington stone as a point of departure. Some of their effigies seem to represent the glorification of the body, for the face bulges in relief from the stone. But others may represent the body, the soul, or both. Some effigies have closed eyes, others open; some frowns and others smiles. It is puzzling to find both smiling and frowning effigies on stones which are otherwise identical. In his study of Plymouth County carving traditions, Peter Benes contends that such expressions reflect the congregation's particular stance in respect to orthodoxy during the tumultuous period of the Great Awakening. New Light congregations emphasize assurance of salvation as a sign of grace by preferring smiling effigies, while conservative congregations prefer dour looks of eschatological uncertainty at the Great Assize.[30] While Benes' thesis is provocative, it is impossible to prove with any certainty due to the lack of contemporary commentary, and it seems unlikely that eschatological systems which have such a long history of survival precisely because they reflect shared beliefs would suddenly become subject to such politicization. Benes is right to point to the generally optimistic cast of effigies in the eighteenth century and the growth of the doctrine of assurance, but an explanation for the particular features of effigies can be found in the eschatological literature of the time, based on agreement rather than disagreement amongst congregations. Given the fact that the Collins family cut stones for congregations running the spectrum of eighteenth-century ecclesiology, we should examine them with reference to shared rather than unshared beliefs.

As we have seen in the eschatology of the Mathers and Edward Taylor, it was commonly held that the saints would return in judgment with Christ at the opening of the Millennium. In his meditation on Matthew 24:27, "So also shall the Coming of the Son of Man be," Taylor imagines this moment:

> Methinks I see, when thou appearest thus,
>   The Clouds to rend, and Skies their Crystall Doore
> Open like thunder for thy pass to us
>   And thy Bright Body deckt with Shine all Ore
>   Flash through the Same like rapid Lightening Waver
>   That gilds the Clouds, and makes the Heavens Quaver.
>
> Proud Sinners now that ore Gods Children crow
>   Would if they could creep into Augur holes,
> Thy Lightening Flashing in their faces so,
>   Melts down their Courage, terrifies their Souls.
>   Thy Rapids Lightning Flashes pierce like darts
>   Of Red hot fiery arrows through their hearts.
>
> Now Glory to the Righteous is the Song.
>   Their dusty Frame drops off its drossiness
> Puts on bright robes, doth jump for joy, doth run
>   To meet thee in the Clouds in lightning Dress.
>   Whose nimble Flashes dancing on each thing
>   While Angells trumpet-musick makes them sing.
>
> Make Sanctifying Grace, my tapestry,
>   My person make thy Lookinglass Lord, clear
> And in my Looking Glass cast thou thine Eye.
>   Thy Image view that stardeth shining there.
>   Then as thou com'st like Light'ning, I shall rise
>   In Glories Dress to meet thee in the Skies.
>   (2:92)

Taylor gives us a composite picture of Christ and saint, resurrected in His image, appearing as judges. The viewer of Collins' stones for Zerviah Buckingham (fig. 43) and Hannah Huntington (fig. 44) is placed dramatically at the imagined moment of the Resurrection, just as Taylor has placed himself in the grave awaiting Christ. While the expression on the face of Collins' tombstones is certainly sober as a judge, the face is a double mask, terrible to sinners and benevolent to saints. The viewer of the stone and the reader of the poem must take the place of the deceased, and the only prayer possible is one for sanctifying grace which will make the saint rise in Christ's image, appearing in judgment dressed like the figures on Collins' stones. The ambiguity of the expression here is essential, for it is the very essence of Puritan eschatology to startle one's senses with the awefulness of the apocalyptic moment. Saints can gain identity and glory only by being a mirror for Christ's image, and it is a test of one's spiritual condition to be able to look on such effigies with confidence. In a meditation on the beauty of the Christ's spouse, each believing member of the church, Taylor comments that the shine of Christ's glory sets "both beauty and terrour on thy face / Pleasant in Christs Eye and terrour to's foes all here / A pleasing Shine to Christ and yet sendst darts / Of Terrour terrifying Wicked hearts" (2:134). Moreover, in his sermon on the Day of Judgment, Taylor contrasts joy and punishment in heaven

> As it is received through, & acts upon the eyes. Oh! that dreadful firy flaming, flashing, sparkling, terrible Majesty of the Judge! how doth it send its firy darts of terror through the very heart to behold. Oh how doth it tear the very eye in pieces to looke upon? & oh those dismall & dreadfull sights, those ghostly, agasting looks of Damned sinners, & Spirits & Divels there! Oh! who is able to immagine what torture . . . upon the sinner, as also beholding the fury of the flames, the fierceness of the fire, & the horror of the place![31]

On some Collins' stones, the wings become indistinguishable from darts or flames, and if the wings were a shorthand for the Resurrection body, then in one image the Collinses represent the two possible Resurrection bodies, one bright with glory, a joy to the soul, the other a bed of flames of torment (figs. 43, 44).

While Taylor and the Collins family associate the power of spiritual eyes with a particular eschatological moment, the aesthetic significance of spiritual eyes extends to their methods of visual presentation. Both Taylor and the Collinses present tableaux which slide into allegorical presentations. Moreover, the dramatic shifts in Taylor's imagery from the glorious to the mundane can be explained in terms of the power of "spiritual eyes." In some poems Taylor concentrates on the power of his new vision to recognize Christ's glory and his own loathsomeness, showing the contrast between human and divine nature, the necessity of leaving the old identity of sin and ugliness for a new self of grace and beauty. A typical example is Meditation 2:27:

> My Mentall Eye, spying thy sparkling Fold
>   Bedeckt, my Lord, with Glories shine alone,
> That doth out do all Broideries of Gold:
>   And Pavements of Rich Pearles, and Precious Stone
>   Did double back its Beams to light my Sphere
>   Making an inward Search, for what springs there.
>
> And in my Search I find myselfe defild:
>   Issues and Leprosies all ore mee streame.

In his more positive moods, however, the spiritual eyes open for Taylor a whole new world of delight, in which individual words and images become alive, with the poet finding himself in a world alive with allegory where before he had met barren images. Notice in this meditation how eyesight gives Taylor access to a metaphor from Scripture which can be translated into a landscape which includes the speaker:

> Lead me, my Lord upon mount Lebanon,
>   And shew me there an Aspect bright of thee.
> Open the Valving Doors, when there upon
>   I mean the Casements of thy Faith in mee.
>   And give my Souls Cleare Eye of thee a Sight
>   As thou shinst its bright looking Glasses bright.
> . . . .
> Then thou hast cleard my Faiths round appled Eye
>   My Souls piert Eye and Lebanon display
> Her Glory and her Excellency high
>   In Sweet perfumes and gaudie bright array
>   And all grow tall, strong, fragrant up from thee
>   And of these Cedars tall I sprung one bee.
>
> Then I shall see these precious square wrought Stones
>   Are to thy Zion brought, foundations laid,
> And all these Cedars Choice, of Lebanon
>   Are built thereon and Spiritual Temples made.
>   And still thy Spirits Breathings makes them grow
>   And forth they flowrish, and their Smell doth flow.
>   (2:125)

Instead of a wooden discussion of cedars, there is Taylor a cedar himself, and he describes a timeless allegory of the fashioning of countless temples breathing, growing, and flowing with Christ's life. Taylor makes his method obvious; once he has cleared eyes, he takes the metaphor Christ has given him to use as a poet ("If I may read thee in its name thou art / The Hill"), and then he embarks on a free-form allegory in which he can imagine himself in terms of images describing Christ. Taylor does not merely tell us that doctrinally and typologically the cedars, Christ's body, and the believer are one in a temple built by Christ's grace: rather he uses the language of scripture as if this association were a given.

One of Taylor's favorite topics for such allegorical enlivening of biblical tableaux is the appearance of the church in Revelation, which Taylor conflates with metaphors from Canticles 6:10. Taylor shared with the emblem tradition and the Collins family a visual imagination which conceived of spiritual truths in a particular tableaux composed of a variety of discrete details which must be "read" properly for an understanding of their organic relationship. Any such visualization contains the liability of becoming a mere wooden and lifeless image once the particular context of the image is lost. The stones cut by the Collinses contain a wide range of elements drawn from Canticles and Revelation imagery—moon, sun, stars, rosettes, flowers or fruitful vines, and a shining crowned and winged effigy. These designs with such a multitude of images are in danger of falling into their discrete elements to a viewer unacquainted with the imaginative act that gave them unity. The viewer has to understand the figurative meanings of each symbol and the relationships between these meanings before their conjunction seems anything but artificial. Of course such understanding was available to a Puritan audience, so the carver or the poet was free to assume a style which did not have to establish precisely the matrix of image-meaning-image but was free to move fluidly from image to image, establishing an allegorical narrative where only discrete metaphors previously existed. For example, Taylor chooses a rather static metaphor, three shining suns, to explicate the three offices of Christ as priest, prophet, and king. But even in presenting this image, Taylor prepares us for his imaginative allegorization of his relationship to Christ's three-in-one authority by adopting a simple cosmological scheme:

> Three Shining Suns rise in the Chyrstall Skies
>   Of Mankinde Orbs, and Orbs Angelicall.
> Whose Rayes out Shine all pimping Stars that rise
>   Within these Spheres and Circuite through them all.
>   These do evigorate all Action done
>   By men and angells right, wherein they run.
> (2:55)

By punning on Chrystall/Christ, with "rise" evoking thoughts of the Resurrection, Taylor has planted the association of these suns with the sun/Son who rose and who in returning would light up the skies once again. Taylor reminds us that Christ "evigorates" both man and angel, and if man would rise into "Chrystall Skies" he must be a member of Christ's body. From a metaphoric description of Christ's offices, Taylor can easily move to an eschatological vision which is no longer static but alive, anticipating the moment when he can, through metaphoric association, rise like the sun/Son:

> O! plant mee in thy Priestly Sunshine, I
>   Shall then be reconcild to God. In mee
> A beame of thy Propheticke Sun imploy.
>   'Twill fill my Spirits Eye with light to see.
>   Make in my heart thy Kingly Sunshine flame.
>   'Twill burn my Sin up, sanctify my frame.
>
> My Gracious-Gracious Lord, shall I be thine?
>   Wilt thou be mine? Then happy, happy mee!
> I shall then be cloath'd with the Sun, and shine,
>   Crown'd with twelve Starrs, Moon under foot too see.[32]

While New England custom would have prohibited the depiction of Christ himself on gravestones, given the example of Taylor we can see how the distinction of metaphoric images of Christ and the saint are so blurred as to allow the viewer to project himself imaginatively into the image of Christ. The images on the Buckingham and Huntington stones (figs. 43, 44) show at once a believer resurrected in the glorious image of Christ and the three offices of Christ which provide for the Resurrection. The tableaux before us is enlivened and allegorized in the same fashion as images in Taylor's poems. On all three stones, the risen saint "outshines" the sun, moon, and stars.[33] Moreover, the light from the effigy shines on a heart, the emblem of divine love to God, so here the sun shines directly into the heart. The priestly office of Christ is represented in sacramental references on the stones, as vines either curl up the pilasters, evoking Christ as the true vine, or flourish with grapes within the tympanum.[34] On the Hannah Huntington stone, what may be a candlestick stands beneath the effigy, as if lit by the shine of the sun-face. Candlesticks were typologically related to the priesthood in the Old Testament temple, and a constant lament in funeral sermons for ministers was over the removal of God's candlesticks from his New Testament temple. The rays of sunshine descending from the face also suggest the Geneva collar, another common gravestone motif emphasizing the priesthood of all believers. Such priestly references are fitting on tombstones, since it is the administration of the Sacrament that symbolizes Christ's priestly function in communicating grace to man, uniting man to His mystical body, thus providing hope of the resurrection of the saint beneath the stone. Finally, the kingly office of Christ is conflated with the believer's resurrection as a king with a crown of life, especially apparent on the Zerviah Buckingham stone (fig. 43).[35] For the Puritan viewer such seemingly static images act out a complex narrative of Christ's offices, His workings of grace in the souls of believers, His relationship to His church, and the glory of these offices redounding to each saint in the Resurrection. It is the personal application of biblical metaphors that sets this narrative in motion, and for both Taylor's poetry and the Collins family carvers, these metaphors transform death into glory.

Figure 33. Noah Grant, 1727, Glastonbury, Connecticut

Figure 34.   Benjamin Madsley, 1719, Westfield, Massachusetts

Figure 35. Nathaniel Williams, 1731(?), Westfield, Massachusetts

Figure 36. Aron Cooke, 1725, Hartford, Connecticut

Figure 38. Reverend Edward Taylor, 1729, Westfield, Massachusetts

Figure 37. Elizabeth Taylor, 1689, Westfield, Massachusetts

Figure 39. Abigail Lothrop, 1735, Norwichtown, Connecticut

Figure 40.   Alice Hart, 1682 (cut ca. 1700), Ipswich, Massachusetts

Figure 41. Sara Leffingwell, ca. 1735, Norwichtown,
Connecticut

Figure 42. Abigail Huntington, 1734, Norwichtown, Connecticut

Figure 43. Zerviah Buckingham, 1748, Columbia, Connecticut

Figure 44.   Hannah Huntington, 1745, Norwichtown, Connecticut

6

Edward Taylor's "Life Metaphoricall"

Heart sick my Lord heart sick of Love to thee!

—Edward Taylor, Meditation 2:165

While biblical descriptions of the last things influenced the content of Taylor's poetry and gravestone carving, Puritan understanding of the nature of biblical language informed the styles of early American artists. Human language, for Puritans, was debased at least as early as the fall of the tower of Babel; people twist words, lie, and pervert the language of the Bible itself by misapprehending its literal truth.[1] Taylor understood that God spoke in special forms of figurative language, such as typology, in order to accommodate divine truth to the limitations of human language and understanding, but as a minister and a poet he distrusted his ability to *know* the truth figurative language signified. Much has been made of Taylor's denigration of metaphorical language, as he follows Ramus in the separation of logical, doctrinal truth and the varnish of metaphorical expressions. Nevertheless, the relationship between metaphor and truth is one of the wellsprings of both Taylor's poetry and the arts of early New England; much of the playfulness and wit of these artists lies in the contrasting of surface and substance, man's language and God's language.

Karl Keller explains Taylor's mixed feelings about metaphor and the art of writing:

> Taylor shows himself in his few comments in his sermons to be of two minds about the art of writing. He had both reservations and excitement about the religious possibilities of such a literary matter as imagery. . . . On the one hand something might be "*onely* Metaphoricall" or "metaphoricall and *not proper*," but on the other hand, it could be a means of realizing truth. He is suspicious of all literary devices yet recognizes in them great relief for man's spiritual desires. In a 1679 sermon he calls the denial of scriptural metaphors "but Rhetoricall Atheism." No doubt it was such interest in the power of metaphor that led him to his poetry.[2]

Taylor assumes that the metaphors chosen by God so to communicate have some inherent fitness for this task, that some suitableness exists between the spiritual truth and the physical image. Man's metaphors, however, do not have such a preordained fitness and are therefore suspect. As Perry Miller explained in his seminal discussion of Puritan American attitudes towards art, the influence of Ramism is clear-cut, for metaphor is seen as a rhetorical dressing for solid logical truths.[3] In an oft-quoted meditation (2:44), Taylor confesses that eloquence is just "Spangled Flowers" picked from "Rhetorick gardens." Indeed, as Norman S. Grabo writes, "metaphor is treated as Taylor treats it rhetorically—a decoration, a shiny varnish used to beautify its object. But at the same time we know that the varnish has to be spiritualized and moralized, that it is a symbolic varnish used by the most glorious of poets to express what otherwise could not be accommodated to human understanding."[4]

Taylor makes several comments in his poetry to the effect that metaphors must be spiritualized; in a meditation on Canticles he writes: "these Metaphors we spiritualized / Speake out the Spouses spirituall Beauty cleare" (2:151). Yet even given these caveats, Taylor's sense of eschatology adds a dimension of significance to metaphor that flavors his understanding of the power of scripture metaphor. In the lines immediately following those just quoted, Taylor ends his meditation with the plea "Make me a member of thy Beautious Bride, / I then shall wear thy lovely Spouses Shine." By becoming one with the spirit in the metaphor, Taylor hopes to become dressed in the "shine" of the metaphor at the Resurrection.

Even during life, the very highest glory in which man can participate is in what Taylor calls "life Metaphoricall," a fulness that involves the saint in the meaning of Christ's words.

> See hence what Course you are to take for Life. You are to goe to the Fountain of Life for Life. If you would live and not dy, you must go to him in whom dwells all the Fulness of Life. Men would fain live and not die: but most take the Way of Death: and not the path of Life. You can never finde Life in the Way of Death: you can never avoide death, out of the way of Life. Christ is the Way: and Christ is the Life, and all Life, and all fulness of Life. If you would have Life naturall: you must have it of him. If you would have Life Spirituall, you must have it from him. If you would have life Eternall you must have it from him. If you Would have Life Metaphoricall, a flourishing prosperous State, a Virtuous, and pleasant Life: If Towns, Societies, Churches, and Families, etc., would be in a peacefull, pleasant, glorious, amiable, Lovely, Thriving, Flourishing State, and Condition, they must go to Christ, Fetch influences from Christ, keep the Channels open and unstopt in which the Waters of Life run from this Spring of Life into the Soul or into the Society.[5]

To be part of Christ's metaphors would be the greatest joy possible, for Taylor knows that Christ's spirit can make the metaphor real, can transform the metaphorical images to take on the qualities of His spirit.

Much of Taylor's poetry concerns the process of going to Christ for "Life Metaphoricall." Taylor moves from the surface varnish of his own metaphors to participation in Christ's metaphors, and in the process hopes to gain the beauty inherent to Christ. The poems often adopt a three-part structure. He admits the inadequacy of his own metaphors to describe Christ, begs Christ to "glaze" his soul with scripture metaphors, and then expresses the hope that he will be able to return the shine of glory to Christ in praise. In one poem Taylor imagines first Christ and then himself as a wanton seductress in the hope that he will be "embedded" in Christ's metaphors:

> Glory, thou Shine of Shining things made fine
>   To fill the Fancy peeping through the Eyes
> At thee that wantons with thy glittering Shine
>   That onely dances on the Outside guise
>   Yet art the brightest blossom fine things bring
>   To please our Fancies with and make them sing.
>
> But spare me, Lord, if I while thou dost use
>   This Metaphor to make thyselfe appeare
> In taking Colours, fancy it to Choose
>   To blandish mine affections with and Cheare
>   Them with thy glory, ever shining best.
>   Thus brought to thee so takingly up dresst.
> (2:101)

He apologizes for his carnal use of biblical metaphors of Christ's spiritual beauty, but as a fallen, sensuous creature he cannot avoid a physical response to physical images. Taylor quickly admits that human beauty is painted makeup in comparison to Christ:

> The Glory bright of Glorified Saints
>   And brightest Glory sparkling out with grace
> Comparde with thine my Lord is but as Paint
>   But glances on them of thy glorious Face.
>   Its weak reflection of thy glories Shine,
>   Painting their Walls not to compare with thine.
> (2:101)

Although he knows he is only a painted strumpet compared to Christ, Taylor hopes that Christ will still "wooe" him, that his painted metaphors will be accepted by a loving Christ.

Taylor's delight in surface can be attributed, in part, to his desire to create a poetic illusion of a glorious, shining, varnished self which Christ might enliven and support with the solid structure of grace. The concern with surfaces identifies Taylor with the baroque style of his age, in which the quick visual play of images and the illusionistic brilliance of surfaces belie the structure of the artifice.

While it has been argued that Taylor is not properly baroque in his sensibilities, it is clear that he shared with his contemporaries the desire to use metaphors to create certain illusions, which are given solidity and strength by the structure, in this case the grace, within.[6] Taylor speaks highly of God as an artist who combines surface with strength and truth, and in a meditation entitled "Full of Truth," Taylor moves through a sustained metaphor to implant himself within the structure of God's art beneath a beautiful surface:

> The Artists Hand more gloriously bright,
>   Than is the Sun itselfe, in'ts shining glory
> Wrought with a stone axe made of Pearle, as light
>   As light itselfe, cut of a Rock all flory
>   Of Precious Pearle, a Box most lively made
>   More rich than gold Brimfull of Truth enlaid.
>
> Which Box should forth a race of boxes send
>   Teemd from its Womb such as itselfe, to run
> Down from the Worlds beginning to its end.
>   But, O! this box of Pearle Fell, Broke, undone.
>   Truth from it flew: It lost Smaragdine Glory:
>   Was filld with Falshood: Boxes teemd of Sory.
>
> The Artist puts his glorious hand again
>   Out to the Worke: His Skill out flames more bright
> Now than before. The worke he goes to gain,
>   He did portray in flaming Rayes of light.
>   A box of Pearle shall from this Sory, pass
>   More rich than that Smaragdine Truth-Box was.
>
> Which Box, four thousand yeares, o'r ere 'twas made,
>   In golden Scutchons lay'd in inke Divine
> Of Promises, of a Prophetick Shade,
>   And in embellishments of Types that shine.
>   Whose Beams in this Choice pearle-made-Box all meet
>   And bedded in't their glorious Truth to keep.
>
> But now, my Lord, thy Humane Nature, I
>   Doe by the Rayes of this Scutcheon sends out, finde
> Is this Smaragdine Box where Truth doth ly
>   Of Types, and Promises, that thee out lin'de.
>   Their Truth they finde in thee: this makes them shine.
>   Their Shine on thee makes thee appeare Divine.

Thou givst thy Truth to them, thus true they bee.
  They bring their Witness out for thee. Hereby
Their Truth appeares emboxt indeed in thee:
  And thou the true Messiah shin'st thereby.
  Hence Thou, and They make One another true
  And They, and Thou each others Glory shew.

Hence thou are full of Truth, and full dost stand,
  Of Promises, of Prophesies, and Types.
But that's not all: All truth is in thy hand,
  Thy lips drop onely Truth, give Falshood gripes.
  Leade through the World to glory, that ne'er ends
  By Truth's bright Hand all such as Grace befriends.

O! Box of Truth! tenent my Credence in
  The mortase of thy Truth: and Thou in Mee.
These Mortases, and Tenents make so trim,
  That They and Thou, and I ne'er severd bee.
  Embox my Faith, Lord, in thy Truth a part
  And I'st by Faith embox thee in my heart.
(2:50)

Taylor's artistry in this poem is brilliant, as he reflects in his use of language the mortice and tenon joinery he exalts. This joint is known for its strength arising from the mutual fit of the two parts. Throughout the poem, Taylor plays with the idea of containment and fulness, as he creates a nest of boxes including Adam, the Bible, Christ, and finally himself. Paradoxically, Christ is the truth that fills all of these boxes, yet the boxes are also contained within Christ. Taylor presents an active surface of imagistic and verbal wit, but the stanzas are solidly morticed and tenoned together with logic, doctrine, and metaphor. In the first stanza, mankind is made out of a rock of pearl, metaphorically Christ. When this box breaks at the Fall, Truth, the image of Christ in the soul, is lost, so the artist has to make a new pearl box, Christ Incarnate from the "sory" mess of mankind. In the fourth stanza, Taylor puns on the notion of the Bible as a box which contains truth by shadowing forth Christ's human nature. But Christ's nature is also a box which contains the truth of the Bible. Taylor's audience would have associated the Bible with a box, since Bibles were customarily kept in carved, painted, or inlaid boxes in the home. In the last three stanzas, Taylor plays with the "Truth" containing all of these boxes—each box is contained in the other, and each truth fills the others with truth.

In the last stanza, Taylor appropriately moves from the pearl box that was Adam, the golden box of the Bible, and the pearly box of Christ, to a homespun form of construction, a wooden, plain, but solid mortice and tenon box to represent his humble faith. This nest of boxes reflects the logic of Taylor's artistry and doctrine, as Taylor hopes his wood-framed faith will be strong enough to contain the fulness of truth which gave glory to the other boxes created by the joiner-Christ. The intricacy of Taylor's language in the last stanza, as he puns on tenent-tenet-tenant, as the musical complexity of the verse locks each word in place by inter-weaving consonant sounds, the repetitions of words, the reciprocity of phrasing (thy-thou, faith-truth) approximating the reciprocity of the mor-tice and tenon joint, makes the stanza a strong structure which supports the surface play of words.

Taylor's playing surface intricacy off structural solidity is also prac-ticed by the artisans of his time. In particular, the Hadley chest, an in-digenous American form of dower chest constructed in and around Hadley, Massachusetts, from 1670 to 1720, reflects a delight in surface detail that belies the heavy construction of the box itself (fig. 45).[7] The basic form of the chest is a three-paneled box with a solid top, placed above one to three drawers. The top of the chest is undecorated pine, while the stiles, rails, posts, and panels are highly carved oak painted red, black, and green. The carved design is a low relief of stylized tulip and lily shapes, leaves, and hearts, with the initials or name of the woman for whom the chest was made often appearing in the central panel or top rail. The carving patterns carry over from panel to rail to stile to drawer, effectively masking the structural units of the chest creating a complex two-dimen-sional surface. The lively splashes of color on both the relief and incised portions of the chest would have further created the impression of a sprawling vegetative growth. But one has merely to lift the lid or pull out a drawer to see the heavily cut mortice and tenon construction to realize that this is a massive piece of furniture built to last centuries despite the delicate and fragile appearance of the decoration.

This illusionistic paradox is a central feature of the Hadley chest, and Taylor, who undoubtedly was familiar with the form, would have appreciated the strength of its joinery, which he celebrates in his medi-tation, and the lightness of its decoration which was finished to shine gloriously in the light. Moreover, he may well have appreciated the inter-play of incised and relief portions of carving which play visual tricks on the viewer. Within the panels of the HS chest (fig. 46), we find leaves arching together to form a heart above the initials, an appropriate deco-ration for a dower chest. Further, on the rail beneath this panel and on the rails of the MM chest (fig. 45), we find a form of visual punning, as the rows of tulips come together at the center of each rail to form a stylized woman's face. The meaning of this pun is appropriate to the occasion of the chest's construction, since the chest itself is a sign of the expected fruitfulness of the woman entering the marriage state.

The method of the creation of this image parallels Taylor's poetic technique of creating the "face" of the saint with metaphorical descriptions of Christ's beauty. The face on the dower chest is a secular manifestation of a theme which Taylor would explore in his meditations on Canticles texts, for this book of the Bible describes the holy marriage between Christ and his spouse which is the pattern for any earthly marriage.

Several of Taylor's poems on Canticles follow the biblical example by taking the metaphorical descriptions drawn from nature to create a beautiful face for the spouse. Taylor would have himself become a looking glass which would reflect the beauty of Christ.[8] He writes,

> If I thy Vally, thou its Lilly bee.
>   My Heart shall be thy Chrystall looking Glass
> Shewing thy Lillies Face most cleare in mee
>   In shape and beauty that doth brightly flash.
>   My Looking glass shall weare thy Lillies Face
>   As tis thy Looking Glass of Every Grace.
> (2:132)

Taylor takes a metaphorical text from Scripture, "He feeds among the Lillies" (Cant. 6:3), takes its images at face value, and constructs a poetic argument by extending fancifully the central metaphor given by Christ. In another meditation on the lilies in Canticles, Taylor expands upon the traditional association of the lily and Christ's humility. Taylor's technique resembles that of the carver of the Hadley chest who uses positive and negative space to create images, since the very presence of the lily, the positive act of Christ, creates a valley in the heart of the believer, the negative space. There is a further blend of positive and negative space in the way in which vegetable and human become metaphorically one as the flower is personified and the heart covered with vegetation:

> How shall my Vallie's Spangling Glory spred,
>   Thou Lilly of the Vallies Spangling
> There springing up? Upon thy bowing Head
>   All Heavens bright Glory hangeth dangling.
>   My Vally then with Blissful Beams shall shine,
>   Thou Lilly of the Vallys, being mine.
> (1:5)

This is a poetic of verbal and imagistic fluidity, as words and images melt into and define one another. For Taylor, this would be a fitting verbal representation of the activities of transforming grace, man's assuming of Christ's beauty. The repetition of words such as spangling, the inter-weaving of sounds (hangeth dangling, blissful beams, lilly, and vally), the counterpoint of thou and mine in the last line to communicate the paradox of two separate beings, one divine and beautiful, the other low and sinful, approximates the visual repetitions and interweavings of images on the Hadley chest. Metaphors have a habit of springing into life in Taylor's verse, as he slips from metaphor to personification to allegory. This vivification represents verbally the kind of "life Metaphoricall" Taylor would have from Christ.

In a delightful allegory based on Canticles 6:11 (2:65), Taylor works up a drama acted by nature, Christ, and his soul which ends with the creation of a lively illusionistic piece reminiscent of the anamorphic paintings popular in the seventeenth century. The grapes and almonds who see Christ's enclosed garden "Are all unmand as tipsy, slink away / As blushing at their manners to behold / Thy Nut trees Gardens buds and flowers unfold." While nature slinks away embarassed by the riches of Christ's spiritual vegetation, the speaker is bold enough to ask Christ to be planted there:

> Make thou my Soule, Lord, thy mount Olivet
>   And plant it with thy Olive Trees fair Green,
> Adorned with Holy Blossoms, thence beset
>   With Heavens Olives, Happy to be seen.
>   Thy Sacred Oyle will then make bright to shine
>   My Soul its face, and all the works of mine.
> . . . .
> The Smiling Dimples on my Fruits Cheeks hung
>   Will as rich jewells adde unto their Shine.

When carved or painted on a solid frame of grace, metaphors glow with spiritual reality, and if the poet's art is morticed and tenoned in Christ, then the poet partakes of a glorious new identity.

Given Taylor's tendency to mix metaphors of earthly grace and heavenly glory, it is not surprising that he also associates the beauty of the spouse on earth with the transcendent glory of the bride of heaven. Design motifs found on Connecticut River valley gravestones suggest that carvers of Hadley chests also made gravestones; while there is not direct reference to a heavenly bridal on the chests, Taylor's treatment of Canticles suggests that metaphorical connections of death and nuptial rites are not unknown to the Puritan imagination. In Taylor's "A Fig for thee Oh! Death," Death is a rapist who ravishes the body in an unholy marriage bed: "My Body, my vile harlot, its thy Mess, / Labouring to drown me into Sin, disguise / By Eating and by drinking such evill joyes, / Though Grace preserv'd mee that I here have / Surprised been not tumbled in such a grave." The soul is preserved for a chaste heavenly marriage, when at the Resurrection the soul and body "as two true lovers / Ery night how do they hug and kiss each other" (*Works*, p. 487). In this eschatological framework, Taylor's meditations on Canticles help to explain a major direction that New England stonecarving takes in the period from Taylor's death until the rise of neoclassical design in the late eighteenth century.

The Bride of Christ

The Song of Solomon, commonly called Canticles by Taylor and his contemporaries, clearly was the poet's favorite book of the Bible,[9] forming the basis for his spiritual and artistic life almost exclusively from 1713 on. As we have seen in the passages cited on Canticles texts above, Taylor's language is filled with spiritual and sensual passion, yet as the meditations progress, Taylor's passion becomes increasingly otherworldly. In his very last meditation, on Canticles 2:5 "I am sick of Love," Taylor adds a new twist to his lifelong habit of belittling his poetry by equating his artistic limitations with his sick wreck of a body which keeps him from Christ. His "parchments ready to crack," and he disdains his "Hidebound gift," both the poems bound in hide he has penned as his gift of praise and his love which is bound in his hide, the body.

Taylor's use of this text to bid farewell to the world is appropriate, for most commentaries on Canticles specified this sickness for Christ's love as one which only death could cure. Taylor may well have also been familiar with popular emblems on this text devised by the Jesuit Hermanus Hugo and "englished" and purged of their Catholic doctrine by Francis Quarles in his popular *Emblems*.[10] Late in the seventeenth century, Edmund Arwaker retranslated the text, and this new edition went through two reprintings. The emblem (fig. 47) shows the spouse in her swoon, and Hugo and Arwaker's texts conclude:

> O then! to slacken this tormenting fire,
> The *Rose of Sharon* only I desire:
> And for an Apple to assvage my grief,
> Give it, oh! give it from the *Tree of Life*!
>
> Then strow them gently on my Virgin-bed!
> And as the withering *Rose* declines its head,
> Compos'd to Death's long sleep, my rest I'll take,
> *Dream of my love, and in his arms awake.*[11]

Taylor's use of Canticles texts has an eschatological flavor even when he meditates on passages not specifically directed to the last things. This is partly the result of his general theory of the eschatological content of metaphoric language discussed above, and partly the result of his personal views on Canticles itself.

As I demonstrated in chapter 2, few books of the Bible generated more controversy over exegetical interpretation than Canticles, and Taylor was certainly aware of the variety of approaches open to him. Whatever sition Taylor takes as a theologian, as an artist he fulfills personal needs in his meditations on Canticles. The book provides him with a vehicle for knowing and praising Christ, for working up his affections in divine love, and finally for expressing his deepest desires to be accepted into mystical marriage with Christ. Taylor reads Canticles as a description of the delights of spiritual marriage on earth and resurrection marriage in heaven with the bridegroom, Christ. As such, the book provided him with a great deal of consolation as he approached death. As John Robotham asserted in his influential commentary, "Thus it is with the Lord Jesus, he hath betrothed himselfe to his Spouse here on earth, and at last the marriage shall be solemnized, *Revel*. 19:17. So that all those riches and dignities the Church now receive in the promise, then shee shall have the fruition of them."[12] A right appreciation of the song was held up as a test of grace by more than one writer. The understanding of the text was like entering into the Holy of Holies, and for John Collinges "In this Song duly understood, a Christian may doubtless see as much of Christ as can be seen of him, on this side Heaven, while *the glorius day* shall come to *break*, and the *dark shadows* which both eclipse the glory of Heaven from us, and darken our eyes as to the visions of God, shall all flee away."[13] While in Taylor's time images from Canticles only make occasional appearances on gravestones, we see in his eschatological approach to the text an aesthetic which would flourish in the fifty years after his death throughout New England stonecarving. Thus it is fitting that we examine Taylor's use of Canticles as a prophecy of things to come, as it was for him a list of joys to be hoped for.

Canticles would have appealed to Taylor's poetic sensibilities on several grounds—voice, decorum, and imagery. Besides the sacramental meditations written on Canticles texts, much of the rest of Taylor's poetry and sermons is imbued with its spirit and imagery. While I will discuss Taylor's use of Canticles metaphors below, it is important to recognize first the appeal of Solomon to Taylor both as a man and a poet. It is traditional to look upon David, the sweet singer of Israel, as the foremost model of a biblical poet for Christian poets of all times, yet in the seventeenth century there developed a school of thought which exalted Solomon above David. A representative voice is that of John Robotham. Robotham locates the excellence of the song in the mixing of modes that occur in other parts of scripture, and the artist who can so mix his songs needs be the greatest in the Bible. After defining the three types of singing found in the Old Testament, he writes "this most excellent song contains them all in one: it is as *a song* for joy and rejoycing: it is as a *hyme* for praise and thanksgiving: it is as a *Psalme* for exhortation and instruction."[14]

Robotham's arguments for Solomon's poetic skill are interesting especially when we consider the qualities of Taylor's verse, including the mixing of modes, which help us to understand some of the differences between his verse and that of his contemporaries in England. First, the subject matter of Canticles excels that of most of David's psalms, since Solomon mystically sings of the love of Christ and his church in the most beautiful metaphors taken from the best things on earth. Second, the very difficulty of the song enhances its artistic value:

> This song admitteth more variety of interpretation then any other: some understand it of the Catholicke Church, some of particular Churches, from *Solomons* time to the last judgment, some of the mutuall affection and love between Christ and every Believer: We deny not, but that there may be usefull truths in each one of these interpretations; but sure it is, that all, or the most passages of this song will very well agree to the spirituall state of the Church in every age of the world.[15]

Far from driving his golden wedges into the cracks and crannies of exegetical disputation over the prophetical, typic, and allegorical modes, Robotham embraces all these modes as long as they are compatible with a spiritual meaning which can inspire every believer. He thus aligns himself with James Durham, who, as we have seen above, presented the most detailed arguments for a spiritual reading of the text. While Taylor wholeheartedly embraced the spiritual interpretation of the text, he also agreed with Robotham that such variety of interpretation was a positive aesthetic quality since it is both edifying and pleasurable to meditate on "all those parabolicall and enigmatical phrases and dark speeches, wherein is contained very divine and heavenly matter."[16]

Given Taylor's acute sense of his own sinfulness, we can imagine him having empathy for Solomon. Solomon's apostasy, great though it was, did not keep God from blessing him with wisdom and renewed faith. Taylor is intensely concerned with his own loathsome sins, and in fact his meditations on Canticles are distinguishable from those of the Catholic mystic St. John of the Cross by the persistence of doubt even when writing on a text celebrating mystical oneness with Christ. For St. John of the Cross, the dark night of the soul is past, but for Taylor it casts a shadow on the saint until death. Even late in his life when one presumes Taylor has gained some assurance of his salvation, he writes,

> Alas! my Soule, Thy Sunburnt Skin looks dun:
>   Thy Elementall jacket's Snake like pi'de.
> I am Deform'd, and uggly all become.
>   Soule Sicknesses do nest in mee: and Pride.
>   I nauseous am: and mine iniquities
>   Like Crawling Worms doe eat on my joys.
>
> All black though plac'de in a White lilly Grove:
>   Not sweet, though in a bed of Lillies rowle,
> Though in Physicians shop I dwell, a Drove
>   Of Hellish Vermin range all ore my Soul.
>   All Spirituall Maladies play rex in mee,
>   Though Christ should Lilly of my Valley bee.
> (2:69)

While many seventeenth-century writers ignored Solomon's apostasy, noting instead his divine wisdom as a type of Christ, others delved deeply into Solomon's fall and recovery as an example of God's mercy to all persons who, no matter how great, are still depraved and in need of grace. Most writers agreed that Ecclesiastes and Canticles were written late in Solomon's life after he had been chastened by God; Ecclesiastes shows him weaning his affections from vain earthly pastimes, and Canticles shows him turning his affections to higher things. As Thomas Ager notes, Solomon's sinful nature did not prevent God from blessing him as a poet:

> *Solomon* was a Man besotted in his Life, and stained with many foul blemishes . . . yet the Lord passed by his great and foul stains, and made choice of *Solomon* to be the Pen-man of his holy Spirit, and an instrument where his Glory should shine. The Lord did not cast off *Solomon* for his stains and blemishes, but had an Eye to that good which was in him, he would make him a worthy Instrument to set forth his Praise.
> . . . .
> For *Solomon*, although he was unworthy and unfit to be chosen for such an Instrument, by reason of his foul stains; yet in regard of his wonderful Wisdom, and great Reach, that the Lord had given him, whereby he was able to borrow Speeches from the nature of Earthly things; to set forth the Lord's mind in Heavenly things, he was a Man excellently fitted.[17]

This last assumption is crucial to an understanding of Taylor's art, for it reveals Puritan approbation of Solomon's use of the things of the earth that had so captured him to express the heavenly glories that had freed him. From an awareness of sin comes an appreciation of glory.

One of the most perplexing features of Canticles to Puritans was the elaborate praise lavished on the spouse by Christ, the bridegroom, who found her so beautiful that He begs her to turn away her eye (Canticles 6:5). Solomon may have learned through his sin how beautiful God is, but how could He see anything but deformity in even the most reformed man? Surely sinful mankind, with even the Elect besotted with imperfection, could not be beautiful to Christ. How then to interpret the words of Christ, who was no silly lover blind to His spouse's sorry history of thousands of years of spiritual fornication with idols?

Puritans had two answers for this question, and in them we see the parameters of Taylor's poetic method. First, the spouse's very recognition of her own degeneracy, a condition that violates the decorum of praise, indicates the presence of grace. Richard Sibbes identifies this paradox by writing

> here is a misterie of Religion, *The Church is never more faire then when she judgeth herselfe to be miserable: never more strong than when she feeles herselfe to be weake, never more righteous then when she feeles herselfe to be most burthened with the guilt of her owne sinnes*, because the sence of one contrary forceth to another, the sence of ill forceth us to the fountaine of good, to have supply thence. . . .[18]

This paradox lends itself to expression in terms of Puritan ways of seeing, since spiritual eyes can simultaneously perceive man's deformity and Christ's beauty. Sibbes instructs believers how to read Christ's praise of his spouse in Canticles with "a double eye, one to set and fixe upon that which is ill in them, to humble them, and another upon that which is supernaturally gracious in them."[19]

When meditating on Canticles, the Puritan can use a variety of voices inspired by the different visions, speaking once as a sinner seeing his deformity, and again as a saint, seeing with Christ's eyes the righteousness Christ has given man. John Collinges launches into a sea of ecstasy in a meditation on Christ's praise of the spouse's face in Canticles:

> Lord! my face? What is more than the face of a dirty worm, a face that hath hardly a line in it of Gods Creation. My eyes are full of vanity, blubbered with unbelief, dirtied with covetousness, bloud shotten with passion; my lips have been blacked with idle filthy words, with murmuring and unbelief. See my face! Lord, I blush to shew my face unto thee, and have hid it from thee through shame. I am ashamed to shew my face to thy people, yet this is the face our Lord will see. . . . Methinks I hear a Soul saying, my dear Saviour, with what eyes dost thou look? I look upon my self in the glass of the Law, I see no *Ethiopian* blacker. I turn and look upon my reflection in the glass of the Gospel, there I see an unbelieving heart full of doubts, ful of fears,

full of reasonings against thy Promises; the World looks upon me, and they see no
comeliness in me, nothing for which I should be desired; and doth my Lord say, *Thy
countenance is comely?* I must now confess that God seeth not as man seeth.[20]

Second, Puritans understood Christ's praise of his spouse as prophetic of beauties promised to his bride. The metaphors of Canticles gain
an eschatological dimension when they are seen as prophetic of the beauties of the church triumphant at the Apocalyptic marriage. The beauty of
the spouse is more than merely metaphorical, since it is "so sure and
permanent that death it self shall not deface it, but rather be the means
of perfecting the same in glory."[21] Thomas Watson affirms,

Here is comfort to them who are by faith married to Christ; this is their glorious
priviledge, Christs beauty and loveliness shall be put upon them; They shall shine by
his beams. . . . The Saints shall not only behold Christs glory, but be transform'd into
it, 1 *John* 3:2. *We shall be like him*; that is, irradiated and enameled with his glory.
Christ is compar'd to the beautiful *Lily*, *Cant.* 1:2. His Lily-whiteness shall be put
upon his Saints. A glorified soul shall be a perfect mirrour, or crystal, where the
beauty of Christ shall be transparent."[22]

Many seventeenth-century commentaries on Canticles anticipate
Taylor by exploiting this text to the fullest in describing millennial glories.
Language from Old Testament prophecies, Canticles, and Revelation slides
together into one allegory of the saint's glory. William Guild reveals the
richness of the range of images that the saint may use to imagine himself
in glory, as an individual identity expands in glory with the acquisition of
powerful biblical image after biblical image:

Hence Observe, *That the Saints have a peerless beauty and purity, communicated to
them from Jesus Christ.* By the communication of this beauty and grace they are the
Jerusalem (spoken of in *Revel.* 21:2) which comes downe from God out of Heaven,
prepared as a Bride trimmed for her husband. . . . The Lord looks upon his Church
not onely as shee is, but also as he meanes to make her hereafter, even all glorious
and beautifull. Againe, he looks on her, not onely as shee is in her selfe, but as she
is in himselfe, that is, washed and cleansed from all impurity, and also decked with
his glory.[23]

Believers are invited to participate in an illusion, one created by mirrors
and language, but an illusion that opens up the possibilities of a glorious
and beautiful marriage with Christ. Through the imagination armed with
biblical metaphors, even a saint deformed by the effects of unavoidable
sin, a saint lying in corruption in the grave, can be seen as a fit spouse
for Christ. The identity and the destiny of Christ and the spouse are
inextricably interwoven both doctrinally and imaginatively, since the imputation of grace gives life and "life metaphoricall."

The emphasis on visual paradox as an aesthetically pleasing experience naturally lent itself to expression in emblem literature as well as gravestone art, since some of the most common devices and emblems exploited visual and verbal puns and paradoxes. Canticles did not escape such treatment, and it is with a comic flair that Francis Quarles used emblems on Canticles texts drawn from a serious Jesuit emblem book, *Pia Desideria*. Quarles writes poetic texts for a series of emblems based on Canticles 3 which narrates the spouse's search for Christ who has left her in the dark night of her distress. As Erwin Panofsky and Mario Praz have shown, the emblems on divine love were the result of a conflation of pagan eros fabliaux with texts on divine love, but Quarles reveals his Calvinist heritage by evoking fears of pollution and rejection similar to those expressed in a child-like, naïve voice by Collinges above.[24] Quarles creates this fear only to dispel it. The spouse speaks as a child at whom the reader can laugh in full knowledge that Christ loves her still. In the emblem, the spouse leaps from bed to seek her beloved, but the viewer can see that Christ hasn't left her at all, for he sleeps quietly on his cross under her bed (fig. 48).[25] The sexual undertones are obvious, as the spouse seeks a lover who is sleeping under her bed, who once noticed only has to be awakened to join her in bed. The implication is that this reunion will be all the more exciting for this momentary separation, with the association between Christ's passion on the cross and the lovers' passionate embrace in the marriage bed. But it is dark, the spouse does not see with Christ's eyes as the viewer does, and so she is off on her fruitless search.

For Hugo and Arwaker, the message of this emblem is that the spouse should seek Christ through the cross, but for the Protestant Quarles, the spouse here learns to seek Christ by examining her contrite and humble heart. Then Christ will ravish the hopeless spouse. Death of the sinful self is followed by marriage:

So when my soul had progress'd ev'ry place,
   That love and dear affection could contrive,
I threw me on my couch, resolv'd t' embrace
   A death for him in whom I ceas'd to live:
     But there injurious Hymen did present
     His landscape joys; my pickled eyes did vent
Full streams of briny tears, tears never to be spent
. . . .

E'en whilst mine eyes were blind, and heart was bleeding,
   He that was sought unfound, was found unsought.
. . . .

O how these arms, these greedy arms did twine
   And strongly twist about his yielding waist!

> The sappy branches of the Thespian vine
>   Ne'er cling their less belov'd elm so fast;
>   Boast not thy flames, blind boy, thy feather'd shot;
>   Let Hymen's easy snares be quite forgot;
> Time cannot quench our fires, nor death dissolve our knot.[26]

The paradox of Canticles imagery exists in the spouse's awestruck disbelief, as she can only see her deformity instead of her imputed righteousness, as she searches for a Christ who is already with her. When she humbly quits her search, Christ is found; even in death Christ will remain with her.

Taylor's meditations on Canticles are suggested by all these precedents, and he dwells both on the ravishing beauty of Christ and on the imputed beauty of the spouse. He lingers over each scriptural metaphor, spiritualizing the text in anticipation of death which will bring him the perfection of a bride of Christ. As Karl Keller notes, Taylor usually adopts the persona of the spouse in his meditations:

> it is not so much the physical features of Christ that are being caressed by loving metaphors (as in verse growing out of the Catholic tradition) as it is the beauty of the idealized self—the pure, beautiful, and beloved person that Taylor desires before God so passionately to be. In that elaborate catalog of descriptions taken from the erotic lines in Canticles (2:116-52), Taylor identifies himself for the most part with the young maiden rather than with the King; that is, with an idealized self whose attributes derive from God but whose identity is separate and passive, rather than with Christ's person itself. . . . Christ, by acting the Divine Lover toward him, can, Taylor desperately hopes, transform him into something beautiful, something worth saving.[27]

From his earliest known use of Canticles texts, Taylor's writing is distinguished by spiritualizing of the text to make intensely personal and eschatological statements. In the sermon Taylor preached at the foundation of his church in Westfield in 1679, a sermon which is a hymn of praise to the metaphorical glories which accrue to each prepared and called person entering the church, Taylor makes much of the persuasiveness of bridegroom-Christ:

> Consider, Souls, that thou art called to enter here, if prepared. Christ speakes unto thee in his Language to his Spouse Can. 2:10,11,12,13, arise, my love, my fair one, & come away for lo, the winter (the time of thy Unregeneracy) is past, the Rain (the means making thee to loath thyselfe as a filthy thing have been effectuall on thee) is over & gone. The flowers (the Sanctifying worke of Gods Spirit) appear on the earth (in thy heart) the time of the Singing of birds (the ground of Spirituall melody) is come, the voice of the Turtle (the holy spirit in the Chh) is heard in our land. The fig tree puteth forth her green. . . . Time with its tender grape (the fruits of new obedience) gives a pleasant smell, are thereby manifested, oh therefore (saith Christ) arise my Love, my fair one, & come away. What sayst thou to this? poore Soule. canst

thou withstand such soul inravishing Rhetorick? Methinks it should be like unto Sweet wine, that causes the lips of him that is asleep to speak & answer. O then attend on the call & reply to the same saying I come Lord.[28]

This passage is interesting for its free-form spiritualizing, as Taylor's voice counterpoints the voice of Christ in the text, reinforcing the sense of the immediacy of the situation, as Taylor's invitation to church membership becomes one with Christ's words to his spouse. Moreover, Taylor's classification of the process of the call as the rhetoric of Christ implies that not only is Christ's word beautiful and affecting, but man's response with his own rhetoric is an absolutely necessary response to Christ the Word. We see in seminal form how Taylor envisions Christ's metaphors to be truly creative and powerful, transforming called persons into spouses as they join His spouse, the church.

Once Taylor has established his church members as spouses of Christ in his enclosed garden, he rhapsodizes for pages in the "Foundation Day" sermon over the privileges redounding to the spouse. Indeed, she is as good as in heaven already, and Taylor explains how fitting it is to imagine the church the glorious New Jerusalem temple, to imagine oneself decked out more gloriously than the High Priest entering the Holy of Holies. Canticles images in particular provide Taylor with metaphors to describe the passage through the veil of death from the inner court, the church on earth, to the Holy of Holies, heaven. In a meditation on Canticles 6:9 "My Dove is One," Taylor describes the dove-like spouse who is "The Sweetest Flower in all thy Paradise," and she is shielded from all harm by Christ's encircling arms.

Taylor's mixing of dove and garden metaphors is analogous to popular designs found on tombstones at the time. John Stevens II of Newport fashioned a stone for the grave of Job Harris who died in 1729 in Providence (fig. 49); on it he cut doves and vegetation in shallow relief, and such designs indicate an awareness of the eschatological import of Canticles imagery. His technique is similar to the method of representation we have analyzed above on the Hadley chest.[29] Stevens has transformed the rigid three-bird crest of the Harris family found on earlier stones to present doves safe in a garden, passing under the shadow of death while protected by a cherub in the tympanum.

Taylor was not unique in associating the spouse's garden in the earthly church and the paradise of heaven.[30] Richard Sibbes represents this commonly-held metaphorical association when he writes on Canticles 6:2:

That is having first planted them *Lillies* here, to gather them, and to transport them out of the garden here, to the garden in Heaven, where there shall be nothing but

Lillies. For the Church of God hath two Gardens or Paradises since the first Paradise (whereof that was a resemblance) the *Paradise* of the Church, and the *Paradise* of Heaven. As Christ saith to the good theefe, this day thou shalt be with me in Paradise. So those that are good plants in the Paradise of the Church, they shall be glorious plants also in the Paradise of Heaven, we must not alway be here, we shall change our soyle and be taken into Heaven: *He is gone into his garden to gather Lillies.*[31]

Taylor develops this conceit in his *Gods Determinations*. He represents the saints as lilies picked from the hothouse of the church and transplanted in heaven; "as they stand / Like Beauties reeching in perfume / a Divine Hand / Doth hand them up to Glories room: / Where each in Sweet'ned Songs all Praises shall / Sing all ore heaven for aye."[32] In two meditations on Canticles texts describing the lover (Christ) entering His garden, Taylor presents the process of transformation by which the dead saint becomes a garden flower. In a passage fraught with Taylor's favorite metaphors, the saint gains a spiritual dress of lilies:

> If I thy Vally, thou its Lilly bee.
> My Heart shall be thy Chrystall looking Glass
> Shewing thy Lillies Face most cleare in mee
> In shape and beauty that doth brightly flash.
> My Looking Glass shall weare thy Lillies Face
> As tis thy Looking Glass of Every Grace.
> (2:132)

If this gracious transformation has grafted the saint into Christ's garden during life, then when Christ comes into his garden, the saint's clay will sprout flowers for Paradise. In a witty blending of eschatological images with Canticles metaphors, Taylor argues for his resurrection:

> Shall this poore baren mould of mine e're bee
> Planted with Spirituall Vines and pomegranates?
> Whose Bud and Blossome flowrish shall to thee?
> And with perfumed joys thee gratiate?
> Then Spiritual joyes flying on Spicy Wings
> Shall entertain thee in thy Visitings.
>
> And if thou makest mee to be thy mold
> Though Clayey mould I bee, and run in mee
> Thy Spirits Gold, thy Trumpet all of gold,
> Though I be Clay Ist thy Gold-Trumpet bee.
> Then in Angelick melody I will
> Trumpet thy Glory and with gracious Skill.
> (2:133)

Not only would Taylor like to be a fruitful part of the new earth, but as poet he would also like to be one of the "trumpets" which sound a fanfare at the Second Coming of Christ.

Canticles imagery of the resurrected bride of Christ finds fullest expression in the work of Zerubbabel Collins and several Connecticut River valley carvers after 1750 (see following, chapter 7, figs. 55-62), but even in the early stages of Hartshorn's work in Taylor's time, there are visual transformations similar to those voiced in Taylor's verse. On a stone Hartshorn cut in 1714 for Skipper Balch in Wenham, Massachusetts (fig. 50), the saint is shown entombed among worms and serpents. The clayey mould which Taylor emphasizes as the body's destiny is graphically depicted. The serpent is a reminder of the duplicity of Satan at the Fall which made death man's legacy, while the worms suggest the very corruption of the body beneath the stone. But the mould is sprouting some new growth beneath the effigy, and when this sprig of vegetation is viewed in conjunction with the two rosettes, an image of a rising new body appears. The rosettes forming the shoulders pun on the conceit of the saint as Christ's rose, who will rise as Christ rose. On the Nathanael Peaslee, Jr., stone, 1730, Haverhill, Massachusetts (fig. 51), the vegetation grows wild beneath the effigy, and the worms are replaced by stars. This is an even more graphic illustration of the saint leaving the mould of the earth for a paradise in the stars. In the pilasters, vines twist and curl, suggesting the spiritual vine into which the saint was grafted in life so that he might grow again after death. The clearest analogy to Taylor's garden motif appears in a highly popular carving tradition in the Connecticut River valley later in the eighteenth century. In Peter Buckland's carving, the effigy is flanked by heart-shaped leaves and clusters of grapes (fig. 52), while the Ama Clark stone presents an effigy with "bodilie eyes" planted among pots of lilies (fig. 53).[33]

The final eschatological system Taylor shares with the gravestone carving tradition is that of representing the face of the spouse as the face of resurrected saints. The logic of Taylor's Canticles series seems based in part on the process whereby the spouse acquires this new face. Taylor starts his long series of meditations on this book (2:115-2:157) with Canticles 5:10, which, as we have seen in the "Day of Judgment" sermon and in the *Christographia*, is interpreted as a description of the spiritual beauties of Christ. As Taylor "sees" Christ in the images of the text, in the dove eyes, pomegranate temple, and so on, he spiritualizes each image to determine the grace it represents. At each recognition of a spiritual truth in Christ's features, the spouse gains a corresponding desire that she, too, may have these graces and these features. Moreover, she gains a corresponding power to respond to each of Christ's beauties with her affections. Meditation on the face of Christ in these metaphors is seen as a fit vehicle for the working up of affections and praise. Taylor is not alone in his method; as Thomas Watson writes,

> let our tongues sing forth the praises of him who is altogether lovely. Daughters of the blood Royal have the pictures of Kings brought to them, and by seeing the pictures, they fall in love with their persons, and are married to them; By our commendations of Christ, we should so paint out Christ to others, and draw his picture, that when they see his picture they may fall in love with him, and the match may be presently struck up.[34]

Through praise and affection the spouse hopes to gain a "spiritual" image or fair copy of each of Christ's features. The face of the spouse gains the dove eyes, the cheeks, the mouth, the temples, and the hair of her lover, sharing His beauty by sharing His grace. For this reason, according to Puritan commentators, the lover and the spouse describe each other in the same metaphors in Canticles itself.

For Taylor, the face is the window to the soul through which the spouse may see Christ's beauty: "Thy Soule Divine arrayde in Splendent Grace, / The Spiritual Temple pinckt with precious Stones: / Like Sparks of Glory glaze thy Spirits Face." The spouse seeks Christ's face, for "That happiness lodg'd in his Glorious face / Will thence when seen slide int'our Hearts with Grace" (2:128). Taylor begins his description of Christ in Meditation 2:116 by lauding God's art which not only remade man's heart to love Christ, but "also madst an object by thy Art / For Love to be laid out upon most Cleare." This is the highest art, capable of firing man with divine love, and Taylor's meditations on Canticles gain momentum as they paint brushstroke by brushstroke a portrait of Christ. The whole series can be read as a word portrait, with each poem deepening the shades and colors of the images of Christ and his spouse.

Taylor's portrait technique explains in part the repetitiveness of his verse, as he dwells upon a single word or phrase; for example, in Meditation 2:119 the words "eye" and "apple" appear six and four times respectively in six lines. There is an unusual delight in image and word here, as Taylor uses the devices of *ploce* and *traductio*, a repetition for the sheer pleasure of acknowledging his admiration of a metaphor. The same dogged repetition is found on gravestones, where image after identical image appears on stones for men, women, and children. But for the carver and the poet, the act of making each image is an invocation of an ideal, a reaffirmation of the connection of the particular saint with a holy pattern, and in effigy and poem alike the repetition of biblical images allies human and divine artistry. Taylor's method is to concentrate intently on a single feature of Christ, such as the eye, until the corresponding spiritual feature is awakened in the soul's face.[35] A typical example is found in his meditation on Canticles 5:12, "His Eyes are as the Eyes of Doves by Rivers of Waters washed with milk and fitly set." Starting with praise for Christ's eye, "My Lord, (my love,) what loveliness doth ly, / In this pert percing fiery Eye of thine? / Thy Dove like Eyes ore varnish gloriously / Thy Face till it the Heavens over shine," Taylor next notes the spiritual qualities of wisdom that make the eye beautiful. Commentators on Canticles are quite specific about what makes an eye fitly set, and Taylor is no exception in describing its apple-like fitness in the socket. As Nathanael Homes writes on this text, "*His eyes were as the eyes of Doves*, (which are not so *hollow, or inward* as the eyes of Batts; nor are such outward goggle-eyes as the eyes of Owls and Hawks."[36] The combination of beauty and wisdom is overpowering to angels and saints alike who "Gastard stare" back at Christ (see figs. 55-62). Taylor ends the meditation by turning to his hope for corresponding spiritual eyes with which to appreciate Christ: "Lord let these Charming Glancing Eyes of thine /Glance on my Soule bright Eye its amorous beams / to fetch as upon golden Ladders fine / My heart and Love to thee in Hottest Steams."

Taylor's portraits of the bride and Christ indicate the passionate attention of the Puritan imagination to the forms of personal glory. In the carving traditions that flourish in the years following Taylor's death, there is a like development of bridal portraiture, as a variety of forms develop to display risen saints as spouses in a paradisial garden. By 1735 in the work of Obadiah Wheeler and the Collins family, the dove-like eyes are the focus of attention, replacing with human expression the hollow-eyed skull of the *memento mori* tradition. While the eyes at first are open in a Taylorean "Gastard stare," as time passes they become softened and affectionate, inspired with dove-like love for the bridegroom, Christ. As in Taylor's profoundly hopeful eschatological vision of personal perfection, the gravestone art of the Great Awakening is fueled by hopes of saintly glory. Taylor is a prophet of this artistry, an artistry inspired by the vision of the wedding of heaven and earth.

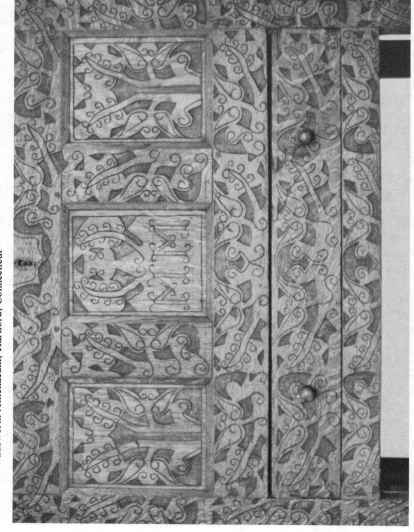

Figure 45. The MM chest, Hadley type, ca. 1690-1710, the Wadsworth Athenaeum, Hartford, Connecticut

Figure 46.   The HS chest, Hadley type, ca. 1690-1710.
Rhode Island School of Design, Museum
Appropriation 19.293

Figure 47. Emblem, Hermanus Hugo, *Pia Desideria: or Divine Adresses, in three books*, trans. Edmund Arwaker, 1686, p. 160, Brown University Library

Figure 48. Emblem, Hermanus Hugo, *Pia Desideria: or Divine Adresses, in three books*, trans. Edmund Arwaker, 1686, p. 122, Brown University Library

By night on my bed, I sought him whom my soul loveth, I sought him, but I found him not. Cant.3.1.

P.122.

Stay me with flagons, comfort me with apples, for I am sick of Love. Cant 2.5. P.160.

Figure 49. Job Harris, 1729, Providence, Rhode Island

Figure 50. Skipper Balch, 1714, Wenham, Massachusetts

Figure 51. Nathaniel Peaslee, 1730, Haverhill, Massachusetts

Figure 52. Deacon Daniel House, 1762, East Glastonbury,
          Connecticut

Figure 53. Ama Clark, 1786, Rockingham, Vermont

7

The Great Awakening:
New Light and "Bodilie Eyes"

My best Beloved keeps his throne
On hills of light, in worlds unknown:
But he descends, and shows his face
In the young gardens of his grace.

—Isaac Watts,
Hymns and Spiritual Songs

While we have seen the importance of the senses, especially "bodilie eyes," in preaching about the Resurrection world, it is only during the Great Awakening of the 1740s that the senses gain preeminence in religious experience. Jonathan Edwards and other architects of the revival wished to replace what they saw as a dead intellectual faith with a faith of mind and body, soul and heart united in delight in holy things. The great debate of the awakening over the proper role of the senses need not concern us here; clearly the awakening added impetus to gravestone carving traditions which already emphasized the sensory nature of heavenly experience. Moreover, fundamental changes in doctrines about the Millennium during the awakening gave gravestone carvers an enlarged repertoire of images of risen saints and renewed nature to place on their stones. By examining the work of Zerubbabel Collins (active around 1750-97) in light of revivalist writings by Jonathan Edwards and Eleazar Wheelock, we can trace the final flowering of "bodilie eyes" designs.

Prior to the Great Awakening, most New Englanders believed in a premillennial eschatology, with millennial heaven on earth coming only after Christ's personal appearance and the Resurrection. They understood that the vision of millennial perfection couched in biblical metaphors would only be realized after Christ's personal appearance. The metaphors did shadow forth a real world, but it was a world as yet inchoate, a world still of the imagination. In Edward Taylor's poetry we have seen metaphorical language forced to the very edge of the distinction between figurative and literal expression, but Taylor never failed to add the caveat that millennial glory could only be anticipated and hoped for before the Apocalypse. During the Great Awakening, however, leading theologians including Jonathan Edwards and Eleazar Wheelock preached a postmillennial eschatology.[1] Christ's millennial reign was spiritual; for 1,000 years his spirit would gradually transform humans and nature into a perfect state. Thus believers could expect to participate in the gradual perfection of the world as promised in biblical metaphors. Radical elements of the New Light revivalists siezed upon postmillennial eschatology. Millennial glory was deemed achievable before the end of the world; biblical metaphors describing resurrected saints were applied to saints who found heaven in their souls. As C. C. Goen has shown, total assurance of salvation became not only possible but essential for the true saint, and the power to see the divine and supernatural light of Christ in all holy things became one of the signs of grace.[2]

Essentially, the distinctions between metaphors of future perfection and descriptions of living "perfect" saints is lost to many of the enthusiastic followers of the Revival. Rather than an imaginative device with which to transfer one's vision from the fallen world to heaven, biblical metaphors are a means to transform the world itself. In the mind of the enthusiast Nathan Cole, a separatist from Connecticut converted by George Whitefield in 1741, biblical promises are spectacles through which to see a millennial world.[3] The mystic no longer distinguishes between the levels of reality in experience, dream vision, and prophecy. For participants in this vision, exciting aesthetic pleasures are available. The world can be a paradise; saints can appear restored in the image of Christ. But for non-participants the whole realm of biblical metaphors takes on a surreal glare, and the world of the Millennium is seen as a fantastic and brittle artifice shattered by common sense.[4] The period of the Great Awakening is especially interesting in the context of this study, for at this time a shared system of metaphorical expression collapses; one camp refuses to distinguish between metaphorical and literal expression and the other denies the millennial doctrines which inform the metaphors themselves. Unfortunately for the developing tradition of gravestone carving, the repertoire of symbols of millennial glory associated with "bodilie eyes" becomes isolated after the awakening in rural areas. With the discrediting of the Revival, the symbols become a liability for areas wishing to show their sophistication and their rationalism by adopting the neoclassical designs popular in Boston stonecarving.

While the formulae of eschatological literature are useful to writers during the American Revolution and beyond, the specific eschatological images on tombstones develop further only in the hothouses of Strict Congregational and Separate Baptist communities until 1810 when neo-classicism becomes an irresistible style.[5] While the tone of epitaphs on these late stones becomes shrill in the insistence on millennial dogma and some of the carvings become confused, there remain truly elegant examples of gravestone art, exotic plants flowering on the New England frontier.

Whatever controversy Jonathan Edwards may have generated with his millennialism, he did not intend to make any innovations in traditional doctrines of the last things. Edwards' most reasonable disciples kept the expectation of Christ's return and a resurrection of saints with "bodilie eyes" alive even while preaching his postmillennialism. Eleazar Wheelock, in whose parish the greatest of New England carvers, Zerubbabel Collins, received the milk of the Gospel, preached concerning the Second Coming, "Christ who is their Life, shall appear and change their vile Bodies, and fashion them like to his own most glorious Body, and they by a transforming view of Christ shall be changed into his Image from Glory to Glory."[6] Wheelock is firmly in the tradition of Perkins, Sibbes, Owen, and Mather when he describes the power of the senses of "separate" souls in Christ's presence:

> The blessed in heaven behold him face to face; yt is, are as sensible of his Presence as we are of the presence of any person whom we look upon with our Eyes. There is doubtless a faculty in spirits, by which they apprehend one another, as our senses do material Objects; and ther is no question but our souls when they are disembodied, or placed in glorified bodies, will by that faculty, in whatever space they reside, be always sensible of the divine presence.[7]

While Wheelock did not have the theoretical mind of an Edwards, he did much to disseminate Edwardsean theology and aesthetics to his congregation and to the rest of New England through his own ministry and that of the Yale graduates who gathered for evangelical training at his Indian school in Lebanon Crank, Connecticut. One of Wheelock's parishioners, a noted local poet named Martha Brewster, wrote on the Last Judgment, "Ye Courtiers of this Lower House, / Lift up your raptur'd Eyes, / Behold, the Bridegroom's on his Way, / Behold he tares the Skys."[8] We can assume that Zerubbabel Collins was steeped in Wheelock and Edwards' eschatology as well.

Edwards' own celebrated postmillennialism did not diminish his belief in a literal resurrection and reign of the saints.[9] Edwards had no trouble integrating traditional New England views on the powers of "bodilie eyes" and Lockean epistemology; the principle that "bodilie eyes" were necessary for the perception of Christ's glorified body was analogous to his own doctrine that saints needed a new sense to perceive the "simple idea" of Christ's beauty.[10] For Edwards, the saint's joy in heaven consists in the continuing apprehension of new glories with new senses: "That the glorified spirits shall grow in holiness and happiness in eternity, I argue from this foundation, that their number of ideas shall increase to eternity."[11] Edwards is insistent when he points to the divine proportion between "bodilie eyes" and Christ's glory:

> They shall see him, as appearing in his glorified human nature, with their bodily eyes; and this will be a most glorious sight. . . . [Y]ea, the eyes of the glorified body will be given chiefly that the saints may behold this sight.
> . . . .
> This seems to be one end of God's assuming a human body, viz. that the saints might see him, not only in understanding, but in every way of seeing of which the human nature is capable; that we might see God as a divine person as we see one another.[12]

Moreover, Edwards maintains that the perception of Christ's beauty conforms to the same laws as does perception with physical eyes in everyday acts of vision and with "spiritual eyes" implanted by grace. Although occuring in different worlds and with different eyes, all vision operates by Lockean principles:

> in all probability the abode of the saints after the resurrection will be so contrived by God that there shall be external beauties and harmonies altogether of another kind from what we perceive here, and probably those beauties will appear chiefly in the bodies of the man Christ Jesus, and of the saints. . . . And it is out of doubt with me that there will be immediate intellectual views of minds, one of antother, and of the Supreme mind, more immediate, clear, and sensible than our views of bodily things with bodily eyes. In this world we behold spiritual beauties only mediately by the intervention of our senses, in perceiving those external actions which are the effect of spiritual proportion. . . . All that wants in order to such an intellectual view, is that a clear and sensible apprehension of what is in mind should be raised in our mind constantly according to such and such laws; for it is by no other way that we perceive with our bodily eyes, or perceive by any of our senses.[13]

Edwards proceeds by arguing the continuities of the saint's experiences in life, heaven, and in the Resurrection world. The transforming power of grace is such that saints under the influence of Christ's unfolding millennial kingdom are swept up into a spiritual heaven on earth.

Edwards' quasi-mystical moments of heavenly enjoyment are described in his "Personal Narrative," and he rhapsodizes over his wife's ability to spend days in rapture.[14] But when Edwards writes, "The church in heaven, and the church on earth are more *one* people, *one* city, and *one* family, than is generally imagined," he always maintains a separation between his aesthetic appreciation of this doctrine and his realization of the distance remaining between heaven and earth.[15] He knows that the saints cannot expect total immersion in divine rapture before death; the moments of joy are all too fleeting, the calls of the world all too disruptive. Edwards looked forward to a heavenly existence in which the saints would have a ringside seat to watch the progress of Christ's kingdom from a perspective free from the confusion of temporary setbacks:

> doubtless the saints that went to heaven, before this remarkable out-pouring of the spirit on this town and other neighbouring towns, especially those that went to heaven from hence, have seen this work and greatly rejoiced at it. And so the saints, that did before the glorious days that are coming at the downfal of antichrist and the calling of the Jews, will rejoice at the conversion of the world to Christianity.[16]

Less sophisticated and, perhaps, more enthusiastic minds would brush aside Edwards' separation of heaven and earth. Some of the first indications of the extent to which revivalists felt that saints could come to a heavenly life on earth are found on gravestones. On the Abigail Ely stone, 1776, of Longmeadow, Massachusetts (fig. 54), the saint's Resurrection body is presented in embryonic form, sleeping with closed, bulging "bodilie eyes." The wings are folded close about the crowned head in an egg-shaped tympanum. For this carver, the saint in life has prepared herself for the Resurrection, and the "bodilie eyes" need only to be opened. The grave is an incubation chamber occupied until the "hatching" of the Resurrection at the cock's crow at the dawning of the Day of Judgment.

The excitable imagination of Nathan Cole creates in literary form a similar picture of immediate gratification of the saint's heavenly desires. His "Spiritual Travels" is a central document in the intellectual and aesthetic history of eighteenth-century separatism; Cole expected biblical metaphors to find embodiment on earth, perhaps with his help. After years of struggle to join a pure separate church, years marked by prosecution and persecution, Cole admits he always expected his dream of perfection to become real:

> the same day that I was Converted my heart and mind were flowing out after God: I had a visionary discovery of A Gospel Church: of the house they met in and the place where it stood; and the behaviour of the people in the house; as clear and real as if I had seen it with my bodily eyes almost the house was built about 4 square; the Chimney at the west end; the lower part divided into Several rooms; and the minister and his family dwelt there, and the whole Chamber was the meeting house; the fore front stood towards the South, and Sun Shined bright in at the windows down on the floor by the Ministers feet, who stood in a praying posture, with his face and his hands lifted up tow'rds heaven and every way the Shape and bigness of Elder Frothingham, there was a small Church in the house with a Solemn sweet Countenance sat upon

their Faces; and one that now is my brother in this Church stood next or near to me in a praying posture; who when I saw him in this Church twenty years after with my bodily eyes, I think I knew him to be the Man.

I had also a view of the Shape of the Land some distance round aforesaid house, of the hills, Valleys highways and brooks, and of the Angels hovering over the house in a light white glimmering Air; Crying the Glory of the Town, the Town.[17]

Cole does not await fulfillment of this vision in heaven; glory comes to earth within twenty years in the form of Frothingham's Separate Church. Cole is convinced that his own pilgrimage will result in the foundation of a pure millennial church after the world is cleansed by fire. In a cryptic comment at the end of his "Spiritual Travels," Cole puns on his name to cast himself in the role of a millennial spark:

i had a sort of visionary trance as i set alone and the Lord seemed to shew what yet should be so clear that i laid it up in my hart until now[,] viz[:] that it was so i was left alone and i was as a poor old coal buryed up in the ashes as if there was no fire to be seen but the Lord seemed to shew that in time a little spark of fire would come out of these ashes from that coal and cat[c]h fire to a brand that was neer and that brand catches fire to some brands that lay hear and there and the fire began to burn more and more and keept increasing until it arose to a much greater height then ever it was before in Kensington etc:—[18]

The willingness of people like Nathan Cole to see their fellow saints filled with the spirit of heaven is matched by the vision of a new paradise emerging in the New England landscape. Edwards again formed the basic doctrinal position which allowed enthusiasts to see nature in terms of biblical descriptions of the Millennium. He saw nature revealing Christ's spirit and beauty on equal terms with the Bible, and in a series of notes known as *Images or Shadows of Divine Things*, he extends typology into nature.[19] Where typology had been used to see the fulfillment of Old Testament shadows with the substance of Christ, so nature could also be seen as a shadow of Christ's glory. As Edwards notes, "We see that even in the material world, God makes one part of it strangely to agree with another, and why is it not reasonable to suppose He makes the whole as a shadow of the spiritual world?"[20]

Martha Brewster reveals the blending of metaphors of natural description, natural types, and the metaphors of growth in grace characteristic of his followers. In the winter section of "An Essay On the four Ages of Man, Resembling the four Seasons of the Year," she adds an apocalyptic flavor to her imagery:

A Snowy Robe adorns instead of Hairs,
And underneath a wither'd Face appears;

And thus she lies benum'd nor strives to rise,
'Till the benign Influence of the Skies,
Destroy's her Foe and gently calls her forth,
In brighter Beauty and with larger Growth:
So may the Son of Righteousness arise,
And the celestial Dove descend the Skies,
And quicken ev'ry Age of mortal Dust,
And make this State more glorious than the first,
Nor let the aged Sinner die accurs'd;
Makes us to Grow 'till we advance so far,
To raise our Feet up high beyond the Stars;
There wholesome Fruitand living Water flows,
There we may bathe, and take a sweet Repose.[21]

Brewster changes from the future to the present and back to the future tense in these lines to emphasize the fact that the "Sun of Righteousness" brings millennial life to souls as well as to nature, and this life blurs distinctions between this world and the next.

The gravestone carving of Zerubbabel Collins was profoundly affected by this new view of nature.[22] Both in Connecticut and in Vermont after 1778, Collins' work is a marked advance over his father's style. He breaks out of a two-dimensional conception of the carving space to model rounded and fleshy faces, wings, and vegetation. The winged face is buoyed up by the exuberant growth of lilies, roses, and vines which fill the tympanum (fig. 55). Floral motifs were not new to New England stonecarving, and Collins probably saw basket and urn arrangements in books and on carved and painted furniture. Emblematic uses of flowers, such as the cut rose and the heliotrope, was also a well-worn tradition by the 1750s. But Collins' designs are neither purely decorative nor emblematic, but typological, with natural objects functioning as types of Christ and the saint's resurrection. Where vegetation was a secondary motif on earlier stones, it now is a central image of millennial perfection. Collins creates the impression of a saint embowered in the "hortus conclusus" which in the Canticles tradition shadows forth the millennial restoration of paradise. These stones are a fit analog to Edwards' typology. In "Miscellanies, No. 991" appended to Image 166 on the true branch, we find a mixing of vegetation which helps us to explain the seemingly illogical growth on Collins' stones. Edwards writes:

And there remains yet a more dreadful destruction of men than has perhaps ever yet been since the flood, which is spoken of, Rev. 19, at the latter end, just before the setting up of Christ's kingdom through the earth, which will be the greatest and chief pruning of the tree to prepare and make room for the great putting forth of the elect seed, the holy bud that had been preserved in the tree by the special care of providence from the beginning of the world and that had lain hid in the branches of the tree through all ages, being reserved for this appointed time for their germination. And then the tree shall be abundantly watered by the showers of heaven and the holy seed shall flourish as the grass of the earth. They shall spring up as among the grass and as willows by the watercourses. The tree shall blossom abundantly and the fruit of it shall shine like Lebanon. God will be as the dew unto Israel, and he shall grow as the lily and cast forth his roots as Lebanon, his branches shall spread, and his beauty shall be as the olive tree and his smell as Lebanon.[23]

On Collins' stones we find roses, sunflowers, vines, and branches mixed with lilies ending in wisps of flame, and on the Ebenezer Cole stone, 1794, of South Shaftesbury, Vermont (fig. 55), the iconography is "Americanized" by the placement of a pine tree in the design space of the lily. A natural type of Christ, the evergreen, is explicitly linked to a biblical type from Canticles. Even the shape of the stone is new, as a series of serpentine curves form the tympanum and pull the viewer's eye upwards, giving the impression that the spirit moves through stone, nature, and resurrected body alike.

Across the state in Rockingham, Vermont, an even more explicit use of Edwardsean nature typology can be seen on the Margaret Campbell stone, 1779 (fig. 56); here the biblical metaphor of humans being barren fig trees cast into the fire or fruitful trees tended by God is translated into terms from New England's forests. The deciduous tree is barren, but the evergreen grows on. The sun-faced effigy promises new life when the sun/Son returns in the spring/resurrection.

It is in the Canticles tradition that Puritan New England stonecarving achieves its greatest, and last, original expression. Throughout the late eighteenth century, the idealization of saint's portraiture in literature and carving found fertile metaphorical ground in Canticles. The popularity of psalms on Canticles texts adapted by Isaac Watts and others ensured a wide audience for images of the spouse of Christ.[24] Jonathan Edwards provides us with an insight into the mystical associations of Canticles texts after the awakening, as he casts one of his earliest mystical moments in the mold of a verse commonly taken to describe Christ's presence with his church:

Those words Cant. ii. I, used to be abundantly with me, *I am the Rose of Sharon, and the Lilly of the valleys.* The words seemed to me, sweetly to represent the loveliness and beauty of Jesus Christ. The whole book of Canticles used to be pleasant to me, and I used to be much in reading it, about that time; and found, from time to time, an inwards sweetness, that would carry me away, in my contemplations. This I know not how to express otherwise, than by a calm, sweet abstraction of soul from all the concerns of this world; and sometimes a kind of vision, or fixed ideas and imaginations, of being alone in the mountains, or some solitary wilderness, far from all mankind, sweetly conversing with Christ, and wrapt and swallowed up in God. The sense I had of divine things, would often of a sudden kindle up, as it were, a sweet burning in my heart; an ardor of soul, that I knew not how to express.[25]

When Edwards presents his magnificent emblem of the holiness of the soul, he again turns to Canticles. Holiness makes "the soul like a field or garden of God, with all manner of pleasant flowers . . . like a little white flower as we see in the spring of the year . . . standing peacefully and lovingly, in the midst of other flowers round about."[26]

The Collins tradition culminates in Vermont with images celebrating the spouse as lily in Christ's garden and as glorious bride decked out for the apocalyptic marriage. In a series of stones once attributed to Zerubbabel Collins but now identified as the work of Samuel Dwight, the metaphoric associations explored by Edward Taylor find fulfillment in stone.[27] "Bodilie eyes" are prominent on the Constant Barney stone of 1792 (fig. 57). On the Ruth Hard marker, 1801, Arlington, Vermont (fig. 58), an effigy buds from the lilies and tulips symbolic of Christ's enclosed garden. The heart-shaped body of the effigy affirms the divine love of the spouse, the deceased, for her bridegroom; the natural growth of vegetation on the stone may be symbolic of the spiritual growth which will occur when Christ as sun/Son shines on the Resurrection world. On other stones, Dwight's effigies are more fully dressed as brides in a garden. The Jebediah Aylesworth stone of 1795 combines dove eyes, jewels, and breasts in a powerfully prophetic image of the marriage of saints to Christ at the Resurrection (fig. 59). Dwight establishes the eschatological framework of Canticles in his stone for Austin Seeley, 1796, which presents an emblem of proper Christian mourning drawn from images in the text (fig. 60). Doves were common symbols for saintly behavior due to their meekness, purity and steadfast faith, but they were especially used to describe proper mourning. As James Durham notes, the dove-like quality of the spouse in Canticles "is thought to allude to the mourning of one [of a pair of doves], after the other one's death; This shews what a believer should be, and who deserves this name."[28] The hands on the Seeley stone may allude to Canticles 5:14 ("His hands are as gold rings set with the beryl"), a verse which Thomas Brightman glosses as a reference to Christ's controlling hand of providence in the death of saints.[29] Finally, the flaming hearts are popular emblems of divine love. The hieratic arrangement of hands, doves, and hearts would suggest to the Christian viewer that Seeley's death was ordained by God and proper Christian mourning should be dove-like and tempered by a love for God which overcomes the grief of the loss of the loved saint. Only through divine love can come a heavenly marriage to replace the earthly spouse.

While the Collins tradition dominated eastern Connecticut and southern Vermont, other carvers in the Connecticut River valley worked in the Canticles tradition as well. Images of the Resurrection body are found most often in communities dominated by Strict Congregationalists and Separate Baptists. The Sarah Wier marker of 1795, Old East Glastonbury, Connecticut (fig. 61), is a magnificent expression of the church as spouse, with the portrait's one eye and golden chain illustrating Canticles 4:9 ("Thou has ravished my heart, my sister, my spouse; thou hast ravished my heart with one of thine eyes, with one chain of thy neck"). Both Thomas Brightman and Thomas Beverly read this passage as a prophetic description of the Gentile church, which has an eye only for Christ. When the fulness of the Gentiles has been joined to Christ by the neck and chain, "the humanitie of Christ," "which thee / the Gentile church / installs /in Nuptial Rights," Christ will come for his bride.[30] The exquisite technique of this carver and others with his skill (fig. 62) betrays the rise of talented carvers who would soon replace portraits of glorified saints with commemorative busts of the deceased in a variety of neoclassical forms.

By 1800, stonecarving in the portrait tradition examined in this study continued in only a few isolated pockets in New England. The mention of "bodilie eyes" in sermons persisted only among revivalist populations in the nineteenth century. Certainly the nation-wide celebration of America's coming of age after the Revolution which found expression in artistic models borrowed from Greece and Rome contributed to the casting off of the Puritan traditions of stonecarving as old-fashioned. Nevertheless, the vision of a bodily resurrection, the belief in a personal heaven, continued to develop among Christians in America, culminating in the Victorian domestication of heaven after the Civil War.[31] While "bodilie eyes" imagery disappears in tombstone carving, it flourishes in psalm singing. In some ways, the very success of the "bodilie eyes" tradition may have contributed to its demise. By calling attention to the use of the senses in funerary rituals, it contributed to the sentimental response to death associated with the urn and willow school of stonecarving and its literary cousin, the graveyard school of poets. Thus while it cannot be said that the aesthetic of "bodilie eyes" survives intact from the Great Awakening to the nineteenth century, glimmerings of this way of seeing appear in such divergent forms as Shaker spirituals and Emily Dickinson's poems. Dickinson looks forward to seeing her lover in heaven in the image of Christ, and she expects a very physical reunion with him. For more than 150 years, "bodilie eyes" in Puritan eschatological literature and gravestone art provided a way of seeing for New Englanders. It was truly an art which dwelt in possibility.

Figure 54. Abigail Ely, 1776, Longmeadow, Massachusetts

Figure 55. Ebenezer Cole, 1794, South Shaftesbury, Vermont

Figure 56. Margaret Campbell, 1779, Rockingham, Vermont

Figure 57.   Constant Barney, 1792, Arlington, Vermont

Figure 58.   Ruth Hard, 1801, Arlington, Vermont

Figure 59. Jedediah Aylesworth, 1795, Arlington, Vermont

Figure 60. Austin Seeley, 1796, Arlington, Vermont

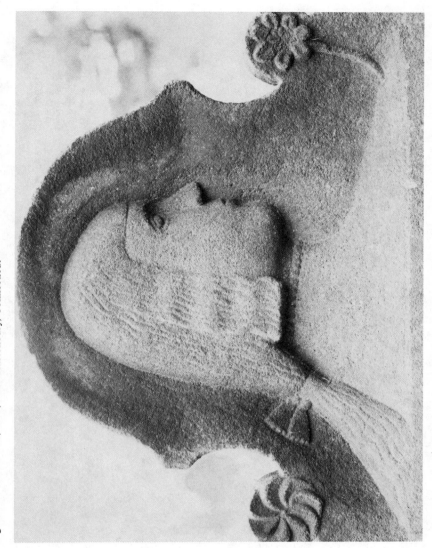

Figure 61.   Sarah Wier, 1795, East Glastonbury, Connecticut

Figure 62. Sarah Storrs, 1798, Longmeadow, Massachusetts

Notes

Notes for the Introduction

1. Erwin Panofsky, *Studies in Iconology* (New York: Oxford University Press, 1939), p. 7.

2. For the view that Essex County, Mass., carving is a degeneration of English provincial styles, see Stephen Foster's "From Significant Incompetence to Insignificant Competence," *Puritan Gravestone Art*, The Dublin Seminar for New England Folklife: Annual Proceedings I (Dublin, N.H.: Boston University and The Dublin Seminar for New England Folklife, 1977), pp. 33-40.

3. Panofsky, p. 11.

4. Henry Glassie, *Folk Housing in Middle Virginia* (Knoxville: University of Tennessee Press, 1975).

5. Philippe Ariès presents a brilliant survey of Western eschatology in *The Hour of Our Death*, tr. Helen Weaver (New York: Knopf, 1981).

6. The best work on the subject is Bryan W. Ball's *A Great Expectation*, Studies in the History of Christian Thought, vol. 12 (Leiden: F. J. Brill, 1975). Other useful works include those by Joseph Hall, *The Revelation Unrevealed, The Works of Joseph Hall, D. D.* (Oxford, 1838), VIII, 507-60; Peter Toon, *Puritans, the Millennium and the Future of Israel* (Cambridge: James Clarke & Co., 1970); John F. Wilson, "Comment on 'Two Roads to the Puritan Millennium,' " *Church History*, XXXII (1963), 339-43, and "Another Look at John Canne," *Church History*, XXXIII (1964), 34-48; Christopher Hill, *Antichrist in Seventeenth-Century England*, Riddell Memorial Lectures, 41st ser. (New York: Oxford University Press, 1971), and *The World Turned Upside Down* (1972; rpt. Baltimore, Md,: Penquin Books, Inc., 1975); Michael Walzer, *The Revolution of the Saints* (Princeton: Princeton University Press, 1966); B. S. Capp, *The Fifth Monarchy Men* (London: Faber, 1972), J. F. Maclear, "New England and the Fifth Monarchy: The Quest for the Millennium in Early American Puritanism," *William and Mary Quarterly*, 3rd ser., XXXII (1975), 223-60; James W. Davidson, *The Logic of Millennial Thought* (New Haven: Yale University Press, 1977); Norman Cohn, *The Pursuit of the Millennium*, 2nd ed. (New York: Harper and Row, 1961), and Ernest Lee Tuveson, *Millennium and Utopia* (Berkeley: University of California Press, 1949). Mason I. Lowance, Jr. relates eschatology and literary theory in *The Language of Canaan* (Cambridge: Harvard University Press, 1980).

7. Ball, p. 229. See *The Humble Advice of The Assembly of Divines . . . Concerning a Confession of Faith . . .* (London, 1658), Chap. XXXIII, and *The Humble Advice of*

The Assembly of Divines . . . Concerning A Larger Catechisme . . . [London, 1658], p. 29.

8. See Aletha Joy Bourne Gilsdorf, "The Puritan Apocalypse: New England Eschatology in the Seventeenth Century" (Ph. D. diss., Yale University, 1965); Sacvan Bercovitch, "Horologicals to Chronometricals: The Rhetoric of the Jeremiad," *Literary Monographs*, III (Madison, Wis.: University of Wisconsin Press, 1970), 3-124; Robert Middlekauff, *The Mathers* (New York: Oxford University Press, 1971); Mason I. Lowance, Jr., "Typology and Millennial Aesthetics in Early New England," *Literary Uses of Typology*, ed. Earl Miner (Princeton: Princeton University Press, 1977), pp. 228-73; Perry Miller, "The End of the World," in *Errand Into the Wilderness* (Boston, 1956; rpt. New York: Harper & Row, 1964), pp. 217-39, *The New England Mind: The Seventeenth Century* (New York, 1939: rpt. Boston: The Beacon Press, 1961), chap. xvi, passim, and *The New England Mind: From Colony to Province* (1953; rpt. Boston: The Beacon Press, 1961), chaps, i-ii, passim; David E. Stannard, "Death and Dying in Puritan New England," *The American Historical Review*, 78 (1973), 1305-30, and *The Puritan Way of Death* (New York: Oxford University Press, 1977); Dickran and Ann Tashjian, *Memorials for Children of Change* (Middletown, Ct.: Wesleyan University Press, 1974).

9. Davidson, chap. one, passim.

10. John Phillips, *The Reformation of Images* (Berkeley: University of California Press, 1973).

11. See *Gravestones of Early New England and the Men who Made Them: 1653-1800* (Boston: Houghton Mifflin Co., 1927).

12. Allan I. Ludwig, *Graven Images* (Middletown, Ct.: Wesleyan University Press, 1966); James Deetz and Edwin S. Dethlefsen, "Death's Head, Cherub, Urn and Willow," *Natural History,*, 76 (March 1967), 28-37.

13. Peter Benes, *The Masks of Orthodoxy* (Amherst: University of Massachusetts Press, 1977).

14. Ball, p. 13.

15. Samuel Willard, *A Compleat Body of Divinity* (Boston, 1726), p. 532. Quoted in Ludwig, p. 33.

16. The Charles Bardin stone, 1773, Newport, R. I. It can be argued that the figure shown here above the sea is not God at the Creation but Moses parting the Red Sea. Crossing the Red Sea from the land of bondage was read as an allegory of the passage from the bondage of flesh and the grave into life and heaven.

17. Ludwig, p. 34.

18. See J. F. Maclear, "Anne Hutchinson and the Mortalist Heresy," *The New England Quarterly*, LIV, no. 1 (March 1981), 74-103. Denial of the resurrection of the body resurfaced in various sects of the eighteenth and nineteenth centuries in New England, such as the Shakers. These sects generally simplified burial rituals and eschewed gravestone imagery.

19. For a discussion of the emblem tradition in Puritan England, see Rosemary Freeman, *English Emblem Books* (London, 1948; rpt. New York: Octagon Books, 1966), and Barbara K. Lewalski, *Protestant Poetics and the Seventeenth-Century Religious Lyric* (Princeton: Princeton University Press, 1979), chap. 6.

20. For a discussion of these ideas, see Lewalski, *Protestant Poetics*, chap. 3, and Perry Miller, *The New England Mind: The Seventeenth Century* (New York, 1939; rpt. Boston: The Beacon Press, 1961), chap. 5.

21. Jesper Rosenmeier, " 'Clearing the Medium': A Reevaluation of the Puritan Plain Style in Light of John Cotton's *A Practicall Commentary Upon the First Epistle Generall of John*," *William and Mary Quarterly*, Third Series, XXXVII, no. 4 (Oct. 1980), 577-91. For the anti-Platonic nature of Puritan symbolism, see Lowance, *The Language of Canaan*, p. 5.

22. Tashjian, pp. 3-12. Robert Daly repeats the Tashjian argument and applies it to Puritan poetics in his "Puritan Poetics: The World, the Flesh, and God," *Early American Literature*, 12 (1977), 136-62.

23. Ibid., pp. 9-10.

24. *The Whole Book of Psalmes* (n.p., 1640), n.p.

Notes for Chapter 1

1. For the history of English iconoclasm, see Phillips, *The Reformation of Images*, op. cit. David Leverenz, in *The Language of Puritan Feeling* (New Brunswick: Rutgers University Press, 1980), offers a psychological interpretation of similar Puritan rhetoric directed at the theater.

2. *Certayne Sermons appoynted by the Quenes Maiestie* . . . (n.p., n.d. [1559-63]), fol. 78v-78r.

3. Henry Ainsworth, *An Arrow Against Idolatry* (Nova Belgia [London], 1640), chap. 2, p. 2. William Perkins, *A Golden Chaine*, in *The Workes of . . . William Perkins* (Cambridge, 1608-09), I, 35.

4. Daniel Featley, *Clavis Mystica* (London, 1636), p. 221.

5. Samuel Chidley, *Thunder from the Throne of God Against the Temples of Idols*, (London, 1653), pp. 3-4.

6. William Guild, *The Sealed Book Opened* (London, 1656), pp. 251-52.

7. Joseph Mede, *The Apostasy of the Latter Times*, in *The Works of the Pious and Profoundly-Learned Joseph Mede, B.D.* (London, 1663-64), Bk. III, 794. See John Cotton, *The Churches Resurrection* (London, 1642), pp. 8-9, and *The Powring oyt of the Seven Vials* (London, 1642), pp. 12-26.

8. Richard Sibbes, *The Brides Longing for her Bride-groomes second coming* (London, 1638).

9. John Calvin, *The Institutes of the Christian Religion*, The Library of Christian Classics, vols. 20-21, ed. John T. McNeill (Philadelphia: Westminster Press, 1960), I, 675-84.

10. In so doing, Puritans went against what anthropologists see as one of the most basic human beliefs. See Richard Huntington and Peter Metcalf, *Celebrations of Death* (New York: Cambridge University Press, 1979).

11. Anon., *A Suruey of the Booke of Common Prayer* (n.p., 1606), p. 143.

12. Dwalphintramis, *The Anatomy of the Service-Book* (n.p., n.d. [c. 1641]), pp. 35-36.

13. See F. E. Brightman, *The English Rite*, 2 vols. (London: Rivingtons, 1915).

14. Dwalphintramis, *The Anatomy of the Service-Book*, pp. 36-37.

15. John Weever, *Ancient Fvneral Monvments* (London, 1631), p. 51.

16. Thomas Comber, *The Occasional Offices* . . . (London, 1679), p. 469.

17. [K. Guernsey], *The Orders for Ecclesiastical Discipline* (London, 1642), pp. 15-16.

18. John Dunton, *The Sick Mans Passing Bell Rung Out*, in *A Mourning Ring* . . . (London, 1692), p. 151.

19. William Perkins, *A Salve for a Sicke Man*, in *The Works of that Famovs and Worthie Minister of Christ, in the Universitie of Cambridge, M. W. Perkins* . . . (Cambridge, 1603), p. 608.

20. See Phillips, chap. 1, passim.

21. Ibid., p. 41.

22. Quoted by Phillips, p. 97. For a further discussion of the effects of the Reformation on tomb sculpture, see Katherine A. Esdaile, *English Church Monuments, 1510 to 1840* (London: Lutterworth Press, 1946), and Frederick Burgess, *English Churchyard Memorials* (London: Lutterworth Press, 1963).

23. Phillips, p. 117.

24. *Certayne Sermons appoynted by the Quenes Maiestie* . . . , fol. 13.

25. Henriette s'Jacob, *Idealism and Realism* (Leiden: E. J. Brill, 1954), p. 17.

26. George Fox, *Iconoclastes* (n.p., 1621 [1671]), pp. 3-4; Edmund Gurnay, *Toward the Vindication of the Second Commandment* (Cambridge, 1639).

27. Perkins, *A Salve for a Sicke Man*, pp. 580, 682-83.

28. Perkins, *The Arte of Prophecying*, trans. Thomas Tuke, in *The Workes of . . . William Perkins* (Cambridge, 1608), II, 731-62.

29. Mede, *Apostasy*, p. 775. The subtitle of Mede's work neatly summarizes its contents: "*the Gentile's Theology of Daemons Revived in the Latter Times amongst Christians, in Worshipping of Angels, Deifying and Invocating of Saints, Adoring of Reliques, Bowing down to Images and Crosses, &c.*"

30. Ibid., pp. 778-79.

31. s'Jacob, pp. 155-56.

32. Ibid., p. 25.

33. Burgess, chap. 1, passim.

34. See Frederick Burgess, op. cit. and Peter Benes, "Additional Light on Wooden Grave Markers," *Essex Institute Historical Collections*, 111 (January 1975), 53-64.

35. Perry Miller, *The New England Mind: The Seventeenth-Century*, p. 358. The best response to Miller's thesis is by Norman S. Grabo, "The Veiled Vision: the Role of Aesthetics in early American Intellectual History," *The William and Mary Quarterly*, Third Series, XIX (1962), 493-510.

36. *Gurnay Redivivus, Or an Appendix unto the Homily Against Images in Churches* (London, 1660), pp. 82-83.

37. John Weever, *Ancient Fvneral Monvments* (London, 1631). This work, cited by Ludwig, Esdaile, Burgess, Phillips, and others, is the primary source of information on seventeenth-century English attitudes towards tomb sculpture.

38. Ibid., p. 7.

39. Ibid., p. 9.

40. Ibid., p. 9.

41. See Phillippe Ariès, *Western Attitudes Toward Death*, tr. Patricia M. Panun (Baltimore: The Johns Hopkins University Press, Md., 1974).

42. Ezekiel Hopkins, *A Sermon Preached at the Funeralls of the Honourable Algernon Grevil, Esq.* (London, 1663), p. 5. The best discussion of didacticism and artistry in the Protestant funeral sermon can be found in Barbara K. Lewalski's *Donne's Anniversaries and the Poetry of Praise* (Princeton: Princeton University Press, 1973), chap. VI, passim.

43. Perkins, *A Salve for a Sicke Man*, in *Workes*, I, 490.

44. Nancy Lee Beaty, *The Craft of Dying*, Yale Studies in English, 175 (New Haven: Yale University Press, 1970).

45. Thomas Becon, *The Sicke Mans Salve* (1561; London, 1631), p. 341. Becon's volume set the pattern for death bed ritual for Puritans for the next 200 years. See, for example, Robert Fern, *A Treatise Of the Celestial Work and Worship* (London, 1721), p. 38.

46. Becon, pp. 349-50.

47. Lewalski, chap. VI, passim.

48. Ibid., p. 9.

49. Richard Sibbes, *Bowels Opened* (London, 1639), p. 341. See also, Daniel Burgess, *The Death and Rest, Resurrection and Blessed Portion of the Saints* (London, 1692), p. 63.

50. Samuel Mather, *The Figures or Types of the Old Testament*, 2nd. ed. (London, 1705).

51. The subject of typology has received extensive treatment in recent years. My discussion of typology is indebted to several useful secondary sources, including Barbara K. Lewalski, *Milton's Brief Epic* (Providence: Brown University Press, 1966), pp. 165-321, and "*Samson Agonistes* and the 'Tragedy' of the Apocalypse," *PMLA*, 85 (1970), 1050-61; William Madsen, *From Shadowy Types to Truth* (New Haven: Yale University Press, 1968), pp. 27-53; Sacvan Bercovitch, "Typology in Puritan New England: The Williams-Cotton Controversy Reassessed," *American Quarterly*, 19 (1967), 167-91; Mason I. Lowance, Jr., "Typology and Millennial Aesthetics in Early New England," in *Literary Uses of Typology*, ed. Earl Miner (Princeton: Princeton University Press, 1977; chapters by Thomas M. Davis, Richard Reinitz, and Mason I. Lowance, Jr. in *Typology and Early American Literature*, ed. Sacvan Bercovitch (Amherst, Mass.: University of Massachusetts Press, 1972). See the bibliography of primary and secondary sources included in this volume. For discussions of typology and literary theory, see Barbara K. Lewalski, *Protestant Poetics and the Seventeenth-Century Religious*

Lyric (Princeton: Princeton University Press, 1979), chap. 4, and Mason I. Lowance, Jr., *The Language of Canaan* (Cambridge: Harvard University Press, 1980), part three.

52. William Guild, *Loves Entercovrs Between the Lamb & his Bride, Christ and his Church* (London, 1658), p. 165.

53. William Perkins, *A Clovd of Faithfvll Witnesses, Leading to the Heavenly Canaan* (London, 1622).

54. Note John Calvin, *Commentaries on the First Book of Moses called Genesis*, 2 vols., tr. John King (Edinburgh, 1847), p. 63: "Nothing shall we find, I say, above or below, which can raise us up to God, until Christ shal have instructed us in his own school. Yet this cannot be done, unless we, having emerged out of the lowest depths, are borne up above all the heavens, in the chariot of his cross, that there by faith we may apprehend those things which the eye has never seen, the ear never heard, and which far surpass our hearts and minds."

55. Perkins, *A Clovd of Faithful Witnesses*, pp. 5-6.

56. Ibid., pp. 216-18.

57. Ibid., pp. 216-18.

58. In my discussion of Sibbes and traditions of Puritan incarnational theory, I am indebted to U. Milo Kaufman's fine work, *The Pilgrims Progress and Traditions in Puritan Meditation*, Yale Studies in English, vol. 163 (New Haven: Yale University Press, 1966), pp. 139-46, E. Brooks Holifield, *The Covenant Sealed* (New Haven: Yale University Press, 1974), and Ball's *A Great Expectation*, passim.

59. Richard Sibbes, *A Breathing After God* (London, 1638), pp. 164-65.

60. Ibid., pp. 169-70.

61. Richard Sibbes, *A Glance of Heaven* (London, 1638), p. 34.

62. Ibid., p. 16.

63. Ibid., pp. 69; 69-70.

64. Ibid., pp. 125-26.

65. Richard Sibbes, *The Brides Longing for her Bride-groomes second comming* (London, 1638), pp. 4-5.

66. Ibid., p. 48.

67. Ibid., pp. 50-51. Note also Burgess, *The Death and Rest*, p. 103: "Their *Bodies* are *Christ's Members*; so that *He* cannot be said to be *entirely risen*, till *they* are raised. *He himself* is in part under ground, till *they* are above it."

68. See Martz's *The Poetry of Meditation*, Yale Studies in English, vol. 125 (1952: rev. ed. New Haven: Yale University Press, 1962), chap. 4, passim, and his foreword in *The Poems of Edward Taylor*, ed. Donald E. Stanford (New Haven: Yale University Press, 1960), pp. xiii-xxxvii. A perceptive response to Martz's discussion of Baxter can be found in Kaufman, chap. 6, passim.

69. Richard Baxter, *The Saints Everlasting Rest* (Ninth ed., London, 1662), p. 40.

70. See his *The Covenant Sealed*, chap. 7, passim.

71. John Owen, *Meditations and Discourses Concerning the Glory of God* (London, 1691), p. 5.

72. Ibid., p. 199.

73. Ibid., p. 145.

74. Ibid., pp. 150-51.

75. Ibid., p. 156.

76. Ibid., pp. 99-103.

Notes for Chapter 2

1. See J. F. Maclear, "New England and the Fifth Monarchy: The Quest for the Millennium in Early American Puritanism," *William and Mary Quarterly*, 3rd. Ser., 32 (1975), 223-60.

2. John Allin and Thomas Shepard, *A Defence of the Answer* (London, 1648), pp. 62-63.

3. Anon., *The Dolefull Lamentation of Cheapside-Cross* (London, 1642), p. 7.

4. William Bradford, *The History of Plymouth Plantation*, 2 vols. (Boston: Houghton Mifflin, 1908).

5. Dickran and Ann Tashjian, *Memorials for Children of Change* (Middletown: Wesleyan University Press, 1974), chap. 1.

6. Ibid., introduction; Robert Daly, *Gods Altar* (Berkeley: University of California Press, 1978).

7. In the following discussion, I am indebted to two seminal studies by Gerhart B. Ladner, "The Concept of the Image in the Greek Fathers and the Byzantine Iconoclastic Controversy," *Dumbarton Oaks Papers*, 7 (1953), 1-34, and *Ad Imaginem Dei*, Wimmer Lecture 16 (Latrobe, Pa.: Archabbey Press, 1965).

8. Ladner, *Ad Imaginem Dei*, p. 3.

9. Ibid., p. 5.

10. Ibid., p. 2.

11. In discussing Gregory of Nyssa's formulation of this metaphor, Ladner writes: "The *eikon*, the image is the state or condition of primitive creational integrity; the *homoiosis*, the likeness or similitude, was given to man at the time of his creation only potentially, as a disposition still to be fulfilled. The Greek Fathers ever so often compared a man's re-assimilation to the image of God after the fall to the cleansing of a painting, spoiled, but not completely ruined by the application of wrong colors or by the accumulation of dirt. According to Origen, man must implore God to delete these accretions so that the image will shine again in its creational splendor. It will then become as close to its divine archetype as an image in a cleansed and polished mirror. This is a favorite metaphor of Gregory of Nyssa, in which he made use of Plato's and perhaps also of Plotinus' mirror similes." Ibid., pp. 12-13.

12. Ibid., p. 28. See s'Jacob, *Idealism and Realism* (Leiden: E. J. Brill, 1954), for a full explication of these developments.

13. See *Donne's Anniversaries and the Poetry of Praise* (Princeton: Princeton University Press, 1973), chap. IV, passim.

14. John Calvin, *Psychopannychia*, trans. Henry Beveridge, in *Tracts and Treatises of the Reformed Faith*, ed. Thomas F. Torrance (Edinburgh, 1851; rpt. Grand Rapids, Mich.: Eerdmans, 1958), pp. 422-23.

15. John T. McNeill, ed., *Calvin: Institutes of the Christian Religion*, The Library of Christian Classics, vols. 20-21 (Philadelphia: Westminster Press, 1960), I, 186-87.

16. Calvin, *Psychopannychia*, p. 424.

17. *Calvin's Doctrine of the Last Things*, trans. Harold Knight (London: Lutterworth Press, 1955), p. 171. This volume is invaluable to the student of Calvin's eschatology.

18. Quoted by Quistorp, Ibid., p. 168.

19. Thomas Pierce, *Death Consider'd as a Door to a Life of Glory* (London, n.d.), p. 115. See also, Robert Fern, *A Practical Discourse Upon Humane Bodies, Especially in their State of Glorification* (London, 1713), p. 116, and John Dunton, *A Mourning Ring* . . . (London, 1692), pp. 32-33.

20. For a historical overview of English Protestant writings on the Resurrection, see Ball's appendix II, *The Resurrection of the Body*, in *A Great Expectation*.

21. Richard Sibbes, *Beames of Divine Light, Breaking forth from severall places of holy Scripture* (London, 1639), p. 107.

22. Robert Bolton, *Mr. Boltons Last and Learned Worke of the Foure last Things, Death, Ivdgement, Hell, and Heaven*, [ed. Edward Bagshaw] (London, 1633), pp. 112-13.

23. Ibid., p. 128.

24. Ibid., p. 119.

25. Ibid., p. 125.

26. Richard Sibbes, *Light from Heaven* (London, 1638), pp. 111-12.

27. Increase Mather, *Meditations on the Glory of the Heavenly World* (Boston, 1711), p. 154.

28. Bolton, pp. 136-37.

29. For a discussion of Archer, see B. S. Capp and J. F. Maclear, cited above. Other writers of Archer's time whose works hold interest for their eschatological images include: John Brinsley, *Three Sacred Emblems*, in *Two Tracts* (London, 1656); Henry Alsted, *The Beloved City*, tr. William Burton (London, 1643); Thomas Goodwin, *A Glimpse of Sions Glory: or, The Churches Beautie specified* (London, 1641); Hanserd Knollys, *Apocalyptical Mysteries* (London, 1667); and Thomas Brightman's earlier *A Revelation of the Apocalypse* (Amsterdam, 1611).

30. Henry [John] Archer, *The Personall Reign of Christ Vpon Earth* (London, 1642), pp. 4-5.

31. Increase Mather, *The Doctrine of the Kingdom And Personal Reign of Christ Asserted and Explained In An Exposition upon Zach. 14:5, 9* (London, 1669), p. 25.

32. Karen E. Rowe, "Sacred or Profane?: Edward Taylor's Meditations on Canticles," *Modern Philology*, 20 (1974), p. 124. Extended discussions of Puritan exegesis of Can-

ticles and literary theory can be found in Barbara K. Lewalski, *Protestant Poetics and the Seventeenth-Century Religious Lyric* (Princeton: Princeton University Press, 1979), and Mason I. Lowance, *The Language of Canaan* (Cambridge: Harvard University Press, 1980), chap. 3.

33. John Dove, *The Conversion of Saloman* (London, 1613).

34. Thomas Beverly, *An Exposition of the Divinely Prophetick Song of Songs which is Solomons* (London, 1687), sig. Aa3.

35. Thomas Brightman, *A commentary on the Canticles* (London, 1642); John Cotton, *A Brief Exposition of the Whole Book of Canticles, or, Song of Solomon* (London, 1642), and *A Brief Exposition with Practical Observations Upon the Whole Book of Canticles* (London, 1655).

36. Ibid., sig. Aaaaaaaa3.

37. Ball, p. 242.

38. Brightman, p. 981.

39. Ibid., p. 1038.

40. Tuckney, preface to Cotton, *A Brief Exposition* . . . (London, 1655), sig. A5v.

41. Nathanael Homes, *A Commentary Literal or Historical, and Mystical or Spiritual On the whole Book of Canticles, The Works of Dr. Nathanael Homes* (London, 1652), sig. A2.

42. Durham's book (Edinburgh, 1668) was reprinted into the eighteenth century. For Taylor's library, see *The Poetical Works of Edward Taylor*, ed. Thomas H. Johnson (New York: Rockland Editions, 1939), pp. 221-28. Keach's citation of Durham can be found in his edition of 1681, IV, sig. A3v.

43. Ibid., p. 10; pp. 12-13.

44. Ibid., p. 115.

45. Ibid., p. 199.

46. *The Bible: that is, the Holy Scriptures* (London, 1599), one of many versions printed with L. Thomson's revised translation of the New Testament.

47. For previous studies of Temple imagery, see Ludwig, pp. 139-42, and Tashjian, pp. 66-70.

48. "Publick Records of the Church at Westfield," ms. Westfield Athenaeum, p. 90. I have regularized slightly Taylor's text.

49. Increase Mather, *The Mystery of Christ Opened and Applyed* (Boston, 1686), p. 196.

50. "Publick Records," p. 97. Taylor's language here suggests his familiarity with Thomas Goodwin's development of this trope in *A State of Glory for Spirits of Just Men Upon Dissolution Demonstrated* (London, 1657), pp. 65-66.

51. Samuel Mather, *The Figures or Types of the Old Testament*, 2nd. ed. (London, 1705), pp. 330-366.

52. Ibid., p. 346.

53. Ibid., p. 364.

54. "Increase Mather's 'New Jerusalem': Millennialism in Late Seventeenth-Century New England," ed. Mason I. Lowance, Jr., and David Watters, *Proceedings*, American Antiquarian Society, 87 (1977), 363. These three sermons were preached ca. 1686 and were subsequently transcribed by Cotton Mather. It appears from a title page in Increase Mather's hand that they were intended for publication with *A Dissertation Concerning the Future Conversion of the Jewish Nation* (London, 1709).

55. For a discussion of the Temple image and the religious lyric, see Barbara K. Lewalski, *Protestant Poetics*, pp. 100-101, and chap. 9, passim. For a comparison of Herbert and Taylor, see William Scheick, "Typology and Allegory: A Comparative Study of George Herbert and Edward Taylor," *Essays in Literature*, II (Spring 1975), 76-86.

　　For Anglican defenses of the temple as the dwelling place of God, see R. T., *De Templis, A Treatise of Temples* (London, 1638), and William Dugdale, *The History of St. Pauls Cathedral in London, From its Foundation untill thes Times* (London, 1658).

56. In *Major Poets of the Earlier Seventeenth Century*, eds. Barbara K. Lewalski and Andrew J. Sabol (New York: Odyssey Press, 1973), pp. 288-89.

57. *The Poems of Edward Taylor*, ed. Donald E. Stanford (New Haven: Yale University Press, 1960), pp. 114-16.

58. See *A Testimony from the Scripture against Idolatry & Superstition* (Cambridge, 1672).

59. Samuel Mather, *Figures or Types*, p. 412.

60. Increase Mather, *The Mystery of Christ Opened and Applyed* (Boston, 1686), p. 85.

61. Thomas Goodwin, *Christ Set Forth* (London, 1652), p. 105.

62. Samuel Mather, *Figures or Types*, pp. 499; 501-502.

63. Ibid., pp. 501-10.

64. Richard Baxter, *The Saints Everlasting Rest*, p. 639.

65. For Parker's life, see *The National Cyclopaedia*, 12 (1904), 249; *DNB*, *14*, (1917), 277-78; *DAB*, 14 (1934), 241-42; Cotton Mather, *Magnalia Christi Americana* (Hartford, 1853-55; rpt. New York: Russell & Russell, 1967), I, 480-88.

66. John Eliot, *The Christian Commonwealth: Or, the Civil Policy . . . Written Before the Interruption of the Government* (London, 1659).

67. Thomas Parker, *The Visions and Prophecies of Daniel Expounded* (London, 1646), pp. 46; 128.

68. Ibid., p. 147.

69. Ibid., pp. 147-49.

70. Cotton Mather, *Magnalia*, I, 482.

Notes for Chapter 3

1. Kenneth B. Murdock, *Increase Mather: The Foremost Puritan* (Cambridge, Mass.: Harvard University Press, 1925).

2. Robert Middlekauff, *The Mathers* (New York: Oxford University Press, 1971), p. 179. For Mather's literalism, see the introduction to "Increase Mather's 'New Jerusalem':

Millennialism in Late Seventeenth-Century New England," eds. Mason I. Lowance, Jr., and David Watters, *Proceedings,* American Antiquarian Society, 87 (1977), 343-408; Mason I. Lowance, Jr., *The Language of Canaan* (Cambridge: Harvard University Press, 1980), chap. 6.

3. Perry Miller, *The New England Mind: From Colony to Province* (1953; rpt. Boston: The Beacon Press, 1961), p. 185.

4. See James W. Davidson, *The Logic of Millennial Thought* (New Haven: Yale University Press, 1977); Middlekauff, chap. 10; and Lowance, *The Language of Canaan,* part three.

5. Cotton Mather, *A Father Departing* (Boston, 1723), p. 16.

6. For Colman and the Mathers, see Perry Miller's *The New England Mind: From Colony to Province,* pp. 240-43.

7. For a discussion of the jeremiad in general and the jeremidic funeral sermon in particular, see Sacvan Bercovitch's *The American Jeremiad* (Madison: University of Wisconsin Press, 1978).

8. Benjamin Colman, *The Prophet's Death Lamented and Improved* (Boston, 1723), p. 6.

9. Ibid., pp. 7; 12-13.

10. Ibid., p. 15.

11. Ibid., p. 16. Colman's point reflects a common view of prophesy. In *The Arte of Prophesying,* William Perkins wrote, "Prophecie (or Prophecying) is a publicke and solemne speech of the Prophet, pertaining to the worship of God, and to the saluation of our neighbour" (p. 731).

12. Ibid., p. 32.

13. Cotton Mather, *Parentator, Memoirs of Remarkables in the Life and the Death of the Ever-Memorable Dr. Increase Mather* (Boston, 1724), pp. 4-5.

14. Ibid., pp. 64-65.

15. Ibid., pp. 193-94.

16. Ibid., p. 231.

17. James W. Davidson, *The Logic of Millennial Thought,* chap. 2, passim.

18. Perry Miller presented the declension theory in *The New England Mind: From Colony to Province* (1953; rpt. Cambridge: The Beacon Press, 1961). Robert G. Pope debates the theory in *The Half-way Covenant: Church Membership in Puritan New England* (Princeton: Princeton University Press, 1969).

19. Middlekauff, *The Mathers,* pp. 173-74.

20. Increase Mather, *The Mystery of Israel's Salvation* (London, 1669).

21. Increase Mather, *The Mystery of Christ Opened and Applyed* (Boston, 1686), pp. 58, 203; *Meditations on the Glory of the Heavenly World* (Boston, 1711), pp. 121, 157-58.

22. For a typical example of Mather's effusions on this subject, see *The Mystery of Christ,* pp. 202-03: "The bodyes of *Saints* shall have a marvellous Lustre upon them after the Resurrection. . . . But the Body of *Christ is far more glorious than theirs shall be: For*

indeed it is the Exemplar which the bodyes of glorified Saints shall only hold some proportion with *Phil.* 3:21. The Lord Jesus Christ shall change *our* vile body, that it might be Fashioned *like* unto His glorious body.—There is one glory of the *Sun,* and anothere glory of the *Stars* (as the Scripture speakes) Such a difference there is and will be to eternity, between the glory of the humane nature of Jesus Christ and what Believers shall in the world to come attain unto."

23. See Increase Mather, *The Mystery of Christ,* p. 109, and *Meditations on the Glory of the Heavenly World,* p. 59.

24. Note *Meditations on the Glory of the Heavenly World,* p. 239: "An *Impossibility of Sinning* in the Man Christ Jesus, proceeds from the Personal Union of the Humane Nature with the Divine. But in Glorify'd Saints, it proceeds from the *Beatifical Vision.* They are so filled with the Fulness of GOD, and to taken up with GOD, that it is impossible that they should sin *whilest they are* so; and they will be so for ever and ever. It remains then that the Happiness of the Glorify'd in Heaven, consists chiefly in this *Vision of God.*"

25. Increase Mather, *The Mystery of Christ,* p. 209.

26. Increase Mather, *A Disquisition Concerning the State of the Souls of Men, (Especially of Good Men) When Separated from their Bodies* (Boston, 1707), pp. 4-5.

27. Increase Mather, *Angelographia* (Boston, 1686), pp. 27-28. See Thomas Doolittle, *The Saints Convoy to Heaven* (London, 1698), pp. 35-37, for an extended treatment of the soul's journey with guardian angels.

28. Doolittle, *The Saints Convoy,* p. 29.

29. Mather's jeremiads are discussed by Perry Miller, *The New England Mind: From Colony to Province,* chap. 2; by Mason I. Lowance, Jr., *Increase Mather,* Twayne's United States Authors Series 246 (New York: Twayne Publishers, Inc., 1974); by Sacvan Bercovitch, *The American Jeremiad* (Madison: The University of Wisconsin Press, 1978).

30. Increase Mather, *A Discourse Concerning the Death of the Righteous* (Boston, 1711), p. 26.

31. Increase Mather, *Meditations on Death* (Boston, 1707), pp. 122, 125.

32. "An Appendix to the Preceeding Dissertation," in *A Dissertation Wherein the Strange Doctrine* (Boston, 1708), pp. 91-92.

33. Middlekauff, *The Mathers,* p. 183.

34. Increase Mather, *The Mystery of Israel's Salvation, Explained and Applied,* p. 155.

35. Ibid., pp. 153-54.

36. Increase Mather, *Meditations on Death* (Boston, 1707) p. 147.

37. Ibid., p. 169.

38. Increase Mather, *Meditations on the Glory of the Heavenly World* (Boston, 1711), pp. 39-40.

39. Ibid., p. 31.

40. See, for example, "An appendix to the Preceeding Dissertation."

41. Increase Mather, *The Mystery of Israel's Salvation,* pp. 163, 164.

Notes for Chapter 4

 1. These pioneering artisans have received attention as seminal early American designers. See Harriette Merrifield Forbes, "The Lamsons of Charlestown, Stone Cutters," *Old Time New England* 17 (January 1927), 125-39, and *Gravestones of Early New England* (1927; rpt. Princeton: The Pyne Press, 1973), pp. 21-28; 34-39; chap. IV; Allan Ludwig, *Graven Images* (Middletown: Wesleyan University Press, 1966), pp. 287; 296-300; 300-13; Dickran and Ann Tashjian, *Memorials for Children of Change* (Middletown: Wesleyan University Press, 1974), pp. 63-71; 91-92, 170-73; 176-80.

 2. For interpretations of the Temple, see above, chapter 2.

 3. Increase Mather, *The Mystery of Christ Opened and Applyed* (Boston, 1686), p. 196.

 4. Ibid., p. 85.

 5. Increase Mather, *Meditations on Death* (Boston, 1707), p. 16.

 6. For discussions of the Charlestown Carver, see above, note 1.

 7. Tashjian, *Memorials for Children of Change,* p. 67.

 8. *Angelographia* (Boston, 1696), pp. 27-28.

 9. Samuel Mather, *Figures or Types of the Old Testament* (London, 1705), pp. 330-66.

10. Ibid. p. 346.

11. For a discussion of the image of the High Priest, often found with temple imagery, see my "A Priest to the Temple," in *Puritan Gravestone Art II* (1978), 32-36.

12. Increase Mather, *Meditations on Death,* pp. 46-47; "Increase Mather's 'New Jerusalem,' " p. 365.

13. Ibid., p. 370.

14. Cotton Mather, *The Temple Opening. A Particular Church Considered as a Temple of the Lord* (Boston, 1709), pp. 1-2.

15. Kenneth Silverman, ed., *Colonial American Poetry* (New York: Hafner Publishing Co., 1968), pp. 143-44.

16. Cotton Mather, *Magnalia Christi Americana* (Hartford, 1853-55), I, 439.

17. Ibid., I, 440.

18. Ludwig, p. 160.

19. While several JN stones are dated in the 1680s, probate records reveal that they were not placed before 1693. The backdating of stones was a common practice in the colonial period.

20. See Forbes, *Gravestones of Early New England,* pp. 34-39; Ludwig, *Graven Images,* pp. 296-300; Tashjian, *Memorials for Children of Change,* pp. 89-92.

21. Ludwig, pp. 296, 300.

22. Tashjian, p. 92.

23. Allan I. Ludwig suggests these figures may represent "degenerate cherubs" in "Eros and Agape: Classical and Early Christian Survivals in New England Stonecarving," *Puritan Gravestone Art,* The Dublin Seminar for New England Folklife, Annual Proceedings, I (1976), 41-56.

24. Thomas Heywood, *The Hierarchie of the Blessed Angels* (London, 1635).

25. Ibid., pp. 40-41.

26. Thomas Wilson, *A Complete Christian Dictionary* (London, 1654), p. 473.

27. Otto Van Veen, *Amoris Divini Emblemata Stvdio et Aere Othonis Vaeni Concinnata* (Antwerp, 1640), pp. 112-13.

28. Barbara Lewalski, *Protestant Poetics and the Seventeenth-Century Religious Lyric* (Princeton: Princeton University Press, 1979), pp. 190-91.

29. See John Gregory, *Notes and Observations upon some passages of Scripture* (Oxford, 1646), pp. 123-26, and Jane Donahue Eberwein, " 'In a book, as in a glass': Literary Sorcery in Mather's Life of Phips," *Early American Literature,* X, no. 3 (Winter 1975-76), 289-300.

30. Increase Mather, *A Discourse Concerning Faith and Fervency in Prayer* (Boston, 1710), p. 60.

31. In *Seventeenth-Century American Poetry,* ed. Harrison T. Meserole (Garden City, New York: Doubleday & Co., Inc., 1968), pp. 42-54.

32. Increase Mather, *A Discourse Concerning Faith and Fervency in Prayer,* p. 65.

33. Ibid., pp. 57-58.

34. Increase Mather, *Some Important Truths About Conversion* (London, 1674), pp. 19-20.

35. Increase Mather, *The Mystery of Israel's Salvation,* p. 139.

36. Increase Mather, *Meditations on the Glory of the Heavenly World,* p. 9.

37. Ibid., pp. 269-70.

38. Joseph Sewall, *Believers invited to Come to Christ As the Author of their Resurrection and Life* (Boston, 1716), pp. 7-8.

39. Increase Mather, *A Discourse Concerning the Death of the Righteous,* p. 10.

40. For the history of the Lamson family, see Harriette Merrifield Forbes, "The Lamsons of Charlestown, Stone Cutters," *Old Time New England* 17 (January 1927), 125-29.

41. Tashjian, *Memorials for Children of Change,* pp. 83-88.

42. Ludwig, *Graven Images,* pp. 223, 225. See also, Ludwig, "Eros and Agape," note 23, above.

43. Increase Mather, *The Mystery of Christ,* p. 110.

44. Increase Mather, *Angelographia,* p. 95.

45. Ibid., p. 95.

46. *The Poems of Edward Taylor,* ed. Donald E. Stanford (New Haven: Yale University Press, 1960), p. 162.

47. Ludwig, *Graven Images*, p. 140.

48. Increase Mather, *A Father Departing*, p. 23. David Leverenz sees in such images the desire of ministers to play a feminine, nurturing role which the culture denied to men. See *The Language of Puritan Feeling* (New Brunswick: Rutgers University Press, 1980).

49. Increase Mather, *A Dissertation Wherein the Strange Doctrine* (Boston, 1708). For the Stoddard-Mather controversy, see Robert Middlekauff, *The Mathers* (New York: Oxford University Press, 1971).

50. Ms. American Antiquarian Society (Worcester, Mass.), pp. 56-57.

51. Increase Mather, "New Jerusalem," p. 378.

52. See Increase Mather, *The Mystery of Israel's Salvation*, pp. 122-24.

53. Cotton Mather, "Problema Theologicum," ms. American Antiquarian Society (Worcester, Mass.), p. 59.

54. For a sensitive discussion of this aspect of Mather's personality, See David Levin, *Cotton Mather* (Cambridge: Harvard University Press, 1978), chaps. 6 and 9.

55. Cotton Mather, "Problema Theologicum," pp. 83, 67, 82.

56. Cotton Mather, "Triparadisus," III, 28.

57. Ibid., II, 38-39.

58. Ibid., II, 11.

59. Ibid., III, 30-31.

60. Ibid., III, 32.

61. For a discussion of this aspect of Gnosticism, see Carolyn Merchant, *The Death of Nature* (San Francisco: Harper & Row, 1980), chap. 1.

62. Cotton Mather, "Triparadisus," III, 32-33.

Notes for Chapter 5

1. Karl Keller, *The Example of Edward Taylor* (Amherst: University of Massachusetts Press, 1975), p. 7. For Taylor's biography see also *The Poems of Edward Taylor*, ed. Donald E. Stanford (New Haven: Yale University Press, 1960), introduction, and Norman S. Grabo, *Edward Taylor*, Twayne United States Authors Series 8 (New Haven: College and University Press, 1961), chap. 1.

2. The exact relationship of the process of composition of the poems, the sermons, and the ritual itself has been the subject of much debate. For the relationship of Taylor's sacramental theory to his poetic, see Kathleen Blake, "Edward Taylor's Protestant Poetic: Nontransubstantiating Metaphor," *American Literature* 43 (1971), 1-24; Norman S. Grabo, ed., *Edward Taylor's Treatise Concerning the Lord's Supper* (Lansing: Michigan State University Press, 1966), introduction; Barbara K. Lewalski, *Protestant Poetics and the Seventeenth-Century Religious Lyric* (Princeton: Princeton University Press, 1979), chap. 12.

3. The relationship of Taylor's poetry and gravestone art has received scant critical at-

tention. Allan Ludwig, in *Graven Images* (Middletown: Wesleyan University Press, 1966), and the Tashjians, in *Memorials for Children of Change* (Middletown: Wesleyan University Press, 1974), use his poetry to elucidate a few carving motifs. Jeff Hammond and Thomas M. Davis in "Edward Taylor: A Note on Visual Imagery," *Early American Literature*, 8 (1973), 126-31 treat Taylor's use of the image of the death's head. Lynn Haims uses Taylor's poetry in her fascinating exploration of Puritan iconography in "The Face of God: Puritan Iconography in Early American Poetry, Sermons, and Tombstone Carving," *Early American Literature*, XIV (Spring, 1979), 15-47.

4. For an overview of Taylor's eschatology, see Donald E. Stanford, "The Imagination of Death in the Poetry of Philip Pain, Edward Taylor, and George Herbert," *Studies in the Literary Imagination*, 9, ii (1976), 53-67. Stanford describes Taylor's belief in the imminence of the Second Coming and writes, "Taylor is the doctrinaire predestinarian, high Calvinist who believed in a narrow interpretation of the Westminster Confession and whose narrow dogmatism generated an intensity of feeling expressed in a powerful rhetoric. . . ." (pp. 61-62). Taylor did not refrain, however, from the hairsplitting logic of millennial thought, as can be seen in his playful letter on the sixth vial to Samuel Sewall. Sewall argued that the vial would be poured on Spanish America, thus indicating the centrality of America in the Millennium. Sewall argued his position fully in his classic *Phaenomena Quaedam Apocalyptica* (Boston, 1697). Taylor took the traditional English view that the vial would be poured upon the Turks, revealing his fervent attachment to the idea of a mystical, universal church which transcends nationality. See Mukhtar Ali Isani's "The Pouring of the Sixth Vial: A Letter in a Taylor-Sewall Debate," Massachusetts Historical Society, *Proceedings*, 83 (1971), 123-39, and for Sewall's response, *The Letter-Book of Samuel Sewall*, Massachusetts Historical Society, *Collections*, 6th ser., I (1886), 171-78.

5. Thomas M. and Virginia L. Davis, "Edward Taylor on the Day of Judgment," *American Literature*, 43 (1972), p. 526.

6. Ibid., p. 529. Taylor affirms that the Resurrection is personally effected by Christ in the *Christographia*, ed. Norman S. Grabo (New Haven: Yale University Press, 1962), pp. 62-63. Moreover, like Increase Mather he parts with Calvin on the presence of Christ's human nature after the Millennium. Taylor feels that His human nature would be needed to mediate between God and man even in Heaven (pp. 412-14).

7. Ibid., p. 538.

8. Ibid., pp. 530, 531.

9. Ibid., p. 540.

10. *The Poems of Edward Taylor*, ed. Donald E. Stanford (New Haven: Yale University Press, 1960), p. 71. Subsequent citations from this edition will be followed with poem number or title in parentheses. Several critics note that the formula of attempting to praise the unpraiseable supplies both wit and intensity to Taylor's art. See Barbara K. Lewalski, *Protestant Poetics*, chap. 12; Michael North, "Edward Taylor's Metaphors of Promise," *American Literature*, 51 (1979), 1-16; Parker H. Johnson, "Poetry and Praise in Edward Taylor's *Preparatory Meditations*," *American Literature*, 52 (March 1980), 84-96.

11. Davis, "Edward Taylor on the Day of Judgment," p. 535.

12. See for example Meditation 2:44 and sermons one and three in the *Christographia*.

13. Keller, p. 265.

14. In the *Christographia* Taylor notes, "This Church consists of the whole Body of the Elect of God both men and Angells, in all times and places of the world wheresoever" (p. 301). Subsequent citations from this text will be followed by "*C*" and the page number in parentheses.

15. See *Edward Taylor's Treatise Concerning the Lord's Supper*, ed. Norman S. Grabo (East Lansing, Mich.: Michigan State University Press, 1966), pp. 51, 94, 184. Taylor's views can be contrasted with the position of Jerome [*The Jerome Biblical Commentary*, eds. Raymond E. Brown, Joseph A. Fitzmyer, Roland E. Murphy, 2 vols. (Englewood Cliffs, N.J., 1968), II, 258]. Catholics rejected the position of the Greeks as theosophism, holding instead that the "perfect" were perfect in charity [*The New Catholic Encyclopedia* (New York, 1967), XI, 126-27].

16. *Christographia*, pp. 89-90. Note also p. 327, "For the Body is glorified by the Crown, which the head doth weare. The head is not Crowned without its body: nor can enjoy any fulness of glory Separated from its body. And hence the Whole body is made to partake of the heads glorie so long as the glory of the head last: and this being everlasting, you will enjoy this everlastingly: and this is Sweet Consolation."

17. For the best discussions of this "personalizing" of typology by Taylor, see Norman S. Grabo, *Edward Taylor*, p. 99; Mason I. Lowance, Jr., *The Language of Canaan* (Cambridge: Harvard University Press, 1980), chap. 5; Robert Reiter, "Poetry and Typology: Edward Taylor's *Preparatory Meditations*, Second Series, Numbers 1-30," *Early American Literature*, V (1970), 111-23.

18. Charles W. Mignon, ed., "Christ the Glory of all Types: The Initial Sermon from Edward Taylor's 'Upon the Types of the Old Testament,' " *William and Mary Quarterly*, Third Series, XXXVII, 2 (April 1980), p. 299.

19. Taylor's attacks on Stoddard continued for at least twenty-five years. Norman S. Grabo has discussed the controversy extensively in "Edward Taylor on the Lord's Supper," *Boston Public Library Quarterly* 12 (1960), 22-36; "The Poet to the Pope: Edward Taylor to Solomon Stoddard," *American Literature* 52 (1960), 197-201; *Edward Taylor's Treatise*, pp. xix-xxxii. Subsequent quotations from this text are followed by *TCLS* and page number in parentheses.

20. See Thomas M. Davis, ed., "Solomon Stoddard's Sermon on the Lord's Supper as a Converting Ordinance," *Resources for American Literary Study*, 4 (1971), p. 219.

21. Elsewhere (p. 148) Taylor cites Isaiah 52:1-2 as a text describing the invitation to the Lord's Supper, but Increase Mather reads this text as a description of the millennial feast in his "New Jerusalem." See Mason I. Lowance, Jr., and David Watters, eds., "Increase Mather's 'New Jerusalem': Millennialism in Late Seventeenth-Century New England," *Proceedings*, American Antiquarian Society, 37 (1977), p. 343.

22. This tradition has received considerable attention. For Hartshorne (active ca. 1690-1734), see James A. Slater, Ralph L. Tucker and Daniel Farber, "The Colonial Gravestone Carvings of John Hartshorne," *Puritan Gravestone Art II (1978)*, 79-146; Peter Benes "Lt. John Hartshorn: Gravestone Maker of Haverhill and Norwich," *Essex Institute Historical Collections*, 109 (1973), 152-64; Ludwig, pp. 358-68, 373-80; Tashjian, pp. 190-201. For Obadiah Wheeler (active 1726-49) see Ludwig, pp. 380-82; Tashjian, pp. 201-08; James A. Slater and Ernest Caulfield, "The Colonial Gravestone Carvings

of Obadiah Wheeler," American Antiquarian Society, *Proceedings*, 84 (1974), 73-103. For Benjamin (active 1726-55), Julius (active 1739-58?), and Zerubbabel Collins (active 1755?-97), see Ernest Caulfied, "Connecticut Gravestones: IX," *Connecticut Historical Society Bulletin*, 28 (1963), 22-29; Ludwig, pp. 382-89; Tashjian, pp. 100-06.

23. John H. Lockwood notes Taylor's habit of studying with local ministers and speculates that he met Elizabeth Fitch during such a stay with her father [*Westfield and Its Historic Influences* (Springfield, Mass., 1922), I, 156]. The similarities between these two communities is attested to by the consultation of Fitch by Taylor on the proper method of forming the Westfield Church. The best biographical information on Taylor can be found in Donald E. Stanford's "An Edition of the Complete Poetical Works of Edward Taylor" (Diss. Stanford University, 1953).

24. Benjamin Lord, *Heaven, a Glorious Retreat and Rest; from all that is Burdensome and Afflicting. A Funeral Sermon for Mrs. Anne Lord* (New London, 1751), pp. 21-22.

25. For the establishment of this important church, see C. C. Goen's *Revivalism and Separatism in New England, 1740-1800* (New Haven: Yale University Press, 1962), p. 108.

26. See Ernest Caulfied, "Connecticut Gravestones V," *Connecticut Historical Society Bulletin*, 21 (1956), 1-13, and "Connecticut Gravestones VII," *Connecticut Historical Society Bulletin* 25 (1960), 1-6, for discussion of these carvers.

27. See Ernest Caulfied, "Connecticut Gravestones II," *Connecticut Historical Society Bulletin*, 16 (1951), 25-31.

28. Critics of Taylor have related his emphasis on vision to Edwardsean epistemology, but Taylor's concern is less with the logic of perceiving divine things than it is with the glories of the vision itself. See Norman S. Grabo's introduction to *Edward Taylor's Treatise*, pp. xxxvi-xxxix, and Karl Keller, *The Example of Edward Taylor*, pp. 149, 1760. Taylor is closest to Thomas Shepard and John Owen (whose *Meditations and Discourses Concerning the Glory of Christ* was in Taylor's library) on the power of vision.

29. For a discussion of this practice, see Peter Benes' *The Masks of Orthodoxy* (Amherst, Mass.: University of Massachusetts Press, 1977), p. 42.

30. Benes, *The Masks of Orthodoxy*, pp. 178-83.

31. Davis, pp. 544-45.

32. See also Meditations 2:142, 143 for this image of the saint cloathed in images of cosmological glory from Revelation. Taylor discusses the three offices of Christ at length in Meditations 1:14-17. We know that Taylor conceived of this robe as the Resurrection body rather than as a robe of sanctifying grace from Meditation 1:25: "But, my sweet Lord, what glorious robes are those / That thou hast brought out of thy Grave for thine? / They do outshine the Sun-Shine, Grace the Rose. / I leape for joy to thinke, shall these be mine? / Such are, as waite upon thee in thy Wars, / Cloathd with the Sun, and Crowned with twelve Stars."

33. The biblical sources for this conceit are Isaiah 24:23 and Rev. 21:23.

34. For a detailed discussion of the image of the priest on gravestones, see my "A Priest to the Temple," *Puritan Gravestone Art II* (1978), 45-57.

35. Taylor describes the crown of life in Meditations 1:43-45.

Notes for Chapter 6

1. Puritan attitudes towards language have received much critical attention. For an overview of the subject, See Barbara K. Lewalski, *Protestant Poetics and the Seventeenth-Century Religious Lyric* (Princeton: Princeton University Press, 1979). For Taylor's attitude, see Willaim J. Scheick, *The Will and the Word* (Athens: University of Georgia Press, 1974).

2. Keller, p. 121. In his discussion of metaphor as the primary mode of the Puritan imagination (pp. 163-67), Keller follows the lead of Austin Warren's "Edward Taylor's Poetry: Colonial Baroque," *Kenyon Review*, 3 (1941), 355-71. Norman S. Grabo, in his *Edward Taylor*, also pointed to Taylor's ambivalence towards metaphoric expression, while he was the first critic to identify the relationship of Taylor's thoughts on metaphor and theanthropy: "Basically Taylor's view of symbols is twofold, as may be seen in his comments about metaphor. When his attention is humbly to compare the best he can do with the glory of his Lord, he minimizes the nature and function of metaphor; he makes it a tassel on the robe of speech. . . . The dignity arises, appropriately, from his consideration of the personal union of the divine and human natures in Christ. Contending that both natures are united in one person, he offers several arguments to the effect that anything one can say about one nature is equally applicable to the other" (p. 99).

3. Perry Miller, *The New England Mind: The Seventeenth Century* (New York, 1939; rpt. Boston: The Beacon Press, 1961), p. 360.

4. Norman S. Grabo, *Edward Taylor*, p. 100.

5. *Edward Taylor's Christographia*, ed. Norman S. Grabo (New Haven: Yale University Press, 1962), p. 192.

6. The most extensive treatment of Taylor as a baroque poet is in Karl Keller's chapter "*Preparatory Meditations*: Towards a Wilderness Baroque," in *The Example of Edward Taylor*, pp. 161-88. Besides Austin Warren's article cited above, the baroque style in early American poetry has been discussed by Harold S. Jantz, *The First Century of New England Verse* (Worcester, Mass.: The Society, 1944), and Calvin Israel, "American Puritan Literary Theory: 1620-1660" (Ph.D. diss., University of California, Davis, 1970).

7. The makers of Hadley chests included Samuel Belden, Sr., and Jr., of Hadley, John Allis (grandnephew of master joiner Nicholas Disbrowe) of Hadley, his son Ichabod of Hatfield, John Hawkes of Deerfield, and John Pease of Enfield. Prototypes of these chests were carved in Ipswich by John Dennis, a lineage which reinforces our sense of the influence of this design area on central New England. The seminal study of the Hadley chest is by Clair Frank Luther, *The Hadley Chest* (Hartford, Ct.: The Case, Lockwood & Brainerd Co., 1935). See also Patricia E. Kane, "The Seventeenth-Century Furniture of the Connecticut Valley: The Hadley Chest Reappraised," *Arts of the Anglo-American Community in the Seventeenth Century*, ed. Ian M. G. Quimby, Winterthur Conference Report 1974 (Charlottesville: The University Press of Virginia, 1975), pp. 79-122.

8. Taylor may also have seen emblems with mirrors held up by cherubs to see the reflection of the human heart. See fig. 4.

9. All but three of Meditations 2:115–2:165 are on Canticles texts. For Taylor's use of this text, see above, chap. 2.

10. *Emblems Divine and Moral* (London, 1635). For the history of this immensely popular book, see Rosemary Freeman's *English Emblem Books* (London, 1948; rpt. New York: Octagon Books, 1966).

11. Arwaker, *Pia Desideria* (London, 1690), p. 162. Quarles joins Hugo and Arwaker by including an epigraph on this text, "O happy sickness, where the infirmity is not to death, but to life."

12. John Robotham *An Exposition on the Whole Book of Solomons Song, Commonly Called the Canticles* (London, 1651), p. 3.

13. John Collinges, *The Intercourses of Divine Love Betwixt Christ and the Church, or the Particular Believing-soul* (London, 1676), sig. A4. For a discussion of this aspect of Taylor's poetic, see Barbara K. Lewalski, *Protestant Poetics*, p. 69.

14. Robotham, *An Exposition* . . . , p. 6.

15. Ibid., p. 9.

16. Ibid., p. 10.

17. Thomas Ager, *A Paraphrase on the Canticles, or Song of Solomon* (London, 1680), p. 8.

18. Sibbes, *Bowels Opened* (London, 1639), pp. 339-40. James Durham concurs: "We may see, That believers are never more beautifull in Christ's eyes, than when their own spots are most discernible to themselves; and oftimes when they are sharpest in censuring themselves, he is most ready to absolve and command them" (p. 105).

19. Ibid., p. 341.

20. Collinges, *The Intercourses of Divine Love* . . . , pp. 352-53.

21. William Guild, *Loves Entercovrs Between the Lamb & his Bride, Christ and his Church* (London, 1658), p. 76.

22. Thomas Watson, *Christs Lovelinesse* (London, 1659), p. 467.

23. Guild, *Loves Entercovrs* . . . , pp. 448-49.

24. See Erwin Panofsky's *Studies in Iconology* (New York: Oxford University Press, 1939), chap. IV, and Mario Praz's *Studies in Seventeenth Century Imagery*, Studies of the Warburg Institute, vol. 3 (London: The Warburg Institute, 1939), I, chap. 3. Rosemary Freeman discusses Quarles' use of Canticles texts in her *English Emblem Books*, p. 140.

25. Quarles, *Emblems*, Book IV, emblem 11.

26. Quarles, *Emblems*, Bk. IV, emblem 12.

27. Keller, p. 216.

28. "The Publick Records of the Church at Westfield," ms. Westfield Athenaeum, p. 98.

29. For a discussion of the sources of Stevens' imagery, see the fine discussion of his shop in Tashjian, pp. 212-30.

30. This trope is examined in detail by Stanley N. Stewart in *The Enclosed Garden* (Madison: University of Wisconsin Press, 1966).

31. *Bowels Opened*, p. 432.

32. *Works*, "The Glory of an Grace in the Church set out," p. 457.

33. For the Buckland family, see Ernest Caulfield, "Connecticut Gravestones XIV," ed. Peter Benes, *The Connecticut Historical Society Bulletin*, 41 (1976), 33-56. Clearly Buckland was influenced by William Stanclift who carved Edward Taylor's stone.

34. Watson, p. 466.

35. James Durham comments on this process: "bodily members or parts, are not to be here looked unto, but believers have an inner-man, as well as an outward, a new man as well as an old; and so that inner man hath, as it were, distinct parts and members as the natural body hath, which art in reference thereto, with some analogy to these members in the natural body. . . . As the new or inner-man sets forth the new nature and habitual grace in the believer; so the particular parts, eyes, lips, &c. signifie parts of that new nature" (*Clavis Cantici*, p. 199).

36. *A Commentary Literal or Historical, and Mystical or Spiritual on the Whole Book of Canticles*, in *The Works of Dr. Nathanael Homes* (London, 1652), p. 381.

Notes for Chapter 7

1. For Edwards' main treatises on the awakening, see *The Great Awakening*, ed. C. C. Goen, in *The Works of Jonathan Edwards*, vol. 5 (New Haven: Yale University Press, 1972). Goen's introduction to this volume treats the controversy over Edwards' views. For radical variations on Edwardsean theology during and after the awakening, see C. C. Goen's *Revivalism and Separatism in New England, 1740-1800* (2nd ed. New York; Archon Books, 1969), and Edwin Scott Gaustad's *The Great Awakening in New England* (New York, 1957; rpt. Chicago: Quadrangle Books, Inc., 1968). For discussion of Edwards millennialism, see Stephen J. Stein, ed. *Jonathan Edwards: Apocalyptic Writings*, The Works of Jonathan Edwards, vol. 5 (New Haven: Yale University Press, 1977), and Mason I. Lowance, Jr., *The Language of Canaan* (Cambridge: Harvard University Press, 1980), chap. 8.

2. *Revivalism and Separatism*, pp. 44-45.

3. "The Spiritual Travels of Nathan Cole," ed. Michael J. Crawford, *The William and Mary Quarterly*, 3rd. ser., 33 (1976), 89-126.

4. Charles Chauncy reacts to the mysticism of the awakening in *Enthusiasm Described and Caution'd against* (Boston, 1742).

5. For millennial themes in the literature of the Revolution, see Alan Heimert's *Religion and the American Mind from the Great Awakening to the Revolution* (Cambridge, Mass.: Harvard University Press, 1966), and Mason I. Lowance, Jr.'s "Typology and Millennial Eschatology in Early New England," in *Literary Uses of Typology*, ed. Earl Miner (Princeton: Princeton University Press, 1977), pp. 228-73.

6. Ms. sermon, ca. 1760, in *The Microfilm Edition of The Papers of Eleazar Wheelock togethe Early Archives of Dartmouth College & Moor's Indian Charity School and Records of the Town of Hanover, New Hampshire through the year 1779.* (Hanover, N.

H.: Dartmouth College Library, 1971), reel 13. For Wheelock's life and influence, see David M'Clure and Elijah Parish's *Memoirs of the Rev. Eleazar Wheelock* (Newburyport, Mass., 1811), and James Dow McCallum's *Eleazar Wheelock*, Manuscript Series, No. 4 (Hanover, N. H.: Dartmouth College Publications, 1939).

7. Ms. Sermon on Psalm 32:1, preached 1760-61, in *Papers*, reel 13.

8. Martha Brewster, *Poems On divers Subjects* (New London, 1757; rpt. Boston, 1758), p. 7.

9. Edwards' most detailed statements on the last things can be found in *A History of the Work of Redemption*, in *The Works of President Edwards* (New York, 1830), VII, 414-20, and in "Sermon VIII," in vol. VIII, 227-79.

10. See "Beauty in Jesus Christ," in Roland Andre Delattre's *Beauty and Sensibility in the Thought of Jonathan Edwards* (New Haven: Yale University Press, 1968), pp. 156-61.

11. *Heaven*, in *The Works of President Edwards* (New York, 1830), VIII, 529.

12. "Sermon VIII," pp. 261-62; 265.

13. *Heaven*, p. 531.

14. "Personal Narrative," in *Jonathan Edwards*, eds. Clarence H. Faust and Thomas H. Johnson, rev. ed., American Century Series (New York: Hill and Wang, 1962), pp. 57-72. For Edwards on Sarah Pierrepont, see *Jonathan Edwards*, p. 56, and *The Great Awakening*, pp. 331-41.

15. *Heaven*, p. 538.

16. "Sermon VIII," p. 243.

17. Cole, p. 121.

18. Cole, pp. 125-26.

19. Ed. Perry Miller (New Haven: Yale University Press, 1948). For a discussion of Edwards' nature typology, see Mason I. Lowance, Jr., *The Language of Canaan*, chap. 10.

20. *Images or Shadows*, p. 44.

21. Brewster, p. 6.

22. For Collins' work, see chapter 6, above.

23. *Images or Shadows*, p. 117.

24. See *The Psalms, Hymns, and Spiritual Songs of the Rev. Isaac Watts, D. D.*, ed. Samuel Worcester (Boston, 1864), pp. 324-31. Allan I. Ludwig and David D. Hall, in "Aspects of Music, Poetry, Stonecarving and Death in Early New England," *Puritan Gravestone Art II*, The Dublin Seminar for New England Folklife Annual Proceedings, 3 (1978), 18-24, argue that it is in the psalm tradition that Puritan eschatology persists into the nineteenth century.

25. "Personal Narrative." p. 60.

26. Ibid., p. 63.

27. Nancy Buckeye, "Samuel Dwight: Stone Carver of Bennington County, Vermont," *Vermont History*, 43 (1975), 208-16, and William E. Harding, "Zerubbabel Collins'

Successor and his work in Bennington County, Vermont," *Puritan Gravestone Art*, The Dublin Seminar for New England Folklife Annual Proceedings, I (1976), 14-22.

28. *Clavis Cantici* (Edinburgh, 1668), p. 140.

29. *A Commentary on the whole Book of Canticles, or Song of Salomon*, in *The Workes of that Famous, Reverend and Learned Divine, Mr. Tho: Brightman* (London, 1644), p. 1039.

30. Brightman, p. 1030; Thomas Beverly, *An Exposition of the Divinely Prophetic Song of Songs which is Solomon's* (London, 1687), chap. 4.

31. For example, see Elizabeth Stuart Phelps, *The Gates Ajar* (1868: Cambridge: Harvard University Press, 1964).

Bibliography

Primary Works

Ager, Thomas. *A Paraphrase on the Canticles, or, Song of Solomon*. London, 1680.

Ainsworth, Henry. *An Arrow Against Idolatry*. Nova Belgia [London], 1640.

Allin, John and Thomas Shepard. *A Defence of the Answer made unto the Nine Questions or Positions sent from New England*. . . . London, 1648.

Alsted, Henry, *The Beloved City, or The Saints Reign on earth a thousand yeares, Asserted and Illustrated, from LXV places of Holy Scripture*. Trans. William Burton. London, 1643.

Anon. *Certayne Sermons appoynted by the Quenes Maiestie, to be declared and read, by all Persons, Vycars, and Curates, euery Sonday and holy dayes, in theyr Churches*. . . . N.p., 1559-63.

Anon. *The dolefull Lamentation of Cheapside-Cross: Or old England sick of the Staggers*. London, 1642.

Anon. *A Suruey of the Booke of Common Prayer, By way of 197. Queres grounded vpon 58 places, ministring iust matter of question, with a View of London Ministers exceptions*. . . . London, 1606.

Archer, John. *The Personall Reign of Christ Vpon Earth. In a treatise, wherein is fully and largely laid vpon and proved, that Jesus Christ, together with the saints shall visibly possesse a monarchicall state and kingdome in this world*. London, 1642.

Bagshaw, Edward. *The Doctrine of the Kingdom and Personal Reign of Christ Asserted and Explained in An Exposition upon Zach. 14:5, 9*. London, 1669.

Baxter, Richard. *The Saints Everlasting Rest: or, a Treatise of the Blessed State of the Saints in their enjoyment of God in Glory*. 9th ed. London, 1662.

Becon, Thomas. *The Sicke Mans Salve*. . . . 1561; London, 1631.

Beverly, Thomas. *An Exposition of the Divinely Prophetick Song of Songs which is Solomons*. London, 1687.

The Bible and Holy Scriptures conteyned in the Olde and Newe Testament. Geneua, 1560.

The Bible: that is, the Holy Scriptures. . . . Trans. L. Thomson. London, 1587.

Bolton, Robert. *Mr. Boltons Last and Learned Worke of the Foure last Things, Death, Ivdgement, Hell, and Heaven*. [Ed. Edward Bagshaw]. London, 1633.

Bradford, William. *The History of Plymouth Plantation*. 2 vols. Boston: Houghton Mifflin, 1908.

Brewster, Martha. *Poems on divers subjects, viz*. . . . New London, 1757; rpt. Boston, 1757.

Brightman, F. E. *The English Rite Being a Synopsis of the Sources and Revisions of the Book of Common Prayer With an Introduction and an Appendix*. 2 vols. London: Rivingtons, 1915.

Brightman, Thomas. *A Commentary on the whole Book of Canticles, or Song of Salomon*, in *The Workes of that Famous, Reverend and Learned Divine, Mr. Tho: Brightman*. London, 1644.

_____ . *A Revelation of the Apocalypse*. Amsterdam, 1611.

Brinsley, John. *Three Sacred Emblems*. In *Two Tracts*. London, 1656.

Burgess, Daniel. *The Death and Rest, Resurrection and Blessed Portion of the Saints*. London, 1692.

Calvin, John, *Commentaries on First Book of Moses Called Genesis*. Trans. John King. 2 vols. Edinburgh, 1847.

_____ .*The Institutes of the Christian Religion*. Ed. John T. McNeill. The Library of Christian Classic, vols. 20-21. Philadelphia: Westminster Press, 1960.

_____ *Psychopannychia*. In *Tracts and Treatises of the Reformed Faith*. Ed. Thomas F. Torrance. Tr. Henry Beveridge. Vol. 3. Edinburgh, 1851; rpt. Grand Rapids, Mich.: Eerdmans, 1958.

Chauncy, Charles, *Enthusiasm Described and Caution'd against*. Boston, 1742.

Chidley, Samuel. *Thunder from the Throne of God Against the Temples of Idols*. [London, 1653].

Cole, Nathan. "The Spiritual Travels of Nathan Cole." Ed. Michael J. Crawford. *The William and Mary Quarterly*, 3rd ser., 33 (1976), 89-126.

Collinges, John. *The Intercourses of Divine Love Betwixt Christ and the Church, or the Particular Believing-soul; as metaphorically expressed by Solomon in the first chapter of the Canticles, opened, and improved in several lecture-sermons*, London, 1676.

Colman, Benjamin. *The Prophet's Death; Lamented and Improved in a Sermon Preached . . . After the Funeral of Their Venerable and Aged Pastor Increase Mather, D. D., and Now Published at the Desire of Many in the Audience*. Boston, 1723.

Comber, Thomas. *The Occasional Offices of Matrimony, Visitation of the Sick, Burial of the Dead, Churching of Women, and the Commination, Explained in the Method of the Companion to the Temple: Being the Fourth and Last Part*. London, 1679.

Cotton, John. *A Brief Exposition of the whole Book of Canticles, or Song of Solomon; Lively describing the Estate of the Church in all the Ages thereof, both Jewish and Christian, to this day: and Modestly pointing at the Gloriousnesse of the restored Estate of the Iewes, and the happy accesse of the Gentiles, in the approaching daies of Reformation, when the Wall of Partition shall be taken away*. London, 1642.

_____ . *A Brief Exposition with Practical Observations Upon the Whole Book of Canticles*. London, 1655.

_____ . *The Churches Resurrection, or The Opening of the Fift and Sixt verses of the 20th. Chap. of the Revelation*. London, 1642.

_____ . *An Exposition Upon The thirteenth Chapter of the Revelation*. London, 1656.

_____ . *The Powring Ovt of the Seven Vials: or an Exposition, or the 16 Chapter of the Revelation, with an Application of it to our Times*. London, 1642.

_____ . *A Practical Commentary, Or An Exposition With Observations, Reasons, and Vses Upon the First Epistle Generall of John*. London, 1656.

[Cotton, John and Richard Mather.] *The Whole Book of Psalmes*. N.p., 1640.

Doolittle, Thomas. *The Saints Convoy to Heaven. A Discourse (on Luke 16:22) Occasioned by . . . the death . . . of Mr. D. Lindsey, Who deceased, the 21st of February, 1697*. London, 1698.

Dugdale, William. *The History of St. Pauls Cathedral in London, From its Foundation untill thes Times. . . .* London, 1658.

Dunton, John. *A Mourning-Ring, In Memory of your Departed Friend. . . .* London, 1692.

Durham, James, *Clavis Cantici: or, and Exposition of the Song of Solomon*. Edinburgh, 1668.

Dwalphintramis. *The Anatomy of the Service-Book, Dedicated to the High Court of Parliament*. N.p., n.d. [ca. 1641].

Edwards, Jonathan. *Images or Shadows of Divine Things*. Ed. Perry Miller. New Haven; Yale University Press, 1948.

_____. *Jonathan Edwards: Apocalyptic Writings*. Ed. Stephen J. Stein. *The Works of Jonathan Edwards*, vol. 5. New Haven; Yale University Press, 1977.

_____. "Personal Narrative." *Jonathan Edwards*. Eds. Clarence H. Faust and Thomas H. Johnson. Rev. ed., American Century Series. New York: Hill and Wang, 1962. Pp. 57-72.

_____. *The Works of Jonathan Edwards*. Eds. Perry Miller and John Smith (gen. eds.). 5 vols. New Haven: Yale University Press, 1958-.

_____. *The Works of President Edwards: With a Memoir of his Life*. Ed. Sereno E. Dwight. 10 vols. New York, 1830.

Eliot, John. *The Christian Commonwealth: Or, The Civil Policy . . . Written Before the Interruption of the Government*. London, 1659.

Featley, Daniel. *Clavis Mystica: A Key Opening Divers Difficult and Mysterious Texts of Holy Scripture*. London, 1636.

Fern, Robert. *A Practical Discourse Upon Humane Bodies, Especially in their State of Glorification*. London, 1713.

Fox, George. *Iconoclastes: or a Hammer to Break Down all Invented Images, Image-Makers and Image-Worshippers*. N.p., 1621 [London?, 1671].

Goodwin, Thomas. *Christ Set Forth in His Death, Resurrection, Ascension, Sitting at Gods Right Hand, Intercession as the Cause of Iustification. Object of Iustifying Faith*. London, 1652.

_____. *A Glimpse of Sions Glory: or, the Churches Beautie specified*. London, 1641.

_____. *A State of Glory For Spirits of Just Men Upon Dissolution Demonstrated*. London, 1657.

G., I. [John Gregory]. *Notes and Observations vpon some passages of Scripture*. Oxford, 1646.

[Guernsey, K.]. *The Orders for Ecclesiastical Discipline*. London, 1642.

Guild, William. *Loves Entercovrs Between the Lamb & his Bride, Christ and his Church*. London, 1658.

_____. *The Sealed Book Opened, or A clear Explication of the Prophecies of the Revelation*. London, 1656.

Gurnay, Edmund. *Toward the Vindication of the Second Commandment*. Cambridge, 1639.

Hall, Joseph. *The Revelation Unrevealed* in *The Works of Joseph Hall, D. D.* Vol. 8. Oxford, 1838.

Heywood, Thomas. *The Hierarchie of the Blessed Angells. . . .* London, 1635.

Homes, Nathanael. *A Commentary Literal or Historical, and Mystical or Spiritual on the Whole Book of Canticles*. In *The Works of Dr. Homes*. London, 1652.

Hopkins, Ezekiel. *A Sermon Preached at the Funeralls of the Honorable Algernon Grevil, Esq*. London, 1663.

Jantz, Harold S. *The First Century of New England Verse*. Worcester, Mass.: The Society, 1944.

Keach, Benjamin. *Tropologia. A Key to Open Scripture-Metaphors; Wherein the Most Significant Tropes . . . Respecting the Father, Son & Holy Spirit, as Also Such as Respect the Sacred Word of God, are Opened*. London, 1681.

Knollys, Hanserd. *Apocalyptical Mysteries*. London, 1667.

Lord, Benjamin. *Heaven, a Glorious Retreat and Rest; from all that is Burdensome and Afflicting. A Funeral Sermon for Mrs. Anne Lord. . . .* New London, 1751.

Mather, Cotton. *A Father Departing. A Sermon on the Departure of the Venerable and Memorable Dr. Increase Mather, who Expired Aug. 23, 1723. In the Eighty Fifth Year of His Age.* Boston, 1723.

_____. *Magnalia Christi Americana; or, The Ecclesiastical History of New-England from Its First Planting in the Year 1620 Unto the Year of Our Lord 1698, in Seven Books.* Hartford, 1853-55; rpt. New York: Russell & Russell, 1967.

_____. *Parentator. Memoirs of Remarkables in the Life and the Death of the Ever-Memorable Dr. Increase Mather.* Boston, 1724.

_____. "Problema Theologicum." Manuscript, American Antiquarian Society, Worcester, Mass.

_____. *The Temple Opening. A Particular Church Considered as a Temple of the Lord.* Boston, 1709.

_____. "Triparadisus." Manuscript, American Antiquarian Society, Worcester, Mass.

Mather, Increase. *Angelographia, or A Discourse Concerning the Nature and Power of the Holy Angels, and the Great Benefit which the True Fearers of God Receive by Their Ministry.* Boston, 1696.

_____. *A Discourse Concerning Faith and Fervency in Prayer, And the Glorious Kingdom of the Lord Jesus Christ, on Earth, Now Approaching.* Boston, 1710.

_____. *A Discourse Concerning the Death of the Righteous.* Boston, 1711.

_____. *A Disquisition Concerning the State of the Souls of Men, (Especially of Good Men) When Separated from Their Bodies, In Which Some Late Very Remarkable Providences Relating to Apparitions are Considered.* Boston, 1707.

_____. *A Dissertation Wherein the Strange Doctrine. . . .* Boston, 1708.

_____. *Ichabod. Or, A Discourse Shewing What Cause There is to Fear that the Glory of the Lord, is Departing from New-England.* Boston, 1702.

_____. "Increase Mather's 'New Jerusalem': Millennialism in Late Seventeenth-Century New England." Eds. Mason I. Lowance, Jr. and David Watters. American Antiquarian Society. *Proceedings,* 87 (1977), 344-405.

_____. *Meditations on Death,* Boston, 1707.

_____. *Meditations on the Glory of the Heavenly World.* Boston, 1711.

_____. *The Mystery of Christ Opened and Applyed. In Several Sermons, Concerning the Person, Office, and Glory of Jesus Christ.* Boston, 1686.

_____. *The Mystery of Israel's Salvation, Explained and Applied: or, A Discourse Concerning the General Conversion of the Israelitish Nation.* London, 1669.

_____. *Some Important Truths About Conversion, Delivered in Sundry Sermons.* London, 1674.

Mather, Samuel. *The Figures or Types of the Old Testament, by Which Christ and the Heavenly Things of the Gospel were Preached and Shadowed to the People of God of Old; Explain'd and Improv'd in Sundry Sermons.* 2nd ed. London, 1705.

_____. *A Testimony from the Scripture Against Idolatry & Superstition.* Cambridge, 1672.

Mede, Joseph. *The Apostasy of the Latter Times; . . . or, the Gentile's Theology of Daemons Revived in the Latter Times amongst Christians, in Worshipping of Angels, Deifying and Invocating of Saints, Adoring of Reliques, Bowing down to Images and Crosses, &C.* In *The Works of the Pious and Profoundly-Learned Joseph Mede, D. D..* London, 1663-64, II, bk. 3.

Owen, John. *Meditations and Discourses Concerning the Glory of Christ.* London, 1691.

Parker, Thomas. *The Visions and Prophecies of Daniel Expounded: Wherein the Mistakes of former Interpreters are modestly discovered, and the true meaning of the Text made plain.* London, 1646.

Perkins, William. *The arte of Prophecying. Or A Treatise Concerning the Sacred and Onely Trve Manner and Methode of Preaching.* In *The Workes of . . . William Perkins.* Trans. Thomas Tuke. Cambridge, 1608-09, II, 731-62.

_____. *A Clovd of Faithfvll Witnesses, Leading to the Heavenly Canaan: Or, A Commentary vpon the eleuenth Chapter to the Hebrewes.* London, 1622.

_____. *A Golden Chaine: Or the Description of Theologie.* In *The Workes of . . . William Perkins.* Cambridge, 1608-09, I, 9-118.

_____. *A Reformed Catholicke: Or, a Declaration Shewing how Neere we may come to the Present Church of Rome in Sundry Points of Religion: and Wherein we must for ever depart from them.* In *The Works of . . . William Perkins.* Cambridge, 1608-09, I, 549-618.

_____. *A Salve for a Sicke Man: or, A Treatise containing the nature, differences, and kinds of death; as also the right manner of dying well.* In *The Workes of . . . Willaim Perkins.* Cambridge, 1608-09, I, 484-509.

_____. *A Warning Against the Idolatrie of the Last Times.* In *The Workes of . . . William Perkins.* Cambridge, 1608-09, I, 549-618.

Phelps, Elizabeth Stuart. *The Gates Ajar.* 1868; Cambridge: Harvard University Press, 1964.

Pierce, Thomas. *Death Consider'd as a Door To A Life of Glory.* London, n.d.

Quarles, Francis. *Emblems Divine and Moral.* London, 1635.

Robotham, John. *An Exposition on the Whole Booke of Solomons Song, Commonly Called the Canticles.* London, 1651.

Sewall, Joseph. *Believers invited to Come to Christ As the Author of their Resurrection and Life.* Boston, 1716.

_____. *Letter-Book of Samuel Sewall [1685-1729]. Massachusetts Historical Society Collections,* 6th ser., I (1886), 171-78.

_____. *Phaenomena Quaedam Apocalyptica Ad Aspectum Novi Orbis Configurata. Or, Some Few Lines Towards a Description of the New Heaven, as it makes to Those who Stand Upon the New Earth.* Boston, 1697.

Sibbes, Richard. *Beams of divine Light, breaking forth from severall places of holy Scripture, as they were learnedly opened, in XXI. sermons.* London, 1639.

_____. *Bowels Opened: or a Discovery of the Neere and Deere Love, Union and Communion between Christ and the Church. . . .* London, 1639.

_____. *A Breathing After God. Or a Christians Desire of God's Presence.* London, 1639.

_____. *The Brides Longing for her Bridegrooms second comming. A Sermon preached at the Funerall of . . . Sir T. Crew.* London, 1638.

_____. *A Glance of Heaven. Or a pretious Taste of a Glorious Feast. Wherein thou mayest taste and see those things which God hath Prepared for Them that Love Him.* London, 1639.

_____. *Light from Heaven: Discovering the Fountaine Opened; Angels acclamations; Churches Riches; Rich Povertie.* London, 1638.

Stoddard, Solomon. "Solomon Stoddard's Sermon on the Lord's Supper as a Converting Ordinance." *Resources for American Literary Study,* 4 (1971), 211-26.

T., R. *De Templis, A Treatise of Temples: Wherein is discovered the Ancient Manner of Building, Consecrating, and Adorning of Churches.* London, 1638.

Taylor, Edward. "Christ the Glory of all Types: The Initial Sermon from Edward Taylor's 'Upon the Types of the Old Testament.' " *William and Mary Quarterly,* Third Series, XXXVII, 2 (April 1980), 289-306.

_____. "Edward Taylor on the Day of Judgment." Eds. Thomas M. and Virginia Davis. *American Literature,* 43 (1972), 525-47.

_____. *Edward Taylor's Christographia.* Ed. Norman S. Grabo. New Haven: Yale University Press, 1962.

_____. *Edward Taylor's Treatise Concerning the Lord's Supper*. East Lansing, Mich.: Michigan State University Press, 1966.

_____. *The Poems of Edward Taylor*. Ed. Donald E. Stanford. New Haven: Yale University Press, 1960.

_____. *The Poetical Works of Edward Taylor*. Ed. Thomas H. Johnson. New York: Rockland Editions, 1939.

_____. "The Publick Records of the Church at Westfield." Ms. Westfield Athenaeum.

Torrey, Samuel. "Epitaph." *Colonial American Poetry*, Ed. Kenneth Silverman. New York: Hafner Publishing Co., 1968, Pp. 143-44.

Watson, Thomas. *Christs Lovelinesse; or, a Discovrse Setting forth the Rare Beauties of the Lord Jesus, Which may both amaze the eye, and draw the heart of a Sinner to him*. In *Three Treastises*. London, 1659.

Watts, Isaac. *The Psalms, Hymns, and Spiritual Songs of the Rev. Isaac Watts, D. D.* Ed. Samuel Worcester. Boston, 1864.

Weever, John. *Ancient Fvneral Monvments with in the Vnited Monarchie of Great Britaine, Ireland, and the Ilands adjacent*. London, 1631.

Wheelock, Eleazar. *The Microfilm Edition of The Papers of Eleazar Wheelock together with the Early Archives of Dartmouth College & Moor's Indian Charity School and Records of the Town of Hanover, New Hampshire through the year 1779*. Hanover, N. H.: Dartmouth College Library, 1971.

Wigglesworth, Michael. "God's Controversy with New England." *Seventeenth-Century American Poetry*. Ed. Harrison T. Meserole. Garden City: Doubleday & Co., Inc., 1968. Pp. 42-54.

Secondary Works

Aries, Philippe *The Hour of Our Death*. Trans. Helen Weaver. New York: Knopf, 1981.

_____. *Western Attitudes Toward Death: From the Middle Ages to the Present*. Trans. Patricia M. Ranum. Baltimore, Md.: The Johns Hopkins University Press, 1974.

Ball, Bryan W. *A Great Expectation. Eschatological Thought in English Protestantism to 1660*. Studies in the History of Christian Thought, vol. 12. Leiden: E. J. Brill, 1975.

Beaty, Nancy Lee. *The Craft of Dying: A Study in the Literary Tradition of the Ars Moriendi in England*. Yale Studies in English, 175. New Haven: Yale University Press, 1970.

Bercovitch, Sacvan. *The American Jeremiad*. Madison: University of Wisconsin Press, 1978.

_____. "Horologicals to Chronometricals: The Rhetoric of the Jeremiad." *Literary Monographs*, 3. Madison, Wisconsin: University of Wisconsin Press, 1970.

_____, Ed. *Typology and Early American Literature*. Amherst, Mass.: University of Massachusetts Press, 1972.

_____. "Typology in Puritan New England: The Williams-Cotton Controversy Reassessed." *American Quarterly*, 19 (1967), 167-91.

Blake, Kathleen. "Edward Taylor's Protestant Poetic: Nontransubtantiating Metaphor." *American Literature*, 43 (1971), 1-24.

Bushman, Richard L. *From Puritan to Yankee: Character and the Social Order in Connecticut, 1690-1765*. Cambridge, 1967; rpt. New York: W. W. Norton & Co., Inc., 1970.

Capp, B. S. *The Fifth Monarchy Men: A Study in Seventeenth-century English Millenarianism*. London, 1972.

Cohn, Norman. *The Pursuit of the Millennium: Revolutionary Messianism in Medieval and Reformation Europe and Its Bearing on Modern Totalitarian Movements*. 2nd ed. New York: Harper and Row, 1961.

Daly, Robert. *God's Altar: The World and the Flesh in Puritan Poetry*. Berkeley: University of California Press, 1978.

_____. "Puritan Poetics: The World, the Flesh, and God." *Early American Literature*, 12 (1977), 136-62.

Davidson, James West. *The Logic of Millennial Thought: Eighteenth-Century New England.* New Haven: Yale University Press, 1977.

Delattre, Roland Andre. *Beauty and Sensibility in the Thought of Jonathan Edwards: An Essay in Aesthetics and Theological Ethics.* New Haven: Yale University Press, 1968.

Eberwein, Jane Donahue. " 'In a Book, as in a glass': Literary Sorcery in Mather's Life of Phips." *Early American Literature*, 12 (Winter, 1975-76), 289-300.

Freeman, Rosemary. *English Emblem Books.* London, 1948; rpt. New York: Octagon Books, 1966.

Gaustad, Erwin Scott. *The Great Awakening in New England.* New York, 1957; rpt. Chicago: Quadrangle Books, Inc., 1968.

Gilsdorf, Aletha Joy Bourne. "The Puritan Apocalypse: New England Eschatology in the Seventeenth Century." Diss. Yale University, 1965.

Glassie, Henry. *Folk Housing in Middle Virginia.* Knoxville: University of Tennessee Press, 1975.

Goen, C. C. *Revivalism and Separatism in New England, 1740-1800: Strict Congregationalists and Separate Baptists in the Great Awakening.* New Haven: Yale University Press, 1962.

Grabo, Norman S. *Edward Taylor.* Twayne United States Authors Series, 8. New Haven: College and University Press, 1961.

_____, ed. *Edward Taylor's Christographia.* New Haven: Yale University Press, 1962.

_____. "Edward Taylor on the Lord's Supper *Boston Public Library Quarterly*, 12 (1960), 22-36.

_____, ed. *Edward Taylor's Treatise Concerning the Lord's Supper.* East Lansing, Mich: Michigan State University Press, 1966.

_____. "The Poet to the Pope: Edward Taylor to Solomon Stoddard." *American Literature*, 52 (1960), 197-201.

_____. "The Veiled Vision: The Role of Aesthetics in Early American Intellectual History." *The William and Mary Quarterly*, Third Series, XIX (1962), 493-510.

Haims, Lynn. "The Face of God: Puritan Iconography in Early American Poetry, Sermons, and Tombstone Carving." *Early American Literature*, XIV (Spring, 1979), 15-47.

Hammond, Jeff, and Thomas M. Davis. "Edward Taylor: A Note on Visual Imagery." *Early American Literature*, 8 (1973), 126-31.

Heimert, Alan. *Religion and the American Mind: From the Great Awakening to the Revolution.* Cambridge, Mass.: Harvard University Press, 1966.

Hill, Christopher. *Antichrist in Seventeenth-Century England.* Riddell Memorial Lectures, 41st Series. New York: Oxford University Press, 1971.

_____. *The World Turned Upside Down: Radical Ideas During the English Revolution.* 1972; rpt. Baltimore, Md.: Penguin Books, Inc., 1975.

Holifield, E. Brooks. *The Covenant Sealed: The Development of Puritan Sacramental Theory in Old and New England, 1570-1720.* New Haven: Yale University Press, 1974.

Huntington, Richard and Peter Metcalf, *Celebrations of Death: The Anthropology of Mortuary Ritual.* New York: Cambridge University Press, 1979.

Isani, Muktar Ali. "The Pouring of the Sixth Vial: A Letter in a Taylor-Sewall Debate." *Proceedings.* Massachusetts Historical Society, 93 (1970), 123-29.

Israel, Calvin. "American Puritan Literary Theory: 1620-1660." Ph.D. diss. University of California, Davis 1970.

Jantz, Harold S. "Introduction." *The First Century of New England Verse.* Worcester; The Society, 1944.

The Jerome Biblical Commentary. Eds. Raymond B. Brown, Joseph A. Fitzmyer, Roland

E. Murphy. 2 vols. Englewood Cliffs, N. J.: 1968.

Johnson, Parker H. "Poetry and Praise in Edward Taylor's *Preparatory Meditations.*" *American Literature*, 52 (1979), 84-96.

Kane, Patricia E. "The Seventeenth-Century Furniture of the Connecticut Valley: The Hadley Chest Reappraised." *Arts of the Anglo-American Community in the Seventeenth Century*. Ed. Ian M. G. Quimby. Winterthur Conference Report 1974. Charlottesville: The University Press of Virginia, 1975. Pp. 79-122.

Kaufman, U. Milo. *The Pilgrims Progress and Traditions in Puritan Meditation*. Yale Studies in English, vol. 163. New Haven: Yale University Press, 1966.

Keller, Karl. *The Example of Edward Taylor*. Amherst, Mass.: University of Massachusetts Press, 1975.

Ladner, Gerhart B. *Ad Imaginem Dei: The Image of Man in Medieval Art*. Wimmer Lecture, 16. Latrobe, Pa.: Archabbey Press, 1965.

—————. "The Concept of the Image in the Greek Fathers and the Byzantine Iconoclastic Controversy." *Dumbarton Oaks Papers*, 7 (1953), 1-34.

Leverenz, David. *The Language of Puritan Feeling*. New Brunswick: Rutgers University Press, 1980.

Levin, David. *Cotton Mather: The Young Life of the Lord's Remembrancer, 1663-1703*. Cambridge: Harvard University Press, 1978.

Lewalski, Barbara K. *Donne's Anniversaries and the Poetry of Praise: The Creation of a Symbolic Mode*. Princeton, N. J.: Princeton University Press, 1973.

—————, and Andrew J. Sabol, eds. *Major Poets of the Earlier Seventeenth Century: Donne, Herbert, Vaughan, Crashaw, Jonson, Herrick, Marvell*. New York: Odyssey Press, 1973.

—————. *Milton's Brief Epic: The Genre, Meaning, and Art of Paradise Regained*. Providence, R. I.: Brown University Press, 1966.

—————. *Protestant Poetics and the Seventeenth-Religious Lyric*. Princeton: Princeton University Press, 1979.

—————. "*Samson Agonistes* and the 'Tragedy' of the Apocalypse." *PMLA*, 85 (1970), 1050-61.

Lockwood, John H. *Westfield and Its Historic Influences*. 2 vols. Springfield, Mass.: By the Author, 1922.

Lowance, Mason I., Jr. *Increase Mather*. Twayne United States Authors Series, 246. New York: Twayne Publishers, Inc., 1974.

—————. *The Language of Canaan: Metaphor and Symbol in New England from the Puritans to the Transcendentalists*. Cambridge: Harvard University Press, 1980.

—————. "Typology and Millennial Aesthetics in Early New England." In *Literary Uses of Typology: From the Late Middle Ages to the Present*. Ed. Earl Miner. Princeton, N. J.: Princeton University Press, 1977.

Lucas, Paul R. *Valley of Discord: Church and Society Along the Connecticut River, 1636-1725*. Hanover, N. H.: University Press of New England, 1976.

Luther, Clair Frank. *The Hadley Chest*. Hartford, Ct.: The Case, Lockwood & Brainard Co., 1935.

McCallum, James Dow. *Eleazar Wheelock: Founder of Dartmouth College*. Manuscript Series, No. 4. Hanover, N. H.: Dartmough College Publications, 1939.

Maclear, J. F. "Anne Hutchinson and the Mortalist Heresy." *The New England Quarterly*, LIV, 1 (March 1981), 74-103.

—————. "New England and the Fifth Monarchy: The Quest for the Millennium in Early American Puritanism." *William and Mary Quarterly*, 3rd ser., 32 (1975), 223-60.

M'Clure, David and Elijah Parish. *Memoirs of the Rev. Eleazar Wheelock, D. D. Founder and President of Dartmouth College and Moor's Indian Charity School; with a Summary History of the College and School, To Which Are Added, copious extracts From Dr. Wheelock's Correspondence*. Newburyport, Mass., 1811.

Madsen, Willaim. *From Shadowy Types to Truth: Studies in Milton's Symbolism*. New Haven: Yale University Press, 1968.

Martz, Louis. Foreword. *The Poems of Edward Taylor*. Ed. Donald E. Stanford. New Haven: Yale University Press, 1960.

_____. *The Poetry of Meditation: A Study in English Religious Literature of the Seventeenth Century*. Yale Studies in English, vol. 125. 1954; rev. ed. New Haven: Yale University Press, 1962.

Merchant, Carolyn, *The Death of Nature*. San Francisco: Harper & Row, 1980.

Middlekauff, Robert. *The Mathers: Three Generations of Puritan Intellectuals, 1596-1728*. New York; Oxford University Press, 1971.

Miller, Perry. "The End of the World." In *Errand Into the Wilderness*. Boston, 1956; rpt. New York: Harper & Row, 1964, 217-39.

_____. *The New England Mind: from Colony to Provine*. 1953; rpt. Boston: The Beacon Press, 1961.

_____. *The New England Mind: The Seventeenth Century*, New York, 1939; rpt. Boston: The Beacon Press, 1961.

Miner, Earl, ed. *Literary Uses of Typology: From the Late Middle Ages to the Present*. Princeton, N.J.: Princeton University Press, 1977.

North, Michael. "Edward Taylor's Metaphors of Promise." *American Literature,* (1979), 1-16.

Panofsky, Erwin. *Studies in Iconology: Humanistic Themes in the Art of the Renaissance*. New York: Oxford University Press, 1939.

"Parker, Thomas." *DAB,* 14 (1934), 241-42.

_____. *DNB,* 14 (1917), 277-78.

_____. *The National Cyclopaedia,* 12 (1904), 249.

Phillips, John. *The Reformation of Images: Destruction of Art in England, 1535-1660,* Berkeley: University of California Press, 1973.

Pope, Robert G. *The Half-way Covenant: Church Membership in Puritan New England*. Princeton: Princeton University Press, 1969.

Praz, Mario. *Studies in Seventeenth Century Imagery*. Studies of the Warburg Institute, vol. 3. 2 vols. London: The Warburg Institute, 1939.

Quistorp, Heinrich. *Calvin's Doctrine of the Last Things*. Trans. Harold Knight. London: Lutterworth Press, 1955.

Reiter, Robert. "Poetry and Typology: Edward Taylor's *Preparatory Meditations,* Second Series, Numbers 1-30." *Early American Literature,* 5 (1970), 111-23.

Rosenmeier, Jesper. " 'Clearing the Medium': A Reevaluation of the Puritan Plain Style in Light of John Cotton's *A Practicall Commentary Upon the First Epistle Generall of John*." *William and Mary Quarterly,* Third Series, no.4 (October 1980), 577-91.

_____. " 'Gospel Simplicity': John Cotton and the Puritan Plain Style." Special Session 28, MLA Convention. New York, 27 Dec. 1976.

Rowe, Karen. "Sacred or Profane?: Edward Taylor's Meditations on Canticles." *Modern Philology,* 20 (1974), 123-38.

Scheick, William J. *The Will and the Word: The Poetry of Edward Taylor*. Athens: University of Georgia Press, 1974.

Shea, Daniel B., Jr. *Spiritual Autobiography in Early America*. Princeton, N. J.: Princeton University Press, 1968.

Stanford, Donald E., Jr. "An Edition of the Complete Poetical Works of Edward Taylor." Diss. Stanford University, 1953.

―――――――. "The Imagination of Death in the Poetry of Phillip Pain, Edward Taylor, and George Herbert." *Studies in the Literary Imagination*, 9 (1976), 53-67.

―――――――. "Introduction." *The Poems of Edward Taylor*, Ed. Donald L. Stanford. New Haven: Yale University Press, 1960.

Stannard, David E. "Death and Dying in Puritan New England." *The American Historical Review*, 78 (1973), 1305-30.

―――――――. *The Puritan Way of Death: A Study in Religion, Culture, and Social Change*. New York: Oxford University Press, 1977.

Stewart, Stanley N. *The Enclosed Garden: The Tradition and the Image in Seventeenth-Century Poetry*. Madison: University of Wisconsin Press, 1966.

Toon, Peter, ed. *Puritans, the Millennium and the Future of Israel: Puritan Eschatology 1600 to 1660*. Cambridge: James Clarke & Co., 1970.

Tuveson, Ernest Lee. *Millennium and Utopia: A Study in the Background of the Idea of Progress*. Berkeley: University of California Press, 1949.

Walzer, Michael. *The Revolution of the Saints*. Princeton, N. J.: Princeton University Press, 1966.

Warren, Austin. "Edward Taylor's Poetry: Colonial Baroque." *Kenyon Review*, 3 (1941), 355-71.

Watters, David H. "Emerson, Dickinson and the Atomic Self." *Emily Dickinson Bulletin*, 8 (1977), 25-38.

Wilson, John F. "Another Look at John Canne." *Church History*, 33 (1964), 34-48.

―――――――. "Comment on 'Two Roads to the Puritan Millennium.' " *Church History, 32 (1963), 339-43*.

Gravestone Studies

Benes, Peter. "Additional Light on Wooden Grave Markers." *Essex Institute Historical Collections*, 111 (January 1975), 53-64.

―――――――. "Lt. John Hartshorn: Gravestone maker of Haverhill and Norwich." *Essex Institute Historical Collections*, 109 (1973), 152-64.

―――――――. *The Masks of Orthodoxy: Folk Gravestone Carving in Plymouth County, Massachusetts, 1689-1805*. Amherst, Mass.: University of Massachusetts Press, 1977.

Buckeye, Nancy. "Samuel Dwight: Bennington County Stone Carver." *Vermont History*, 43 (1975), 208-16.

Burgess, William. *English Churchyard Memorials*. London: The Lutterworth Press, 1963.

Caulfield, Ernest. "Connecticut Gravestones II." *Connecticut Historical Society Bulletin*, 16 (1951), 25-31.

―――――――. "Connecticut Gravestones V." *Connecticut Historical Society Bulletin*, 21 (1956), 1-13.

―――――――. "Connecticut Gravestones VII." *Connecticut Historical Society Bulletin*, 25 (1960), 1-6.

―――――――. "Connecticut Gravestones: IX." *Connecticut Historical Society Bulletin*, 28 (1963), 22-29.

―――――――. "Connecticut Gravestones: XII." *Connecticut Historical Society Bulletin*, 32 (1967), 65-79.

―――――――. "Connecticut Gravestones XIV." Ed. Peter Benes. *Connecticut Historical Society Bulletin*, 41 (1976), 33-56.

Deetz, James and Edwin S. Dethlefsen. "Death's Head Cherub Urn and Willow." *Natural History*, 76:3 (1967), 38-37.

Forbes, Harriette Merrifield. *Gravestones of Early New England and the Men Who Made Them: 1653-1800*. Boston: Houghton Mifflin Co., 1927.

_____. "The Lamsons of Charlestown, Stone Cutters." Old Time New England, 17 (January 1927), 125-39.

Foster, Stephen C. "From Significant Incompetence to Insignificant Competence." In *Puritan Gravestone Art*. The Dublin Seminar for New England Folklife Annual Proceedings I. (1976), 33-40.

Hall, David D. "The Gravestone Image as a Puritan Cultural Code." In *Puritan Gravestone Art*. The Dublin Seminar for New England Folklife: Annual Proceedings I. (1976), 23-32.

Harding, William E. "Zerubbabel Collins' Successor and his Work in Bennington County, Vermont." *Puritan Gravestone Art II*. The Dublin Seminar for New England Folklife Annual Proceedings I (1976), 14-22.

s'Jacob, Henriette. Idealism and Realism: A Study of Sepulchral Symbolism. Leiden: E. J. Brill, 1954.

Ludwig, Allan I. "Eros and Agape: Classical and Early Christian Survivals in New England Stonecarving." *Puritan Gravestone Art*. The Dublin Seminar for New England Folklife Annual Proceedings I (1976), 41-56.

_____. *Graven Images: New England Stonecarving and its Symbols, 1650-1815*. Middletown, Ct.: Wesleyan University Press, 1966.

Slater, James A., Ralph L. Tucker, and Daniel Farber. "The Colonial Gravestone Carvings of John Hartshorne." *Puritan Gravestone Art II*. The Dublin Seminar for New England Folklife Annual Proceedings III (1978), 79-146.

_____, and Ernest Caulfield, "The Colonial Gravestone Carvings of Obadiah Wheeler," American Antiquarian Society. *Proceedings*, 84 (1974), 73-103.

Tashjian, Dickran and Ann. *Memorials for Children of Change: The Art of Early New England Stonecarving*. Middletown, Ct.: Wesleyan University Press, 1974.

Watters, David H. "A Priest to the Temple." *Puritan Gravestone Art II*. The Dublin Seminar for New England Folklife Annual Proceedings III (1978), 45-57.

Index

The names of gravestones appear in boldface.